Sunset

Good Cook's Handbook

By the Editors of Sunset Books
and Sunset Magazine

Lane Publishing Co. ▪ Menlo Park, California

Coordinating Editor
Suzanne N. Mathison

Contributing Editor
Claire Coleman

Design
Williams & Ziller Design

Illustrations
Sally Shimizu
Carole Etow
John Lytle
Ellen Blonder

Photography
Nikolay Zurek

Photo Stylist
JoAnn Masaoka

SUCCESS AT YOUR FINGERTIPS

At what temperature do you roast a turkey? How do you choose a perfect melon? What wine goes best with a veal entrée?

You'll find the answers to these questions and many, many more in the pages of this book. A kitchen reference book extraordinaire, it offers clear, easy-to-read charts, diagrams, and instructions, allowing you to perform every kind of cooking task quickly and with ease.

Whether you're a beginning cook eager to master the fundamentals or a culinary whiz who just needs to double-check an occasional time or temperature, this volume will be an invaluable addition to your kitchen.

We extend special thanks to Rebecca La Brum for editing the manuscript, to Kathy Oetinger for coloring the illustrations, and to Bob Thompson for sharing with us his expertise on wines and cheeses. We're also grateful to Williams-Sonoma for their generosity in sharing props for use in our photographs.

Cover: Design by Williams & Ziller Design. Photograph by Nikolay Zurek. Photo styling by JoAnn Masaoka.

Editor, Sunset Books: David E. Clark
First printing May 1986

CONTENTS

KITCHEN BASICS 4

MEATS & POULTRY 32

FISH & SHELLFISH 50

EGGS & CHEESE 68

PASTA & GRAINS 74

FRUITS & VEGETABLES 82

SPECIAL FEATURES

Kitchen Basics

Good cooks often have differences of opinion. But if there's one thing on which they all agree, it's the importance of knowing the basics. How to select cookware, how to measure ingredients, which herbs and spices to use, what to do if you suddenly run out of a key item in your recipe—these are a few of the fundamental skills which lay the foundation for a lifetime of success in the kitchen.

This chapter offers a lesson in kitchen know-how. If you're already an experienced cook, the following pages will refresh your memory on information basic to food preparation; if you're a beginner, they'll provide the confidence you need to jump right in and start cooking.

KITCHEN EQUIPMENT

A cook's fundamental armory of pots and pans needn't be as extensive as the gleaming displays in the local department store may suggest. It's much wiser to collect quality tools piece by piece than to invest in a decorative set of matching cookware. No matter what you choose, though, buy the best you can afford. A good, strong pan with a riveted handle and thick bottom will perform beautifully for a lifetime. Thin, inexpensive cookware is likely to dent, break, or develop "hot spots" (causing food to burn) within a few months. Make sure your pans have tight-fitting lids, sturdy insulated handles and knobs, and straight sides that curve gently at the bottom so there are no "corners" inaccessible to a spoon or wire whisk.

Below is a brief survey of cookware, each with its virtues and a few failings as well. See pages 7 and 8 for a visual guide to basic cookware.

RANGE-TOP ACCESSORIES

Pots and pans may be made from a variety of materials; the most common types are discussed below.

Aluminum. Good heat conductor (important for browning meat and sautéing), lightweight, and relatively inexpensive. Tends to react chemically with acidic foods (artichokes, citrus fruits, spinach, tomatoes, wine sauces), causing slight metallic flavor and surface pitting of metal.

Cast iron. Evenly distributes and retains heat, extremely durable; heaviest metal used in cooking, yet inexpensive. Season before using; see manufacturer's directions. Prone to rust—must be dried immediately after washing.

Copper. Superb heat conductor, most popular for sensitive temperature control and foods requiring exact timing; weight varies. Some are ultra-expensive (a medium-size frying pan can cost $75); thin, less expensive pans are attractive, but best reserved for baking or serving. Because copper reacts chemically with all foods and moisture and can cause unpleasant tastes (even toxicity), copper pans are always lined—usually with tin. This lining will eventually need replacement (also expensive). Must be polished with special cleaners.

Nonmetal coating. Porcelain (usually bright in color, and frequently mislabeled "enamel") is sometimes bonded to iron, aluminum, or steel; weights vary. Porcelain bonded to iron evenly distributes and retains heat, but when it is bonded to aluminum or steel, heat conduction is spotty. Porcelain won't react with foods; it's easy to clean and resists scratching and staining (use nonmetal utensils), but may chip. Colorful acrylic or polyamide are also available—less expensive than porcelain, but more prone to fading and discoloration.

Stainless steel. Conducts heat unevenly, so food may scorch if pan is placed on very hot burner; best used for cooking liquids. Doesn't react with foods; lightweight, durable. Remains bright and tarnish free, but is dulled by water spots if not dried carefully. Moderately expensive.

BAKEWARE & ACCESSORIES

For cakes and cookies, use shiny aluminum, tin, or stainless steel pans with smooth seams (for ease in cleaning); these distribute heat evenly and give baked goods a golden brown surface. For pies, use glass, ceramic, or dull metal pans, all of which absorb heat and brown the crust. When baking breads, pies, and cakes in glass, reduce specified oven temperature by 25°, because glass absorbs so much heat. Most glass and ceramic bakeware can travel directly from freezer to oven to table, but check the manufacturer's instructions to be sure.

In baking, it's important always to use a pan or dish in the size that's called for in a recipe. If the size isn't marked on the utensil, measure the width, length, and depth from the inside top edges, or check its capacity by measuring the amount of water it holds. An 8- by 8-inch pan holds 1½ quarts; a 9- by 9-inch pan or a 7- by 11-inch pan, 2 quarts; and a 9- by 13-inch pan, 3 quarts.

KNIVES: THE BASIC CUTTING TOOLS

Many otherwise well-equipped kitchens lack a set of good knives—possibly because the cook hasn't yet discovered how expertly a really good knife performs.

A knife's performance depends on the quality of its steel and the excellence of its "grind" (cutting edge). To take and hold a keen edge, a blade must be made of steel with a high carbon content. Carbon content determines the hardness of a blade—and hardness is essential for a sharp edge.

A carbon steel knife, therefore, would seem to be the best choice, but there's one disadvantage—this material tends to turn dark, and it will rust if you don't dry it immediately after each washing. Stainless steel, a combination of carbon steel and chromium, has noncorrosive properties, so it stays shiny. But most stainless steel has a low carbon content and won't keep a sharp edge. You can find high carbon stainless, which takes a good edge, but it's more difficult to sharpen.

The pros and cons of carbon and stainless balance each other fairly well—you'll probably put as much effort into keeping a carbon steel knife clean and rust-free as you would into keeping a stainless steel knife sharp, and if frequently sharpened, the stainless will probably give just as good a cutting edge as the carbon.

Chrome-plated knives look like stainless steel knives, but they don't give anything like the same service. In time, the chromium finish wears off, and the edge is likely to rust.

Test for quality. Usually a knife's cost is directly related to its quality, but there are other tests besides price. Grip the handle to be sure the knife is well balanced, with the center of gravity near the handle (especially important in large knives). Look for a "full tang"—an extension of the blade that runs the full length of the handle. This extension may not be visible, but three rivets in the handle usually indicate a full tang (watch out for knives with fake rivets hiding a tang of only 2 inches or so). The best knives taper from heel to tip, and from the top of the blade to the cutting edge. The bolster protects the grip hand from the blade.

Proper care of knives. Keep your knives in their own protected place—not in a miscellany drawer where edges will be dulled by knocking against other tools. Hang them on a magnetic rack or keep them in a grooved wooden knife block. To preserve their handles, never soak knives in dishwater, and absolutely never subject them to a dishwasher. The water may dry and warp wooden handles, causing the tang to loosen. The best way to care for knives is simply to wash them quickly and dry them immediately. It's perfectly safe to scour carbon knives with abrasives—this actually helps keep them sharp.

Basic knives. Listed below are eight knife types that can handle virtually any kitchen cutting job you're likely to encounter: **paring knife,** for peeling, seeding, and pitting; **utility knife,** for slicing tomatoes and fruit; **boning knife,** for boning meat, fish, and chicken; **slicing knife,** for thinly slicing large cuts of meat; **butcher knife,** for cutting up raw meat and poultry and large foods like watermelon; **French knife,** for chopping and mincing vegetables and for many other uses; **serrated knife,** for cutting bread and baked goods such as angel food cakes; and flexible-bladed **filleting knife,** for boning and skinning fish.

KNIVES

ANATOMY OF A KNIFE

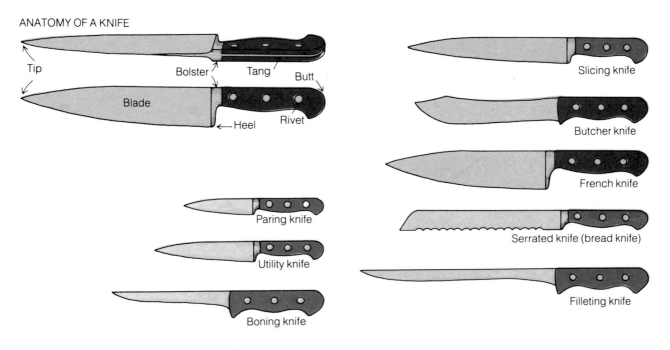

Tip — Bolster — Tang — Butt — Blade — Heel — Rivet

Slicing knife
Butcher knife
French knife
Serrated knife (bread knife)
Filleting knife

Paring knife
Utility knife
Boning knife

COOKWARE & BAKEWARE

RANGE TOP ACCESSORIES

ROASTING & BAKING ACCESSORIES

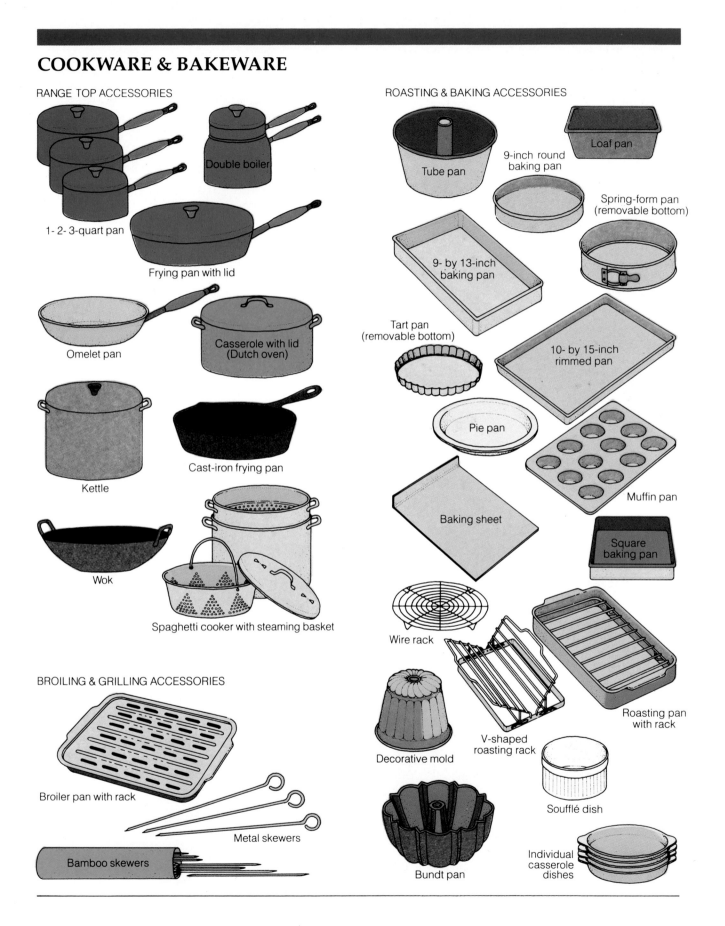

Double boiler

1- 2- 3-quart pan

Frying pan with lid

Omelet pan

Casserole with lid
(Dutch oven)

Kettle

Cast-iron frying pan

Wok

Spaghetti cooker with steaming basket

Tube pan

9-inch round
baking pan

Loaf pan

Spring-form pan
(removable bottom)

9- by 13-inch
baking pan

Tart pan
(removable bottom)

10- by 15-inch
rimmed pan

Pie pan

Baking sheet

Muffin pan

Square
baking pan

Wire rack

Roasting pan
with rack

Decorative mold

V-shaped
roasting rack

Soufflé dish

BROILING & GRILLING ACCESSORIES

Broiler pan with rack

Metal skewers

Bamboo skewers

Bundt pan

Individual
casserole
dishes

OTHER EQUIPMENT

Metal spatulas

Wooden spoons

Rubber spatulas

Ice cream scoop

Utility spoon

Slotted spoon

Ladle

2-tined kitchen fork

Wide metal spatula

Nonmetal spatula

Spaghetti rake

Wire whisks

Mixing bowls

Bottle opener

Can opener

Mallet

Vegetable peeler

Meat thermometers

Bulb baster

Kitchen scissors

Poultry shears

Tongs

Vegetable steamer

Oriental wire skimmer

Strainer

Garlic press

Mortar and pestle

Colander

Sifter

Funnel

Grater

Nutmeg grater

Rolling pins

Pastry bag and tips

Pastry brushes

Pastry blender

Slicing wheel

Pastry wheel

Cookie cutters

SMALL APPLIANCES

Blender

Food processor

Electric mixer

FOOD PROCESSOR TIPS

The food processor is an invaluable addition to any kitchen, streamling food preparation and saving time and energy for the cook. Charts in this book will show you how to use the food processor to chop, slice, shred, and julienne-cut a number of foods with lightning speed. To get the safest, most effective service from your machine, keep the following common-sense rules in mind:

■ Before operating your processor for the first time, read the instruction manual thoroughly to familiarize yourself with the machine's parts, use, and care. Capabilities vary from one machine to another; let the manufacturer's instructions be the final word for your particular model.

■ Handle the metal blade and discs with as much respect as you'd handle a knife; the cutting edges are razor sharp. Be sure to store blades out of reach of children.

■ *Never* insert any blade until the work bowl is locked in place. After inserting a blade or disc, be sure it's down as far as possible on the shaft.

■ *Always* use the pusher when slicing or shredding. *Never* put your fingers in the feed tube.

■ *Always* wait for the metal blade or a disc to stop spinning before you remove the cover.

■ *Never* leave the metal blade soaking in soapy water, planning to return and wash it later. You may forget it's there and be unable to see the sharp edges through the suds. It's best to wash the blade right after using it.

■ When chopping food, insert the metal blade before adding food to the work bowl (this is easy to forget at first). Putting food in first won't cause any damage, but it's a nuisance to empty out the bowl, fit in the blade, and start again.

■ To empty the work bowl filled with dry ingredients, remove the blade first or hold it in place with your fingers as you tip the bowl upside down. (Or, if the work bowl has a hole in the bottom, put one finger in it, then invert the bowl. The blade will stay firmly in place.)

■ To empty the work bowl filled with liquid, hold the blade in place against the bottom of the bowl with a spatula or your hand. This prevents leakage and stops the blade from dropping out and cutting you. To clean the last bit of a liquid mixture off the metal blade, replace the empty work bowl (with blade in place) on the base; put on the cover and turn on the machine for just a few seconds. The blade will be clean, and the remaining liquid mixture can be easily and neatly scraped off the sides of the bowl.

■ A food processor is built with a temperature-controlled circuit breaker that automatically cuts off the current if a machine overheats from mixing a load that's too heavy. If your machine stops, turn it off, then wait the length of time recommended in your manual before starting it again.

WEIGHTS & MEASURES

There's no getting around it—accurate measurement is critical. To achieve consistent results each time you follow a recipe, you must measure correctly.

Measure liquids in standard glass or clear plastic measuring cups designed for liquids. Measure dry or solid ingredients in metal or plastic cups that hold the exact capacity specified in a recipe. Don't shake or pack dry ingredients down—spoon them in, piling the cup high and light, then level off. (Brown sugar is an exception to this rule—press it firmly into the cup with your fingers or a spoon, then level off.)

WEIGHT OR AVOIRDUPOIS EQUIVALENTS

16 ounces = 1 pound
2.2 pounds = 1 kilo

LIQUID MEASURE EQUIVALENTS

3 teaspoons = 1 tablespoon
2 tablespoons = 1 fluid ounce
4 tablespoons = ¼ cup
5 tablespoons + 1 teaspoon = ⅓ cup
8 tablespoons = ½ cup = 4 fluid ounces
10 tablespoons + 2 teaspoons = ⅔ cup
12 tablespoons = ¾ cup
16 tablespoons = 1 cup = 8 fluid ounces
¼ cup + 2 tablespoons = ⅜ cup
½ cup + 2 tablespoons = ⅝ cup
¾ cup + 2 tablespoons = ⅞ cup
2 cups = 16 fluid ounces = 1 pint
4 cups = 2 pints = 1 quart
1 quart = .946 liters (946.3 milliliters)
1 liter = 1.06 quarts
4 quarts = 1 gallon

DRY MEASURE EQUIVALENT

2 pints = 1 quart

Note: Dry measure pints and quarts are approximately ⅙ larger than liquid measure pints and quarts. Dry measure is used for raw fruits and vegetables when measured in large amounts.

EQUIVALENT YIELDS

1 lemon = 3 tablespoons lemon juice
1 medium-size orange = ¼ cup orange juice
8 egg whites = 1 cup
4 ounces firm cheese (Cheddar, jack, Swiss) = 1 cup lightly packed shredded cheese
1½ to 2½ ounces hard cheese (Parmesan, Romano) = ½ cup grated cheese
¼ pound (1 stick) butter or margarine = ½ cup = 8 tablespoons
1 cup (½ pint) whipping cream = 2 cups whipped cream
1 pound granulated sugar = 2⅓ cups
1 pound brown sugar = 2⅓ cups, firmly packed
1 pound powdered sugar = 3¾ cups, unsifted
1 square baking chocolate (semisweet or unsweetened) = 1 ounce
4 ounces almond or walnut meats = 1 cup chopped nuts
1 sandwich-size slice crisp dry bread = ¼ cup fine crumbs
1 sandwich-size slice fresh bread = ½ cup soft crumbs
28 squares saltine crackers = 1 cup crumbs
16 squares graham crackers = 1 cup crumbs
24 two-inch vanilla wafers = 1 cup crumbs
18 two-inch chocolate wafers = 1 cup crumbs
1 package active dry yeast = 1 tablespoon

MEASURING EQUIPMENT

Standard cups for liquid measuring come in 1-, 2-, and 4-cup sizes with pouring spout. Measurement marks are on the sides.

Standard cups for dry measuring come in sets that include ¼ cup, ⅓ cup, ½ cup, and 1 cup.

Standard measuring spoons in sets of four include ¼-, ½-, and 1-teaspoon measures, plus 1 tablespoon. Use for liquid and dry ingredients.

EMERGENCY SUBSTITUTIONS

It's always best to use the exact ingredients called for in a recipe. But if you're in the middle of cooking and find you don't have a particular ingredient on hand, don't despair.

Just look below for a substitute that will give satisfactory results. We recommend, however, that you avoid making more than one substitution in a single recipe.

INGREDIENT	SUBSTITUTION
1 cup cake flour	1 cup all-purpose flour minus 2 tablespoons; or all-purpose flour sifted 3 times, then measured to make 1 cup
¼ cup fine dry bread crumbs	1 sandwich-size slice crisp dry bread, crushed
1 teaspoon baking powder	¼ teaspoon baking soda plus ½ teaspoon cream of tartar
1 package (1 tablespoon) active dry yeast	1 compressed yeast cake, crumbled (water used for dissolving compressed yeast should be about 95°F, as opposed to the 110°F used for dissolving active dry yeast)
1 tablespoon cornstarch (used for thickening)	2 tablespoons all-purpose flour or 1 tablespoon potato, rice, or arrowroot starch
1 cup buttermilk or sour milk	1 tablespoon distilled white vinegar or lemon juice stirred into 1 cup milk and allowed to stand for 5 minutes
1 cup milk	½ cup evaporated milk plus ½ cup water, or ⅓ cup instant nonfat dry milk stirred into 1 cup water
1 cup whipping cream (in soups and sauces)	¾ cup milk plus ⅓ cup butter or margarine, melted and cooled
1 cup corn syrup	1 cup granulated sugar plus ¼ cup liquid*
1 cup honey	1¼ cups granulated sugar plus ¼ cup liquid*
2 egg yolks (used for thickening in custards)	1 whole egg
1 square (1 oz.) unsweetened chocolate	1 envelope (1 oz.) premelted chocolate; or 3 tablespoons unsweetened cocoa plus 1 tablespoon melted butter or margarine
6 squares (6 oz. *total*) semisweet chocolate	1 cup (6 oz.) semisweet chocolate chips
Juice of 1 lemon	3 tablespoons bottled lemon juice
1 teaspoon grated fresh lemon peel or zest of 1 lemon	1 teaspoon dry lemon peel (purchased)
Juice of 1 medium-size orange	¼ cup reconstituted frozen orange juice
1 teaspoon grated fresh orange peel	1 teaspoon dry orange peel (purchased)
1 cup regular-strength chicken or beef broth	1 chicken or beef bouillon cube dissolved in 1 cup boiling water
1 can (1 lb.) tomatoes	2½ cups chopped, peeled fresh tomatoes, simmered for about 10 minutes
1 cup catsup or tomato-based chili sauce	1 can (8 oz.) tomato sauce plus ½ cup granulated sugar and 2 tablespoons distilled white vinegar
1 cup tomato juice	½ cup tomato sauce plus ½ cup water
1 teaspoon Italian herb seasoning	¼ teaspoon *each* dry basil, marjoram leaves, oregano leaves, and thyme leaves
1 teaspoon dry mustard (in wet mixtures)	1 tablespoon prepared mustard
¼ cup minced fresh onion	1 tablespoon instant minced onion (let stand in liquid as directed)
1 medium-size onion	2 teaspoons onion powder
1 clove garlic	⅛ teaspoon garlic powder
2 tablespoons minced fresh parsley	1 tablespoon parsley flakes
½ teaspoon grated fresh ginger	¼ teaspoon ground ginger
2 tablespoons chopped green or red bell pepper	1 tablespoon sweet pepper flakes (let stand in liquid as directed)
¼ cup dry sherry	¼ cup sweet white wine or Marsala
¼ cup dry white wine	¼ cup dry vermouth

*Use a liquid called for in recipe. Equivalence is based on how product functions in recipe, not on sweetness.

STAPLE FOODS

Always keep your kitchen well stocked—it makes meal preparation so much easier and reduces the need for frequent trips to the market just for a quart of milk or a bunch of parsley. Here are some of the items that a well-supplied pantry should contain; your list may differ slightly depending on your cooking habits. Do remember to replenish your supplies *before* they run out; that way, you won't be caught short at an inconvenient time. See pages 16 to 18 for a discussion of herbs and spices and their culinary uses.

IN THE REFRIGERATOR

These ingredients should stock the shelves and crisper unit of your refrigerator.

- ☐ Milk
- ☐ Half-and-half or light cream
- ☐ Whipping cream
- ☐ Sour cream
- ☐ Plain yogurt
- ☐ Butter or margarine
- ☐ Cheeses (Cheddar, jack, Parmesan, Swiss, cream cheese)
- ☐ Eggs
- ☐ Mayonnaise
- ☐ Catsup
- ☐ Chili sauce
- ☐ Prepared mustard
- ☐ Dijon mustard
- ☐ Prepared horseradish
- ☐ Granulated beef or chicken stock base
- ☐ Lemons
- ☐ Bottled lemon juice
- ☐ Salad greens
- ☐ Tomatoes
- ☐ Carrots
- ☐ Celery
- ☐ Green onions
- ☐ Parsley
- ☐ Thin-skinned potatoes
- ☐ Nuts (peanuts, cashews, walnuts, almonds)

IN THE PRODUCE BIN

These don't need refrigeration, but they should be kept in a cool, dark, dry place.

- ☐ Apples
- ☐ Bananas
- ☐ Oranges
- ☐ Garlic
- ☐ Yellow and red onions
- ☐ Russet potatoes

IN THE FREEZER

Keep out-of-season fruit and hard-to-find vegetables in the freezer, so you'll have them when you need them. Breads also keep best when frozen—unless you use them very quickly.

- ☐ Ice cream
- ☐ Raspberries
- ☐ Blueberries
- ☐ Peaches
- ☐ Orange juice concentrate
- ☐ Peas
- ☐ Corn
- ☐ Green beans
- ☐ Breads (white, whole wheat, rye, pumpernickel, English muffins, bagels, dinner rolls)

ON THE PANTRY SHELF

These canned, bottled, and packaged goods are used frequently in a variety of recipes.

- ☐ Canned tomatoes (regular and Italian-style)
- ☐ Tomato sauce
- ☐ Tomato paste
- ☐ Tomato juice
- ☐ Tuna
- ☐ Chopped clams
- ☐ Whole and sliced ripe olives
- ☐ Kidney beans
- ☐ Pineapple chunks and slices in their own juice
- ☐ Sliced pimentos
- ☐ Anchovy fillets
- ☐ Major Grey's chutney
- ☐ Honey
- ☐ Peanut butter
- ☐ Soy sauce
- ☐ Worcestershire sauce
- ☐ Liquid hot pepper seasoning
- ☐ Clam juice
- ☐ Regular-strength beef or chicken broth (or bouillon cubes)
- ☐ Dry sherry
- ☐ Marsala
- ☐ Wine for cooking (red and white)
- ☐ Salad oil
- ☐ Olive oil
- ☐ Vinegar (distilled white, red wine, white wine)
- ☐ Long-grain white rice
- ☐ Cracked wheat and/or bulgur
- ☐ Spaghetti and other pasta
- ☐ All-purpose flour
- ☐ Sugar (granulated, brown, powdered)
- ☐ Salt
- ☐ Baking powder
- ☐ Baking soda
- ☐ Vanilla extract
- ☐ Cornstarch
- ☐ Cornmeal
- ☐ Fine dry bread crumbs
- ☐ Raisins
- ☐ Sweet pickle relish
- ☐ Shredded coconut
- ☐ Semisweet chocolate

FOOD STORAGE

To preserve good flavor, texture, and nutritive value in the foods you buy—as well as for reasons of food safety—it's important to know the basics of food storage. This means knowing how and where to store food, and for how long it will remain fresh.

When you refrigerate or freeze perishable foods, it's especially important to know that you're doing so at the correct temperature. Refrigerator temperature should be 35° to 40°F, freezer temperature 0°F or lower. Use a reliable thermometer to check the temperature if you're not sure it's low enough.

MEATS

For short-term storage, keep uncooked meat in the refrigerator. Ground meats, stew meat, and variety meats (organ meats) are more perishable than other types and should be used within 1 or 2 days; chops, cutlets, roasts, and steaks may be kept for 3 to 5 days. If you wish to keep prepackaged meat in the refrigerator for more than 2 days, discard the original package and store the meat loosely wrapped.

To freeze meat, divide it into serving-size portions and wrap it airtight in moisture-proof material. Frozen ground meats and stew meat should be used within 2 or 3 months; variety meats, chops, and cutlets within 4 months. Use pork or veal roasts and steaks within 8 months; beef or lamb roasts and steaks will keep for up to 12 months.

For more meat storage information, see page 33.

POULTRY

Fresh poultry is highly perishable and should be kept no longer than 3 days in the coldest part of the refrigerator. If you won't use it within that time, freeze it. You can freeze poultry just as it comes from the market—but to prevent any chance of freezer burn, add an extra layer of insulation by enclosing the wrapped poultry in foil, heavy-duty plastic wrap, a plastic bag, or wax-coated freezer paper. Squeeze out as much air as possible before sealing, then mark the package with the type of bird, its weight, and the date. For best results, use frozen poultry within 6 months.

If you buy poultry complete with neck and giblets but don't want to cook them with the bird, freeze them for later use. Freeze neck, heart, and gizzard in one container, collecting them until you have enough for stock or other purposes. Freeze livers in another container, saving them for recipes such as pâté. All frozen giblets should be used within 3 months.

For more information on storing poultry, see page 44.

FISH & SHELLFISH

Fresh fish should be eviscerated, if necessary, then refrigerated in a leakproof wrapper as soon as possible after purchase—even a few hours at room temperature could start spoilage. Cook the fish within 2 days. Fresh shellfish should be eaten the day you buy it; keep it in the coldest part of the refrigerator until cooking time.

You may freeze fish for storage, though we don't recommend it; freezing causes a slight but noticeable loss of moisture and flavor. If you must freeze fish, wrap it airtight in moisture-proof material. Fish of moderate fat content, as well as crab and lobster, may be stored in the freezer for 3 months. Leaner fish and other shellfish (shells removed) may remain frozen for up to 6 months. (See the charts on pages 52 to 55 for information on the fat content of various fish.)

EGGS & CHEESE

Store eggs in the refrigerator, covered to prevent absorption of odors. In general, you can keep them for up to a month; check the date on the carton. Most cheeses should also be refrigerated. Soft cheeses such as ricotta and cottage cheese should be used within a few days, but harder cheeses will keep for several weeks. After opening firm or hard cheeses, wrap them airtight in plastic wrap and store in the coldest part of the refrigerator.

Cheeses other than ricotta or cottage cheese may be frozen if necessary, but this usually causes deterioration in texture. Firm cheeses are generally quite crumbly after thawing and are best used in cooking.

PASTA & GRAINS

Dried pasta, grains, and flours should be kept in a cool, dry place; always store them in tightly closed containers to prevent absorption of moisture or infestation by insects or rodents. Whole-grain products (such as whole wheat flour) are more perishable than refined ones, since the fat contained in the grain's germ can become rancid. For long-term storage, these products should be kept in the refrigerator or freezer.

FRUITS & VEGETABLES

Root vegetables such as potatoes and onions will keep for several weeks in a cool (50°F), dark, dry place. Other types of fresh vegetables, however, require refrigeration and should be used within a few days. Fruits, too, have different storage requirements, depending on the type of fruit and its stage of ripeness when purchased. For specific advice on storage techniques for fruits and vegetables, see the charts on pages 83 to 85 and 88 to 95.

WINE SELECTION GUIDE

Nobody can write rules for matching wines with food. Personal preference governs every time. However, preferences do fall into helpful patterns. Most people find Dover sole pleasing when it is served in cream sauce, but few are fond of the same fish when it swims in chocolate. For similar reasons, most people enjoy Dover sole with Chenin Blanc but have a harder time appreciating either fish or wine when Petite Sirah is the companion.

This chart offers some safe starting points for matching foods and wines, recording some well-established patterns of preference. But the fact is that adventurous pairings can be more pleasing than conventional ones; though the chart doesn't recommend Chardonnay as a partner for beef or lamb, many experienced wine drinkers take pleasure in pairing this sturdy white wine with red meats. Don't feel compelled to follow the chart too closely—even if experiments don't work out to perfection, one learns something useful at very small cost.

Flavor, sweetness, tartness, and astringency are the four major factors making a wine welcome with some foods, less appealing with others.

Flavor is foremost of the four factors. The range of flavors in wine results largely from the grape variety or varieties used to make each wine. Some grapes have intense flavors, while others are quite subtle. In a sense, choosing among wines is much like deciding which vegetable to serve with a steak.

If there is a rule of thumb, it is this: Intensely flavored wines hold up against strong-flavored foods, and vice versa; similarly, subtly flavored wines and delicate-flavored foods enhance each other.

Sweetness in wine is the opposite of dryness. Put another way,

KEY:
■ Good to excellent
★ Outstanding
□☆ Choose light wine of type

	WINES	FLAVOR ASSOCIATION/CHARACTER	Sole and all other mild white fish	Trout	Salmon	Crab	Lobster	Shrimp/prawns	Clams/mussels	Oysters	Chicken	Turkey	
REDS	Barbera	Pleasant fruity flavors. Dry; medium tannin									■	■	
	Cabernet Sauvignon	Strong flavors akin to herbs or tea. Dry; tannic									☆	□	
	Gamay	Pronounced fruity flavors. Dry; moderate tannin									■	■	
	Merlot	Herbaceous cousin of Cabernet. Dry; less tannic than Cabernet									■	■	
	Petite Sirah	Flavor hints of black pepper. Dry; very tannic											
	Pinot Noir	May be faintly raisiny or minty. Dry; soft, due to low tannin									■	■	
	Zinfandel	Berrylike flavors. Dry; medium to strong tannin			□						□	■	
WHITES	Blanc de Noir and Rosé	Made from all above grape varieties. Often off-dry to slightly sweet	■								■	■	
	Chardonnay	Subtle, sometimes hints of peach. Dry			★	■	★	★	★	☆	★		
	Chenin Blanc	Gently fruity. Usually off-dry to slightly sweet	■	■		■	■			■	■		
	French Colombard	Distinct, almost perfumy flavors. Usually off-dry; can be tart	■	■	■				■			■	
	Gewürztraminer	Strongly aromatic, sometimes spicy. Usually off-dry									■	■	
	Pinot Blanc	Subtle, similar to Chardonnay. Usually dry; often tart			■	■	■	■			★	★	
	Sauvignon Blanc	Flavorful. Herby, sometimes floral. Dry or just off; light, tart	■		■				■		★		
	Sémillon	Sometimes described as "figgy." Dry or just off			■						■	■	
	White Riesling (Johannisberg)	Apricot or other definite fruit flavor. Off-dry or slightly sweet	■	■			★		★	★	■		

"dry," as used to describe a wine, implies the absence of sugar; sweetness is a sign of its presence.

Winemakers can leave any amount of "residual sugar" in a wine by stopping fermentation before all the grape sugar has been converted to alcohol and carbon dioxide. Almost all wines with .5 percent or less residual sugar taste dry. Even with 1 percent residual sugar, extra-tart wines will taste dry; less tart ones may have a somewhat less dry flavor but still won't taste truly sweet. At these low levels, residual sugar enhances fruit flavors and makes a wine feel softer and fuller on the palate than it would if it were truly dry.

Most wines with .8 to 1.5 percent residual sugar are called off-dry and are meant to give a slight sug-gestion of sweetness. Those with 1.5 to 2.5 percent are described as slightly sweet, "slightly" meaning easy to notice. Greater than 2.5 per-cent residual sugar usually means wines that are cloying rather than refreshing with a meal, though ex-ceptions exist.

Tartness in grapes comes from their natural acidity, which gives both the fruit and the wines made from it crisp, refreshing qualities. In naturally tart wines—mostly young whites and blush wines and rosés—winemakers leave some re-sidual sugar to achieve a pleasing balance between sweet and tart.

Astringency comes from tannin, another natural component of grapes, and is most noticeable in red wines. Astringent tannins do an excellent job of cutting the fat in meats and cheeses; conversely, fats soften tannic wines, making them seem fuller and rounder. Astrin-gency, more than flavor, is the rea-son why reds are held to go well with meat—and the fattier the meat, the more this is true.

The chart below lists plain foods first, followed with a range of fa-miliar sauces and seasonings. To be certain a wine fits a sauced or sea-soned dish, check to make sure it's listed under both categories.

The chart does not list sparkling wines. Because they are subtly flavored and depend on their bub-bles for texture, they are more ver-satile than most table wines. Bruts and natures are dry; extra-drys have noticeable sweetness. Blanc de blancs are lighter and crisper; blanc de noirs are fuller.

	Duck/goose	Pheasant and other game birds	Rabbit	Veal	Beef	Lamb	Pork	Wild game	Ham, sausages, and smoked meats	Liver	Sweetbreads	Pasta	Butter/light cream	Cheese	Nut (amandine, etc.)	Tomato	Barbecue (smoky flavors)	Brown sauces/gravies	Herb marinades/sauces	Garlic	Onion	Citrus	Mustard	Indian curries	Spicy Mexican	Spicy Chinese	Mild Chinese (Cantonese)
		■	■		■	■	■	■	■			■		■		■		■	■								★
	★	★	■	□	■	★	■	★			☆	□		■		■	★	■	★	■	■		■				
	■		■		■	■	■		■			■				■	■	■				■	■	■		■	
	■	★	★	■	■	■	★	■			■	■		■		■	★	■	■	■	■		■				
	■		■		■	■	□	★	■			■				■	■	■	■				■				
		■	■	■	★	■	■			■	■		■	■				■		■	■						■
	■	■	★	☆	■	■	★	■	□	■		■		■		★	★	■	■	■	■		■		■	□	☆
		■	■			★	■		★			■	■	■	■	■	★		■		■			★	■	■	■
			■	★			■		■				■	★	■	■				■			★			☆	☆
			■				■		■				■	■	■	■			■			■		■	■		■
				■									■	■				■				■	■			■	■
						★													■				■			★	■
			■		■		■						■	★	■	■				■	■					■	■
			■				■						■	■		■				■	★		■	■	■	■	
			■				■						■	■	■						■		■			■	■
			■										■	■	■								■	■	■		■

HERBS & SPICES

One of the keys to good cooking is knowing how to use herbs and spices. For a novice cook, this can be difficult—with hundreds of seasonings to choose from, which ones will be most valuable for everyday use? These three pages take some of the mystery out of herbs and spices, offering a guide to the more common types. We list the available forms of each herb or spice, describe its flavor, and note which foods it enhances. But first, some definitions.

Herbs are nonwoody (herbaceous), low-growing shrubs or plants; they may be annuals, biennials, or perennials. Most are native to temperate climates. In general, only the leaves of these plants are used as seasonings, though some herbs—such as dill and coriander—also produce aromatic seeds used in cooking. In a few cases, just the seeds are used; caraway and poppy fall into this category.

Spices are generally derived from the bark, root, or fruit—not the leaves—of perennial plants and trees. For example, cinnamon is the bark of a tree, ginger the root of a tropical plant. Nutmeg is a fruit, mace the husk of the same fruit; pepper and allspice are both berries. Many spices are tropical in origin; most are used in both whole and ground form.

Allspice. Whole or ground; flavor and aroma like a combination of cinnamon, cloves, and nutmeg. *Compatible foods:* Ham, sweet potatoes, winter squash, sweet pickles and relishes, cakes, cookies

Anise. Seeds; sweet, licorice-like flavor. *Compatible foods:* Cookies, coffeecakes, breads, spicy meat dishes, cabbage salads, pickles

Basil. Fresh or dried leaves; spicy-sweet flavor, heady aroma. *Compatible foods:* Poultry; omelets; tomato-based soups, sauces, and pasta dishes; artichokes, eggplant, spinach, fresh tomatoes, zucchini; salad dressings

Bay leaves. Fresh or dried leaves; pungent flavor and aroma. *Compatible foods:* Meat loaf, stews, soups

Caraway. Seeds; bold, fresh, tangy flavor. *Compatible foods:* Cabbage and cucumber salads, carrots, green beans, potatoes, hearty meat dishes, dark breads

Cardamom. Whole seed pods or ground seeds; flowery-sweet flavor and aroma. *Compatible foods:* Pastries, coffeecakes, cookies, spicy meat dishes, fruit, coffee, punches

Cayenne. Ground; fiery-hot and spicy. *Compatible foods:* Mexican, Spanish, Indian, and Middle Eastern dishes

Celery seeds. Whole or ground; slightly bitter flavor, mildly sweet aroma. *Compatible foods:* Stews, vegetable dishes, soups, salads, poultry, breads

Chervil. Fresh or dried leaves; subtle, aromatic flavor with spicy overtones. *Compatible foods:* Salads, soups, sauces, egg and fish dishes

Chili powder. A blend of ground spices, usually including dried chiles, cumin, coriander, garlic, cloves, paprika, salt, oregano, black pepper, and turmeric; flavor ranges from mildly spicy to quite hot, depending on blend. *Compatible foods:* Chili, cheese dishes, corn, soups, Mexican sauces

Chinese five-spice. A blend of ground cloves, fennel, licorice root, cinnamon, and star anise; some brands also contain Szechuan peppercorns. Warm, pungent, spicy-sweet flavor. *Compatible foods:* Chinese dishes, roast pork

Chives. Fresh, frozen, or freeze-dried; mild, sweet, onionlike flavor. *Compatible foods:* Salmon, mild white fish, scrambled eggs, cheese dishes, chilled soups, baked potatoes, salads, salad dressings

Cilantro (coriander). Fresh or dried leaves, dried whole seeds, or ground. Very pungent, peppery flavor when fresh; sweet, faint lemon flavor when dried. *Compatible foods:* Leaves with Mexican and Chinese dishes, pork, duck, corn; ground with curries, Middle Eastern dishes

Cinnamon. Whole sticks or ground; sweet, spicy flavor. *Compatible foods:* Sweet potatoes, winter squash, fruit compote, custards, cakes, pies, cookies

Cloves. Whole or ground; strong, spicy-sweet flavor. *Compatible foods:* Ham, barbecue sauce, spaghetti sauce, pickles, relishes, cakes, cookies

Crushed red pepper. Flakes of crushed dried red chiles; hot, spicy flavor. *Compatible foods:* Pizza, spaghetti sauce, Middle Eastern and Indian dishes

Cumin. Whole or ground seeds; warm, musky, slightly sweet flavor. *Compatible foods:* Curries; Mexican, Middle Eastern, and Indian dishes

Curry powder. A blend of ground spices, usually including six or more of the following: cumin, coriander, turmeric, ginger, pepper, mace, cardamom, and cloves. Spicy-hot, sharp flavor. *Compatible foods:* Curries, salad dressings, dips, egg and cheese dishes

Dill. Fresh or dried leaves or dried whole seeds; leaves have delicate, refreshing flavor, seeds more pronounced flavor. *Compatible foods:* Salmon, shrimp, omelets, beets, cabbage, thin-skinned potatoes, cucumbers, vegetable salads, dips

Fennel. Seeds; sweet, mild licorice flavor. *Compatible foods:* Breads, spicy meat dishes, sausages, fish

Fines herbes. An herb blend, usually a combination of parsley, chervil, tarragon, and chives. *Compatible foods:* Salads, chilled soups, sauces, fish, egg dishes

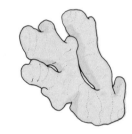

Ginger. Fresh root, crystallized, or ground; hot, spicy-sweet flavor. *Compatible foods:* Fresh with chicken, mild white fish, Asian dishes; crystallized in cookies or ice creams (or serve whole, as a confection); ground in pot roast, glazed carrots, winter squash, breads, cakes, cookies

Italian herb seasoning. A blend of herbs, usually including oregano, basil, marjoram, and thyme. *Compatible foods:* Italian dishes, meats and poultry, salad dressings, marinades

Mace. Ground; aromatic, spicy-sweet flavor, similar to nutmeg but more pungent. *Compatible foods:* Cakes, cookies, pies, fruit, custards

Marjoram. Fresh or dried (crumbled or ground) leaves; sweet, mild flavor. *Compatible foods:* Beef, veal, poultry, omelets, soufflés, vegetable soup, tomato-based soups and sauces, eggplant, summer squash, salad dressings

Mint. Fresh or dried leaves; sweet, fresh flavor. *Compatible foods:* Lamb, veal, fruit salads, carrots, peas, spinach, candies, jellies, iced beverages

Mustard. Whole black or white seeds, or ground; pungent flavor ranging from mild to hot. *Compatible foods:* Seeds in corned beef, sauerkraut, chutneys, relishes, salad dressings; ground in dressings, sauces, hearty meat dishes

Nutmeg. Whole or ground; sweet, aromatic flavor. *Compatible foods:* Ground beef, soufflés, cream-based pasta dishes, white sauce, spinach, custard, cakes, cookies

(Continued on next page)

Oregano. Fresh or dried (crumbled or ground) leaves; strong, aromatic flavor. *Compatible foods:* Grilled meats, stews, poultry stuffing; tomato-based soups, sauces, and pasta dishes; vegetable soups, bell peppers, salad dressings

Paprika. Ground; mild, warm, musky-sweet flavor. *Compatible foods:* Veal, chicken, fish, stews, cream soups, white sauce, vegetable or potato gratins, salad dressings

Parsley. Fresh or dried leaves; fresh, mild flavor. *Compatible foods:* All meats, fish, poultry; soups, stews, omelets, scrambled eggs, pasta dishes, fresh vegetables, salads (cabbage, pasta, potato), salad dressings

Pepper. Black or white (for red pepper, see Cayenne, page 16); whole, cracked, coarsely or finely ground. Warm, pungent flavor (white is milder and sweeter). *Compatible foods:* All meats, poultry, fish; soups, stews, eggs, pasta dishes, vegetables, salads, dressings, sauces

Pickling spice. A blend of whole spices, usually including mustard seeds, bay leaves, whole black and white peppercorns, dill seeds, red chiles, cinnamon, mace, allspice, coriander seeds, and sometimes others; strong, spicy flavor. *Compatible foods:* Pickles, preserved meats; also use as seasoning for vegetables, relishes, and sauces

Poppy seeds. Seeds; rich, nutty flavor. *Compatible foods:* Breads, cookies, cakes, pastries, salad dressings, dips and spreads

Poultry seasoning. An herb blend of sage, thyme, marjoram, summer savory, and sometimes rosemary or other herbs. *Compatible foods:* Poultry, stuffings, soups

Pumpkin pie spice. A blend of ground spices, usually cinnamon, cloves, nutmeg, and ginger; warm, spicy-sweet flavor. *Compatible foods:* Pumpkin pie, puddings, cookies, cakes

Rosemary. Fresh or dried leaves; bold, pungent flavor and aroma. *Compatible foods:* Chicken, lamb, meat marinades, vegetable soups, broccoli, peas, potatoes

Saffron. Ground or dried whole "threads"; earthy, bittersweet flavor. *Compatible foods:* Poultry, seafood, rice, breads, South American and Mediterranean-style dishes

Sage. Fresh or dried (crumbled or ground) leaves; bold flavor and aroma. *Compatible foods:* Veal, sausage, poultry, mild white fish, pork, game, poultry stuffings, lima beans, mushrooms, onions

Sesame seeds. Seeds; rich, nutty flavor. *Compatible foods:* Vegetables, breads, cookies, candies, salads, Middle Eastern and Asian dishes

Summer savory. Fresh or dried leaves; warm, grassy, delicately peppery flavor. *Compatible foods:* Legumes, vegetables, eggs, fish, poultry, meat dishes

Tarragon. Fresh or dried leaves; spicy, aromatic flavor. *Compatible foods:* Veal, lamb, chicken, mild white fish, crab, shrimp, eggs, soufflés, soups, asparagus, mushrooms, béarnaise sauce, salad dressings

Thyme. Fresh or dried (crumbled or ground) leaves; strong flavor, spicy aroma. *Compatible foods:* Beef, pork, poultry, mild white fish, vegetable soups, tomato-based soups and sauces, carrots, green beans, mushrooms, salad dressings

Turmeric. Ground; musky, bittersweet flavor and brilliant yellow color. *Compatible foods:* Indian dishes, pickles, relishes, salad dressings

NUTRITIVE VALUES

The importance of a wholesome diet in maintaining health and physical fitness is well known; almost everyone seems to be interested in limiting fat, cholesterol, or sodium, or in increasing dietary vitamins, iron, or calcium. The following pages will show you exactly what is present in a variety of foods (TR indicates a trace amount). This information is based on material in *Nutritive Value of Foods* (Home and Garden Bulletin Number 72), a publication of the United States Department of Agriculture.

As a reference, at right are the RDAs (Recommended Daily Dietary Allowances) established by the Food and Nutrition Board of the National Research Council. These amounts are considered adequate for the maintenance of good nutrition of healthy persons.

SEX-AGE CATEGORY	CALORIES	PROTEIN (grams)	VITAMIN A (international units)	THIAMIN (milligrams)	RIBOFLAVIN (milligrams)	NIACIN (milligrams)	VITAMIN C (milligrams)	CALCIUM (milligrams)	PHOSPHORUS (milligrams)	IRON (milligrams)
MALES (70″ tall, 154 lbs.)										
Ages 19–22	2900	56	5000	1.5	1.7	19	60	800	800	10
Ages 23–50	2700	56	5000	1.4	1.6	18	60	800	800	10
Ages 50 and over*	2400	56	5000	1.2	1.4	16	60	800	800	10
FEMALES (64″ tall, 120 lbs.)										
Ages 19–22	2100	44	4000	1.1	1.3	14	60	800	800	18
Ages 23–50	2000	44	4000	1.0	1.2	13	60	800	800	18
Ages 50 and over*	1800	44	4000	1.0	1.2	13	60	800	800	10

*After age 75, calorie requirement is 2050 for males and 1600 for females.

Note: Because exact recipes vary from brand to brand, the nutritional values of some purchased prepared foods (such as puddings, packaged baked goods, and so on) may differ from the values listed here. For precise information on a particular brand, consult the package label or write to the manufacturer.

FOOD	CALORIES	PROTEIN (grams)	TOTAL FAT (grams)	SATURATED FAT (grams)	CHOLESTEROL (milligrams)	CARBOHYDRATE (grams)	CALCIUM (milligrams)	IRON (milligrams)	SODIUM (milligrams)	VITAMIN A (international units)	THIAMIN (milligrams)	RIBOFLAVIN (milligrams)	NIACIN (milligrams)	VITAMIN C (milligrams)
ALMONDS, whole shelled (1 oz.)	165	6	15	1.4	0	6	75	1.0	3	0	0.06	0.22	1.0	TR
APPLE JUICE (1 cup)	115	TR	TR	TR	0	29	17	0.9	7	TR	0.05	0.04	0.2	2
APPLESAUCE, canned unsweetened (1 cup)	105	TR	TR	TR	0	28	7	0.3	5	70	0.03	0.06	0.5	3
APPLES, fresh, unpeeled (about 3 per lb.) (1 apple)	80	TR	TR	0.1	0	21	10	0.2	TR	70	0.02	0.02	0.1	8
APRICOT NECTAR (1 cup)	140	1	TR	TR	0	36	18	1.0	8	3300	0.02	0.04	0.7	2
APRICOTS, fresh (about 12 per lb.) (3 apricots)	50	1	TR	TR	0	12	15	0.6	1	2770	0.03	0.04	0.6	11
ARTICHOKES, globe, cooked (1 artichoke)	55	3	TR	TR	0	12	47	1.6	79	170	0.07	0.06	0.7	9
ASPARAGUS, fresh cooked (4 spears)	15	2	TR	TR	0	3	14	0.4	2	500	0.06	0.07	0.6	16
AVOCADOS, California (about 2 per lb.) (1 avocado)	305	4	30	4.5	0	12	19	2.0	21	1060	0.19	0.21	3.3	14
BACON, regular (3 slices)	110	6	9	3.3	16	TR	2	0.3	303	0	0.13	0.05	1.4	6

(Continued on next page)

FOOD	CALORIES	PROTEIN (grams)	TOTAL FAT (grams)	SATURATED FAT (grams)	CHOLESTEROL (milligrams)	CARBOHYDRATE (grams)	CALCIUM (milligrams)	IRON (milligrams)	SODIUM (milligrams)	VITAMIN A (international units)	THIAMIN (milligrams)	RIBOFLAVIN (milligrams)	NIACIN (milligrams)	VITAMIN C (milligrams)
BAGELS, plain or water, enriched (1 bagel)	200	7	2	0.3	0	38	29	1.8	245	0	0.26	0.20	2.4	0
BANANAS (about 2½ per lb.) (1 banana)	105	1	1	0.2	0	27	7	0.4	1	90	0.05	0.11	0.6	10
BEANS, black, dry, cooked (1 cup)	225	15	1	0.1	0	41	47	2.9	1	TR	0.43	0.05	0.9	0
BEANS, green, fresh, cooked (1 cup)	45	2	TR	0.1	0	10	58	1.6	4	830	0.09	0.12	0.8	12
BEANS, lima, dry, cooked (1 cup)	260	16	1	0.2	0	49	55	5.9	4	0	0.25	0.11	1.3	0
BEANS, pinto, dry, cooked (1 cup)	265	15	1	0.1	0	49	86	5.4	3	TR	0.33	0.16	0.7	0
BEEF, ground, lean (3-oz. patty)	230	21	16	6.2	74	0	9	1.8	65	TR	0.04	0.18	4.4	0
BEEF, relatively fat cut, braised, lean only (2.2 oz.)	170	19	9	3.9	66	0	8	2.3	44	TR	0.05	0.17	1.7	0
BEEF, relatively lean cut, braised, lean only (2.8 oz.)	175	25	8	2.7	75	0	4	2.7	40	TR	0.06	0.20	3.0	0
BEEF, roasted, relatively lean cut, lean only (2.6 oz.)	135	22	5	1.9	52	0	3	1.5	46	TR	0.07	0.13	2.8	0
BEEF, roasted, relatively fat cut, lean only (2.2 oz.)	150	17	9	3.6	49	0	5	1.7	45	TR	0.05	0.13	2.7	0
BEEF, steak, broiled, lean only (2.5 oz.)	150	22	6	2.6	64	0	8	2.4	48	TR	0.09	0.22	3.1	0
BEEF LIVER, fried (3 oz.)	185	23	7	2.5	410	7	9	5.3	90	30690	0.18	3.52	12.3	23
BEETS, fresh whole, cooked (2 2-inch beets)	30	1	TR	TR	0	7	11	0.6	49	10	0.03	0.01	0.3	6
BLACKBERRIES, fresh (1 cup)	75	1	1	0.2	0	18	46	0.8	TR	240	0.04	0.06	0.6	30
BLUEBERRIES, fresh (1 cup)	80	1	1	TR	0	20	9	0.2	9	150	0.07	0.07	0.5	19
BREAD, rye, light (1 slice)	65	2	1	0.2	0	12	20	0.7	175	0	0.10	0.08	0.8	0
BREAD, white, enriched (1 slice)	65	2	1	0.3	0	12	32	0.7	129	TR	0.12	0.08	0.9	TR
BREAD, whole wheat (1 slice)	70	3	1	0.4	0	13	20	1.0	180	TR	0.10	0.06	1.1	TR
BROCCOLI, fresh, cooked (1 cup)	45	5	TR	0.1	0	9	177	1.8	17	2180	0.13	0.32	1.2	97
BROWNIES WITH NUTS (1 brownie)	95	1	6	1.4	18	11	9	0.4	51	20	0.05	0.05	0.3	TR
BRUSSELS SPROUTS, fresh, cooked (1 cup)	60	4	1	0.2	0	13	56	1.9	33	1110	0.17	0.12	0.9	96
BUTTER, salted (1 tbsp.)	100	TR	11	7.1	31	TR	3	TR	116	430	TR	TR	TR	0
BUTTERMILK (1 cup)	100	8	2	1.3	9	12	285	0.1	257	80	0.08	0.38	0.1	2
CABBAGE, green, cooked (1 cup)	30	1	TR	TR	0	7	50	0.6	29	130	0.09	0.08	0.3	36
CABBAGE, green, raw shredded (1 cup)	15	1	TR	TR	0	4	33	0.4	13	90	0.04	0.02	0.2	33

FOOD	CALORIES	PROTEIN (grams)	TOTAL FAT (grams)	SATURATED FAT (grams)	CHOLESTEROL (milligrams)	CARBOHYDRATE (grams)	CALCIUM (milligrams)	IRON (milligrams)	SODIUM (milligrams)	VITAMIN A (international units)	THIAMIN (milligrams)	RIBOFLAVIN (milligrams)	NIACIN (milligrams)	VITAMIN C (milligrams)
CABBAGE, red, raw shredded (1 cup)	20	1	TR	TR	0	4	36	0.3	8	30	0.04	0.02	0.2	40
CAKE, yellow, with chocolate frosting (made from mix) (1/16 of 8- or 9-inch layer cake)	235	3	8	3.0	36	40	63	1.0	157	100	0.08	0.10	0.7	TR
CANDY, hard (1 oz.)	110	0	0	0.0	0	28	TR	0.1	7	0	0.10	0.00	0.0	0
CARAMELS, plain or chocolate (1 oz.)	115	1	3	2.2	1	22	42	0.4	64	TR	0.01	0.05	0.1	TR
CARROTS, fresh sliced, cooked (1 cup)	70	2	TR	0.1	0	16	48	1.0	103	38300	0.05	0.09	0.8	4
CARROTS, fresh, raw (1 carrot)	30	1	TR	TR	0	7	19	0.4	25	20250	0.07	0.04	0.7	7
CASHEW NUTS, salted, roasted in oil (1 oz.)	165	5	14	2.7	0	8	12	1.2	177	0	0.12	0.05	0.5	0
CATSUP (1 tbsp.)	15	TR	TR	TR	0	4	3	0.1	156	210	0.01	0.01	0.2	2
CAULIFLOWER, fresh, cooked (1 cup)	30	2	TR	TR	0	6	34	0.5	8	20	0.08	0.07	0.7	69
CAULIFLOWER, fresh, raw (1 cup)	25	2	TR	TR	0	5	29	0.6	15	20	0.08	0.06	0.6	72
CHEESE, blue (1 oz.)	100	6	8	5.3	21	1	150	0.1	396	200	0.01	0.11	0.3	0
CHEESE, Camembert (1⅓ oz.)	115	8	9	5.8	27	TR	147	0.1	320	350	0.01	0.19	0.2	0
CHEESE, Cheddar (1 oz.)	115	7	9	6.0	30	TR	204	0.2	176	300	0.01	0.11	TR	0
CHEESE, cottage, creamed (4% fat), small curd (1 cup)	215	26	9	6.0	31	6	126	0.3	850	340	0.04	0.34	0.3	TR
CHEESE, cottage, lowfat (2% fat) (1 cup)	205	31	4	2.8	19	8	155	0.4	918	160	0.05	0.42	0.3	TR
CHEESE, cream (1 oz.)	100	2	10	6.2	31	1	23	0.3	84	400	TR	0.06	TR	0
CHEESE, feta (1 oz.)	75	4	6	4.2	25	1	140	0.2	316	130	0.04	0.24	0.3	0
CHEESE, mozzarella, part skim (1 oz.)	80	8	5	3.1	15	1	207	0.1	150	180	0.01	0.10	TR	0
CHEESE, Münster (1 oz.)	105	7	9	5.4	27	TR	203	0.1	178	320	TR	0.09	TR	0
CHEESE, Parmesan, grated (1 tbsp.)	25	2	2	1.0	4	TR	69	TR	93	40	TR	0.02	TR	0
CHEESE, pasteurized process, American (1 oz.)	105	6	9	5.6	27	TR	174	0.1	406	340	0.01	0.10	TR	0
CHEESE, ricotta, part skim (1 cup)	340	28	19	12.1	76	13	669	1.1	307	1060	0.05	0.46	0.2	0
CHEESE, Swiss (1 oz.)	105	8	8	5.0	26	1	272	TR	74	240	0.01	0.10	TR	0
CHERRIES, sweet, fresh (10 cherries)	50	1	1	0.1	0	11	10	0.3	TR	150	0.03	0.04	0.3	5
CHICKEN, canned boneless (5 oz.)	235	31	11	3.1	88	0	20	2.2	714	170	0.02	0.18	9.0	3
CHICKEN, cooked light and dark meat, chopped or diced (1 cup)	250	38	9	2.6	116	0	20	1.6	98	70	0.07	0.23	8.6	0
CHICKEN, drumstick, roasted, meat only (2.9 oz. with bones and skin)	75	12	2	0.7	41	0	5	0.6	42	30	0.03	0.10	2.7	0

(Continued on next page)

FOOD	CALORIES	PROTEIN (grams)	TOTAL FAT (grams)	SATURATED FAT (grams)	CHOLESTEROL (milligrams)	CARBOHYDRATE (grams)	CALCIUM (milligrams)	IRON (milligrams)	SODIUM (milligrams)	VITAMIN A (international units)	THIAMIN (milligrams)	RIBOFLAVIN (milligrams)	NIACIN (milligrams)	VITAMIN C (milligrams)
CHICKEN, half breast, roasted, meat only (4.2 oz. with bones and skin)	140	27	3	0.9	73	0	13	0.9	64	20	0.06	0.10	11.8	0
CHICKEN LIVER (1 liver)	30	5	1	0.4	126	TR	3	1.7	10	3270	0.03	0.35	0.9	3
CHOCOLATE, milk, plain (1 oz.)	145	2	9	5.4	6	16	50	0.4	23	30	0.02	0.10	0.1	TR
CHOCOLATE, semisweet chips (6 oz.)	860	7	61	36.2	0	97	51	5.8	24	30	0.10	0.14	0.9	TR
CHOCOLATE, sweet (dark) (1 oz.)	150	1	10	5.9	0	16	7	0.6	5	10	0.01	0.04	0.1	TR
CLAMS, raw, meat only (3 oz.)	65	11	1	0.3	43	2	59	2.6	102	90	0.09	0.15	1.1	9
COCONUT, dried, sweetened shredded (1 cup)	470	3	33	29.3	0	44	14	1.8	244	0	0.03	0.02	0.4	1
COFFEE (brewed) (6 oz.)	TR	TR	TR	TR	0	TR	4	TR	2	0	0.00	0.02	0.4	0
COLA (12 oz.)	160	0	0	0.0	0	41	11	0.2	18	0	0.00	0.00	0.0	0
COOKIES, chocolate chip (4 cookies)	185	2	11	3.9	18	26	13	1.0	82	20	0.06	0.06	0.6	0
COOKIES, shortbread (4 small cookies)	155	2	8	2.9	27	20	13	0.8	123	30	0.10	0.09	0.9	0
CORN, fresh, cooked (1 ear)	85	3	1	0.2	0	19	2	0.5	13	170	0.17	0.06	1.2	5
CORN, frozen whole-kernel, cooked (1 cup)	135	5	TR	TR	0	34	3	0.5	8	410	0.11	0.12	2.1	4
CORN CHIPS (1 oz.)	155	2	9	1.4	0	16	35	0.5	233	110	0.04	0.05	0.4	1
CORNMEAL, degermed, enriched (1 cup)	500	,11	2	0.2	0	108	8	5.9	1	610	0.61	0.36	4.8	0
CRABMEAT, canned (1 cup)	135	23	3	0.5	135	1	61	1.1	1350	50	0.11	0.11	2.6	0
CRACKERS, graham (2½-inch square) (2 crackers)	60	1	1	0.4	0	11	6	0.4	86	0	0.02	0.03	0.6	0
CRACKERS, saltine (4 crackers)	50	1	1	0.5	4	9	3	0.5	165	0	0.06	0.05	0.6	0
CRANBERRY JUICE COCKTAIL (1 cup)	145	TR	TR	TR	0	38	8	0.4	10	10	0.01	0.04	0.1	108
CREAM, light (1 tbsp.)	30	TR	3	1.8	10	1	14	TR	6	110	TR	0.02	TR	TR
CREAM, sour (1 tbsp.)	25	TR	3	1.6	5	1	14	TR	6	90	TR	0.02	TR	TR
CREAM, whipping, unwhipped (1 tbsp.)	50	TR	6	3.5	21	TR	10	TR	6	220	TR	0.02	TR	TR
CROISSANTS, plain (1 croissant)	235	5	12	3.5	13	27	20	2.1	452	50	0.17	0.13	1.3	0
CUCUMBER, unpeeled (6 slices)	5	TR	TR	TR	0	1	4	0.1	1	10	0.01	0.01	0.1	1
DATES, whole pitted (10 dates)	230	2	TR	0.1	0	61	27	1.0	2	40	0.07	0.08	1.8	0
DOUGHNUTS, cake type (1 doughnut)	210	3	12	2.8	20	24	22	1.0	192	20	0.12	0.12	1.1	TR
DOUGHNUTS, raised, glazed (1 doughnut)	235	4	13	5.2	21	26	17	1.4	222	TR	0.28	0.12	1.8	0

FOOD	CALORIES	PROTEIN (grams)	TOTAL FAT (grams)	SATURATED FAT (grams)	CHOLESTEROL (milligrams)	CARBOHYDRATE (grams)	CALCIUM (milligrams)	IRON (milligrams)	SODIUM (milligrams)	VITAMIN A (international units)	THIAMIN (milligrams)	RIBOFLAVIN (milligrams)	NIACIN (milligrams)	VITAMIN C (milligrams)
DUCK, roasted, meat only (½ duck)	445	52	25	9.2	197	0	27	6.0	144	170	0.57	1.04	11.3	0
EGGPLANT, cooked (1 cup)	25	1	TR	TR	0	6	6	0.3	3	60	0.07	0.02	0.6	1
EGGS, large (24 oz. per dozen), whole (1 egg)	80	6	6	1.7	274	1	28	1.0	69	260	0.04	0.15	TR	0
ENGLISH MUFFINS, plain (1 muffin)	140	5	1	0.3	0	27	96	1.7	378	0	0.26	0.19	2.2	0
FLOUNDER OR SOLE, baked with butter and lemon juice (3 oz.)	120	16	6	3.2	68	TR	13	0.3	145	210	0.05	0.08	1.6	1
FLOUR, all-purpose, sifted (1 cup)	420	12	1	0.2	0	88	18	5.1	2	0	0.73	0.46	6.1	0
FLOUR, whole wheat, stirred (1 cup)	400	16	2	0.3	0	85	49	5.2	4	0	0.66	0.14	5.2	0
FRANKFURTER, cooked (1 frankfurter)	145	5	13	4.8	23	1	5	0.5	504	0	0.09	0.05	1.2	12
FRENCH TOAST, homemade (1 slice)	155	6	7	1.6	112	17	72	1.3	257	110	0.12	0.16	1.0	TR
FUDGE, chocolate, plain (1 oz.)	115	1	3	2.1	1	21	22	0.3	54	TR	0.01	0.03	0.1	TR
GINGER ALE (12 oz.)	125	0	0	0.0	0	32	11	0.1	29	0	0.00	0.00	0.0	0
GINGERBREAD (⅑ of 8-inch-square cake)	175	2	4	1.1	1	32	57	1.2	192	0	0.09	0.11	0.8	TR
GRAPE JUICE (1 cup)	155	1	TR	0.1	0	38	23	0.6	8	20	0.07	0.09	0.7	TR
GRAPEFRUIT, fresh (17 oz. whole) (½ grapefruit)	40	1	TR	TR	0	10	14	0.1	TR	10	0.04	0.02	0.3	41
GRAPEFRUIT JUICE, from concentrate (1 cup)	100	1	TR	TR	0	24	20	0.3	2	20	0.10	0.05	0.5	83
GRAPES (10 grapes)	40	TR	TR	0.1	0	10	6	0.1	1	40	0.05	0.03	0.2	6
GUMDROPS (1 oz.)	100	TR	TR	TR	0	25	2	0.1	10	0	0.00	TR	TR	0
HALF-AND-HALF (1 tbsp.)	20	TR	2	1.1	6	1	16	TR	6	70	0.01	0.02	TR	TR
HALIBUT, broiled with butter and lemon juice (3 oz.)	140	20	6	3.3	62	TR	14	0.7	103	610	0.06	0.07	7.7	1
HAM, canned, roasted (3 oz.)	140	18	7	2.4	35	TR	6	0.9	908	0	0.82	0.21	4.3	19
HAM, fresh, roasted, lean only (2.5 oz.)	160	20	8	2.7	68	0	5	0.8	46	10	0.50	0.25	3.6	TR
HERRING, pickled (3 oz.)	190	17	13	4.3	85	0	29	0.9	850	110	0.04	0.18	2.8	0
HONEY, strained or extracted (1 tbsp.)	65	TR	0	0.0	0	17	1	0.1	1	0	TR	0.01	0.1	TR
ICE CREAM, vanilla (about 11% fat) (1 cup)	270	5	14	8.9	59	32	176	0.1	116	540	0.05	0.33	0.1	1
ICE MILK, vanilla (about 4% fat) (1 cup)	185	5	6	3.5	18	29	176	0.2	105	210	0.08	0.35	0.1	1
JAMS (1 tbsp.)	55	TR	TR	0.0	0	14	4	0.2	2	TR	TR	0.01	TR	TR
JELLIES (1 tbsp.)	50	TR	TR	TR	0	13	2	0.1	5	TR	TR	0.01	TR	1
JELLY BEANS (1 oz.)	105	TR	TR	TR	0	26	1	0.3	7	0	0.00	TR	TR	0

(Continued on next page)

FOOD	CALORIES	PROTEIN (grams)	TOTAL FAT (grams)	SATURATED FAT (grams)	CHOLESTEROL (milligrams)	CARBOHYDRATE (grams)	CALCIUM (milligrams)	IRON (milligrams)	SODIUM (milligrams)	VITAMIN A (international units)	THIAMIN (milligrams)	RIBOFLAVIN (milligrams)	NIACIN (milligrams)	VITAMIN C (milligrams)
KALE, fresh, cooked (1 cup)	40	2	1	0.1	0	7	94	1.2	30	9620	0.07	0.09	0.7	53
KIWI FRUIT (about 5 per lb.), peeled (1 kiwi fruit)	45	1	TR	TR	0	11	20	0.3	4	130	0.02	0.04	0.4	74
KOHLRABI, fresh, cooked (1 cup)	50	3	TR	TR	0	11	41	0.7	35	60	0.07	0.03	0.6	89
LAMB, arm chops, braised, lean only (1.7 oz.)	135	17	7	2.9	59	0	12	1.3	36	TR	0.03	0.13	3.0	0
LAMB, leg, roasted, lean only (2.6 oz.)	140	20	6	2.4	65	0	6	1.5	50	TR	0.08	0.20	4.6	0
LAMB, loin chops, broiled, lean only (2.3 oz.)	140	19	6	2.6	60	0	12	1.3	54	TR	0.08	0.18	4.4	0
LEMON JUICE, fresh (1 cup)	60	1	TR	TR	0	21	17	0.1	2	50	0.07	0.02	0.2	112
LEMONADE, from concentrate (6 oz.)	80	TR	TR	TR	0	21	2	0.1	1	10	0.01	0.02	0.2	13
LENTILS, dry, cooked (1 cup)	215	16	1	0.1	0	38	50	4.2	26	40	0.14	0.12	1.2	0
LETTUCE, green leaf, red leaf, romaine (1 cup)	10	1	TR	TR	0	2	38	0.8	5	1060	0.03	0.04	0.2	10
LETTUCE, iceberg (1 cup)	5	1	TR	TR	0	1	10	0.3	5	180	0.03	0.02	0.1	2
LIQUOR (gin, rum, vodka, whiskey), 80 proof (1½ oz.)	95	0	0	0.0	0	TR	TR	TR	TR	0	TR	TR	TR	0
MACARONI, cooked (1 cup)	190	7	1	0.1	0	39	14	2.1	1	0	0.23	0.13	1.8	0
MANGOES (about 1½ per lb.), peeled (1 mango)	135	1	1	0.1	0	35	21	0.3	4	8060	0.12	0.12	1.2	57
MARGARINE, imitation, soft (1 tbsp.)	50	TR	5	1.1	0	TR	2	0.0	134	460	TR	TR	TR	TR
MARGARINE, regular, hard (1 tbsp.)	100	TR	11	2.2	0	TR	4	TR	132	460	TR	0.01	TR	TR
MARGARINE, regular, soft (1 tbsp.)	100	TR	11	1.9	0	TR	4	0.0	151	460	TR	TR	TR	TR
MARSHMALLOWS (1 oz.)	90	1	0	0.0	0	23	1	0.5	25	0	0.00	TR	TR	0
MELON, cantaloupe (2⅓-lb.) (½ melon)	95	2	1	0.1	0	22	29	0.6	24	8610	0.10	0.06	1.5	113
MELON, honeydew (5¼-lb. whole) (1/10 melon)	45	1	TR	TR	0	12	8	0.1	13	50	0.10	0.02	0.8	32
MILK, chocolate lowfat (2% fat) (1 cup)	180	8	5	3.1	17	26	284	0.6	151	500	0.09	0.41	0.3	2
MILK, condensed, sweetened (1 cup)	980	24	27	16.8	104	166	868	0.6	389	1000	0.28	1.27	0.6	8
MILK, dried, nonfat instant (1 envelope, 3.2 oz.)	325	32	1	0.4	17	47	1120	0.3	499	2160	0.38	1.59	0.8	5
MILK, evaporated (whole) (1 cup)	340	17	19	11.6	74	25	657	0.5	267	610	0.12	0.80	0.5	5
MILK, lowfat (2% fat) (1 cup)	120	8	5	2.9	18	12	297	0.1	122	500	0.10	0.40	0.2	2

FOOD	CALORIES	PROTEIN (grams)	TOTAL FAT (grams)	SATURATED FAT (grams)	CHOLESTEROL (milligrams)	CARBOHYDRATE (grams)	CALCIUM (milligrams)	IRON (milligrams)	SODIUM (milligrams)	VITAMIN A (international units)	THIAMIN (milligrams)	RIBOFLAVIN (milligrams)	NIACIN (milligrams)	VITAMIN C (milligrams)
MILK, nonfat (1 cup)	85	8	TR	0.3	4	12	302	0.1	126	500	0.09	0.34	0.2	2
MILK, whole (3.3% fat) (1 cup)	150	8	8	5.1	33	11	291	0.1	120	310	0.09	0.40	0.2	2
MOLASSES (2 tbsp.)	85	0	0	0.0	0	22	274	10.1	38	0	0.04	0.08	0.8	0
MUFFINS, bran (1 muffin)	125	3	6	1.4	24	19	60	1.4	189	230	0.11	0.13	1.3	3
MUSHROOMS, fresh, cooked (1 cup)	40	3	1	0.1	0	8	9	2.7	3	0	0.11	0.47	7.0	6
MUSHROOMS, fresh, raw sliced or chopped (1 cup)	20	1	TR	TR	0	3	4	0.9	3	0	0.07	0.31	2.9	2
MUSTARD, prepared, yellow (1 tsp.)	5	TR	TR	TR	0	TR	4	0.1	63	0	TR	0.01	TR	TR
NECTARINES (about 3 per lb.) (1 nectarine)	65	1	1	0.1	0	16	7	0.2	TR	1000	0.02	0.06	1.3	7
NOODLES, egg, cooked (1 cup)	200	7	2	0.5	50	37	16	2.6	3	110	0.22	0.13	1.9	0
OATMEAL, regular, quick-cooking or instant (nonfortified) (1 cup)	145	6	2	0.4	0	25	19	1.6	2	40	0.26	0.05	0.3	0
OIL, vegetable (1 tbsp.)	125	0	14	1.8	0	0	0	0.0	0	0	0.00	0.00	0.0	0
OLIVES, green (4 medium)	15	TR	2	0.2	0	TR	8	0.2	312	40	TR	TR	TR	0
OLIVES, ripe, pitted (2 large)	15	TR	2	0.3	0	TR	10	0.2	68	10	TR	TR	TR	0
ONIONS, green, without tops (6 onions)	10	1	TR	TR	0	2	18	0.6	1	1500	0.02	0.04	0.1	14
ONIONS, dry, raw chopped or sliced (1 cup)	55	2	TR	0.1	0	12	40	0.6	3	0	0.10	0.02	0.2	13
ORANGE JUICE, fresh (1 cup)	110	2	TR	0.1	0	26	27	0.5	2	500	0.22	0.07	1.0	124
ORANGE JUICE, from concentrate (1 cup)	110	2	TR	TR	0	27	22	0.2	2	190	0.20	0.04	0.5	97
ORANGES (about 2½ per lb.) (1 orange)	60	1	TR	TR	0	15	52	0.1	TR	270	0.11	0.05	0.4	70
OYSTERS, raw, meat only (1 cup)	160	20	4	1.4	120	8	226	15.6	175	740	0.34	0.43	6.0	24
PANCAKES, plain (1 4-inch pancake)	60	2	2	0.5	16	8	36	0.7	160	30	0.09	0.12	0.8	TR
PEACHES, fresh (about 4 per lb.) (1 peach)	35	1	TR	TR	0	10	4	0.1	TR	470	0.01	0.04	0.9	6
PEANUT BUTTER (1 tbsp.)	95	5	8	1.4	0	3	5	0.3	75	0	0.02	0.02	2.2	0
PEANUTS, salted, roasted in oil (1 oz.)	165	8	14	1.9	0	5	24	0.5	122	0	0.08	0.03	4.2	0
PEARS, fresh, Bartlett (about 2½ per lb.) (1 pear)	100	1	1	TR	0	25	18	0.4	TR	30	0.03	0.07	0.2	7
PEAS, edible-pod, fresh, cooked (1 cup)	65	5	TR	0.1	0	11	67	3.2	6	210	0.20	0.12	0.9	77
PEAS, green, frozen, cooked (1 cup)	125	8	TR	0.1	0	23	38	2.5	139	1070	0.45	0.16	2.4	16
PECANS, halves (1 oz.)	190	2	19	1.5	0	5	10	0.6	TR	40	0.24	0.04	0.3	1

(Continued on next page)

FOOD	CALORIES	PROTEIN (grams)	TOTAL FAT (grams)	SATURATED FAT (grams)	CHOLESTEROL (milligrams)	CARBOHYDRATE (grams)	CALCIUM (milligrams)	IRON (milligrams)	SODIUM (milligrams)	VITAMIN A (international units)	THIAMIN (milligrams)	RIBOFLAVIN (milligrams)	NIACIN (milligrams)	VITAMIN C (milligrams)
PEPPERS, bell (1 pepper)	20	1	TR	TR	0	4	4	0.9	2	390	0.06	0.04	0.4	95
PICKLES, dill (1 medium)	5	TR	TR	TR	0	1	17	0.7	928	70	TR	0.01	TR	4
PICKLES, sweet (1 small)	20	TR	TR	TR	0	5	2	0.2	107	10	TR	TR	TR	1
PIE, apple (9-inch) (⅙ of pie)	405	3	18	4.6	0	60	13	1.6	476	50	0.17	0.13	1.6	2
PIE, cream (9-inch) (⅙ of pie)	455	3	23	15.0	8	59	46	1.1	369	210	0.06	0.15	1.1	0
PINEAPPLE JUICE, canned unsweetened (1 cup)	140	1	TR	TR	0	34	43	0.7	3	10	0.14	0.06	0.6	27
PINEAPPLE, canned in juice, chunks or tidbits (1 cup)	150	1	TR	TR	0	39	35	0.7	3	100	0.24	0.05	0.7	24
PINEAPPLE, canned in juice, slices (1 slice)	35	TR	TR	TR	0	9	8	0.2	1	20	0.06	0.01	0.2	6
PINEAPPLE, canned in syrup, chunks or tidbits (1 cup)	200	1	TR	TR	0	52	36	1.0	3	40	0.23	0.06	0.7	19
PINEAPPLE, fresh, diced (1 cup)	75	1	1	TR	0	19	11	0.6	2	40	0.14	0.06	0.7	24
PLUMS, fresh (about 6½ per lb.) (1 plum)	35	1	TR	TR	0	9	3	0.1	TR	210	0.03	0.06	0.3	6
POPCORN, popped in oil, salted (1 cup)	55	1	3	0.5	0	6	3	0.3	86	20	0.01	0.02	0.1	0
PORK, loin chops, pan-fried, lean only (2.4 oz.)	180	19	11	3.7	72	0	3	0.7	57	10	0.84	0.22	4.0	TR
PORK, ribs, roasted, lean only (2.5 oz.)	175	20	10	3.4	56	0	8	0.7	33	10	0.45	0.22	3.8	TR
PORK, shoulder cut, braised, lean only (2.4 oz.)	165	22	8	2.8	76	0	5	1.3	68	10	0.40	0.24	4.0	TR
POTATO CHIPS (10 chips)	105	1	7	1.8	0	10	5	0.2	94	0	0.03	TR	0.8	8
POTATOES, russet (about 2 per lb.), baked, with skin (1 potato)	220	5	TR	0.1	0	51	20	2.7	16	0	0.22	0.07	3.3	26
POTATOES, sweet (about 2½ per lb.), baked in skin, peeled (1 potato)	115	2	TR	TR	0	28	32	0.5	11	24880	0.08	0.14	0.7	28
POTATOES, thin-skinned (about 3 per lb.), boiled, peeled (1 potato)	120	3	TR	TR	0	27	7	0.4	5	0	0.14	0.03	2.0	18
PRESERVES (1 tbsp.)	55	TR	TR	0.0	0	14	4	0.2	2	TR	TR	0.01	TR	TR
PRETZELS, thin twisted (10 pretzels)	240	6	2	0.4	0	48	16	1.2	966	0	0.19	0.15	2.6	0
PRUNE JUICE (1 cup)	180	2	TR	TR	0	45	31	3.0	10	10	0.04	0.18	2.0	10
PRUNES, cooked (1 cup)	225	2	TR	TR	0	60	49	2.4	4	650	0.05	0.21	1.5	6
PRUNES, dried (5 large prunes)	115	1	TR	TR	0	31	25	1.2	2	970	0.04	0.08	1.0	2
PUDDING, chocolate, cooked (½ cup)	150	4	4	2.4	15	25	146	0.2	167	140	0.05	0.20	0.1	1

FOOD	CALORIES	PROTEIN (grams)	TOTAL FAT (grams)	SATURATED FAT (grams)	CHOLESTEROL (milligrams)	CARBOHYDRATE (grams)	CALCIUM (milligrams)	IRON (milligrams)	SODIUM (milligrams)	VITAMIN A (international units)	THIAMIN (milligrams)	RIBOFLAVIN (milligrams)	NIACIN (milligrams)	VITAMIN C (milligrams)
PUDDING, vanilla, cooked (½ cup)	145	4	4	2.3	15	25	132	0.1	178	140	0.04	0.18	0.1	1
RAISINS, seedless (1 cup)	435	5	1	0.2	0	115	71	3.0	17	10	0.23	0.13	1.2	5
RASPBERRIES, fresh (1 cup)	60	1	1	TR	0	14	27	0.7	TR	160	0.04	0.11	1.1	31
RICE, brown, cooked (1 cup)	230	5	1	0.3	0	50	23	1.0	0	0	0.18	0.04	2.7	0
RICE, white, enriched, cooked (1 cup)	225	4	TR	0.1	0	50	21	1.8	0	0	0.23	0.02	2.1	0
ROLLS, frankfurter or hamburger (1 roll)	115	3	2	0.5	TR	20	54	1.2	241	TR	0.20	0.13	1.6	TR
ROLLS, hard (1 roll)	155	5	2	0.4	TR	30	24	1.4	313	0	0.20	0.12	1.7	0
ROOT BEER (12 oz.)	165	0	0	0.0	0	42	15	0.2	48	0	0.00	0.00	0.0	0
SALAMI, dry (2 thin slices)	85	5	7	2.4	16	1	2	0.3	372	0	0.12	0.06	1.0	5
SALMON, baked (red) (3 oz.)	140	21	5	1.2	60	0	26	0.5	55	290	0.18	0.14	5.5	0
SALMON, canned (pink), solids and liquid (3 oz.)	120	17	5	0.9	34	0	167	0.7	443	60	0.03	0.15	6.8	0
SALMON, smoked (3 oz.)	150	18	8	2.6	51	0	12	0.8	1700	260	0.17	0.17	6.8	0
SARDINES, canned in oil, drained (3 oz.)	175	20	9	2.1	85	0	371	2.6	425	190	0.03	0.17	4.6	0
SAUCE, soy (1 tbsp.)	10	2	0	0.0	0	2	3	0.5	1029	0	0.01	0.02	0.6	0
SAUSAGE, bologna (2 oz.)	180	7	16	6.1	31	2	7	0.9	581	0	0.10	0.08	1.5	12
SAUSAGE, braunschweiger (2 oz.)	205	8	18	6.2	89	2	5	5.3	652	8010	0.14	0.87	4.8	6
SAUSAGE, brown-and-serve, cooked (1 link)	50	2	5	1.7	9	TR	1	0.1	105	0	0.05	0.02	0.4	0
SHERBET (about 2% fat) (1 cup)	270	2	4	2.4	14	59	103	0.3	88	190	0.03	0.09	0.1	4
SHRIMP, canned, drained (3 oz.)	100	21	1	0.2	128	1	98	1.4	1955	50	0.01	0.03	1.5	0
SOYBEANS, dry, cooked (1 cup)	235	20	10	1.3	0	19	131	4.9	4	50	0.38	0.16	1.1	0
SPAGHETTI, cooked (1 cup)	190	7	1	0.1	0	39	14	2.0	1	0	0.23	0.13	1.8	0
SPINACH, fresh, cooked (1 cup)	40	5	TR	0.1	0	7	245	6.4	126	14740	0.17	0.42	0.9	18
SPINACH, fresh, raw chopped (1 cup)	10	2	TR	TR	0	2	54	1.5	43	3690	0.04	0.10	0.4	15
SQUASH, summer (all varieties), fresh, cooked (1 cup)	35	2	1	0.1	0	8	49	0.6	2	520	0.08	0.07	0.9	10
SQUASH, winter (all varieties), fresh, cooked (1 cup)	80	2	1	0.3	0	18	29	0.7	2	7290	0.17	0.05	1.4	20
STRAWBERRIES, fresh (1 cup)	45	1	1	TR	0	10	21	0.6	1	40	0.03	0.10	0.3	84
SUGAR, brown (1 cup)	820	0	0	0.0	0	212	187	4.8	97	0	0.02	0.07	0.2	0

(Continued on next page)

FOOD	CALORIES	PROTEIN (grams)	TOTAL FAT (grams)	SATURATED FAT (grams)	CHOLESTEROL (milligrams)	CARBOHYDRATE (grams)	CALCIUM (milligrams)	IRON (milligrams)	SODIUM (milligrams)	VITAMIN A (international units)	THIAMIN (milligrams)	RIBOFLAVIN (milligrams)	NIACIN (milligrams)	VITAMIN C (milligrams)
SUGAR, granulated (1 tbsp.)	45	0	0	0.0	0	12	TR	TR	TR	0	0.00	0.00	0.0	0
SUGAR, powdered, sifted (1 cup)	385	0	0	0.0	0	100	1	TR	2	0	0.00	0.00	0.0	0
SYRUP, chocolate-flavored (2 tbsp.)	85	1	TR	0.2	0	22	6	0.8	36	TR	TR	0.02	0.1	0
SYRUP, maple (2 tbsp.)	122	0	0	0.0	0	32	1	TR	19	0	0.00	0.00	0.0	0
TANGERINES (about 4 per·lb.) (1 tangerine)	35	1	TR	TR	0	9	12	0.1	1	770	0.09	0.02	0.1	26
TEA (brewed) (8 oz.)	TR	TR	TR	TR	0	TR	0	TR	1	0	0.00	0.03	TR	0
TOFU (bean curd) (2½- by 2¾- by 1-inch piece)	85	9	5	0.7	0	3	108	2.3	8	0	0.07	0.04	0.1	0
TOMATO JUICE, canned (1 cup)	40	2	TR	TR	0	10	22	1.4	881	1360	0.11	0.08	1.6	45
TOMATOES, canned (1 cup)	50	2	1	0.1	0	10	62	1.5	391	1450	0.11	0.07	1.8	36
TOMATOES, fresh (1 small tomato, about 4 oz.)	25	1	TR	TR	0	5	9	0.6	10	1390	0.07	0.06	0.7	22
TORTILLAS, corn (1 tortilla)	65	2	1	0.1	0	13	42	0.6	1	80	0.05	0.03	0.4	0
TROUT, broiled with butter and lemon juice (3 oz.)	175	21	9	4.1	71	TR	26	1.0	122	230	0.07	0.07	2.3	1
TUNA, chunk light, in oil, drained (3 oz.)	165	24	7	1.4	55	0	7	1.6	303	70	0.04	0.09	10.1	0
TUNA, solid white, in water, drained (3 oz.)	135	30	1	0.3	48	0	17	0.6	468	110	0.03	0.10	13.4	0
TURKEY, cooked light and dark meat, chopped or diced (1 cup)	240	41	7	2.3	106	0	35	2.5	98	0	0.09	0.25	7.6	0
TURKEY, dark meat, roasted, meat only, each piece 2½ by 1⅝ by ¼ inch (4 pieces)	160	24	6	2.1	72	0	27	2.0	67	0	0.05	0.21	3.1	0
TURKEY, light meat, roasted, meat only, each piece 4 by 2 by ¼ inch (2 pieces)	135	25	3	0.9	59	0	16	1.1	54	0	0.05	0.11	5.8	0
VEAL, cutlet, braised or broiled (3 oz.)	185	23	9	4.1	109	0	9	0.8	56	TR	0.06	0.21	4.6	0
VEAL, roasted (rib) (3 oz.)	230	23	14	6.0	109	0	10	0.7	57	TR	0.11	0.26	6.6	0
WALNUTS, English, pieces (1 cup)	770	17	74	6.7	0	22	113	2.9	12	150	0.46	0.18	1.3	4
WATERMELON (1 wedge, 4 by 8 inches)	155	3	2	0.3	0	35	39	0.8	10	1760	0.39	0.10	1.0	46
WINE, red table (3½ oz.)	75	TR	0	0.0	0	3	8	0.4	5	*	0.00	0.03	0.1	0
WINE, white table (3½ oz.)	80	TR	0	0.0	0	3	9	0.3	5	*	0.00	0.01	0.1	0
YOGURT, lowfat, fruit-flavored (8 oz.)	230	10	2	1.6	10	43	345	0.2	133	100	0.08	0.40	0.2	1
YOGURT, lowfat, plain (8 oz.)	145	12	4	2.3	14	16	415	0.2	159	150	0.10	0.49	0.3	2

*Value not determined.

GLOSSARY OF COOKING TERMS

Acidulated water: Water to which vinegar or lemon juice has been added; used to prevent discoloration and darkening of certain foods.

Al dente: Italian term used to describe pasta cooked until tender but still firm to the bite.

Au jus: French term meaning served in natural unthickened meat juices (from roasting).

Bake: To cook, covered or uncovered, by dry heat (usually in an oven). When applied to meats and poultry cooked uncovered, the process is called roasting.

Bake blind: To bake a pastry shell empty, without a filling.

Baste: To brush or spoon pan drippings, other fat, or a liquid mixture over food as it cooks, to keep the surface moist and add flavor.

Batter: A semiliquid mixture (containing flour and other ingredients) that can be dropped from a spoon or poured.

Beat: To stir or mix rapidly, adding air with a quick, even, circular motion to make a mixture smooth, light, or fluffy. When using a spoon or wire whisk, lift mixture up and over with each stroke.

Blanch: To immerse food briefly in boiling water, either to help loosen the skin or to precook briefly to set color and flavor.

Blend: To thoroughly combine two or more ingredients.

Boil: To cook liquid rapidly so that bubbles constantly rise and break on the surface. To cook food in boiling liquid.

Bone: To remove bones from meat, poultry, or fish.

Bouquet garni: Bundle of several herbs tied into cheesecloth; used to flavor soups and stews.

Braise: To cook slowly in liquid in a covered pan or casserole. Food may or may not be browned first in a small amount of fat.

Bread: To coat with bread or cracker crumbs before cooking, usually after first dipping food into egg or other liquid so crumbs will adhere.

Broil: To cook below direct heat in the broiler of an electric or gas range.

Broth: Liquid in which meat, poultry, fish, vegetables, or a combination of these has been cooked.

Brown: To cook in a small amount of fat until browned on all sides, giving food an appetizing color and, in meats, sealing in natural juices.

Butterfly: To cut a piece of meat, fish, or poultry in half horizontally, leaving one side attached.

Caramelize: To melt sugar over low heat, without scorching or burning, until it turns golden brown and develops characteristic flavor. To cook onions until sweet and golden.

Chill: To refrigerate food or let stand in ice or ice water until cold.

Chop: To cut food into small pieces.

Coat: To cover a food with a surface layer of another ingredient, such as beaten egg or flour, by sprinkling, dipping, or rolling.

Coat a spoon: Stage reached by a thickened liquid mixture when it leaves a thin film on the back of a metal spoon.

Condiment: A sauce, relish, or spice used to season food at the table.

Core: To remove the center of a fruit or vegetable.

Cream: To beat with a spoon or an electric mixer until soft, smooth, and fluffy, as in blending butter and sugar.

Cube: To cut into small cubes (about ½ inch). In meats, to tenderize by pounding with a special tool that imprints a small checkered pattern on the surface, breaking meat fibers to increase tenderness.

Curdled: Separated into a liquid containing small solid particles (caused by overcooking or too much heat or agitation).

Cut in: To distribute solid fat into dry ingredients with a pastry blender (or 2 knives, used scissor-fashion) until particles are desired size.

Dash: A very small amount, less than ⅛ teaspoon.

(Continued on next page)

Deep-fry: To cook immersed in hot fat, in a large, deep, heavy pan.

Deglaze: To loosen drippings from bottom of roasting or frying pan by adding wine, stock, or other liquid.

Degrease: To skim fat from surface of a liquid.

Dice: To cut into very small pieces (about ⅛ to ¼ inch).

Dot: To scatter bits of an ingredient, such as butter, over surface of food.

Dough: A thick, pliable mixture of flour and liquid ingredients, firm enough to be kneaded or shaped with the hands.

Dredge: To coat or cover food lightly but completely with flour, sugar, or other fine substance.

Drippings: Melted fat and juices given off by meat or poultry as it cooks.

Drizzle: To pour melted fat, sugar syrup, or other liquid in a fine stream, making a zigzag pattern over food surface.

Dust: To sprinkle lightly with powdered sugar or flour. (Shake off excess after dusting meats, poultry, or fish with flour.)

Emulsion: A liquid mixture in which fatty particles are suspended.

Entrée: The main dish of a meal.

Fat: Generic term for butter, margarine, lard, solid vegetable shortening; also the rendered drippings of meat or poultry.

Fillet: A piece of meat or fish that is naturally boneless or has had all bones removed.

Fines herbes: Equal amounts of fresh or dried herbs, usually parsley, tarragon, chervil, and chives.

Flake: To lightly break into small, thin pieces, often using tines of a fork.

Floweret: A small flower, one of a cluster of composite flowers, as in broccoli or cauliflower.

Flute: To make decorative indentations around edge of pastry; to cut indentations into a vegetable or fruit.

Fold in: To gently combine a light, delicate, aerated substance (such as whipped cream or beaten egg whites) with a heavier mixture, using an over-and-under motion.

Freeze: To chill rapidly at 0°F until solid.

Fry: To cook in hot fat. Pan-frying is done in a frying pan, using very little fat; deep-frying is done in a heavy pan, with the food immersed in fat.

Garnish: To decorate a completed dish, making it more attractive.

Gel: To congeal, becoming firm enough to retain shape of container.

Glaze: To coat with smooth mixture, giving food a sheen.

Gluten: Protein part of wheat or other cereal that gives flour its elastic properties—essential in bread making.

Grate: To rub solid food against a metal object that has sharp-edged holes, reducing food to thin shreds.

Grease: To rub fat or oil on surface of a utensil to prevent food from sticking.

Grill: To cook on a rack over direct heat (gas, electricity, or charcoal); to cook on a grill.

Hull: To remove stems and hulls (as from strawberries).

Julienne strips: Matchstick pieces of vegetables, fruits, meats, or other foods.

Knead: To work dough with hands in a fold-and-press motion.

Line: To cover inside or bottom of baking dish or pan with foil, parchment paper, wax paper, or crumbs.

Marinade: A seasoned liquid (usually containing acid such as vinegar or wine) in which food soaks. Marinating helps to tenderize meats, enhances flavor of all foods.

Marinate: To soak in a marinade.

Mash: To crush to a pulpy, soft mixture.

Mask: To cover completely with a sauce, aspic, mayonnaise, or cream.

Meringue: Stiffly beaten egg whites combined with sugar.

Mince: To cut or chop into very fine particles.

Pan-broil: To cook, uncovered, in an ungreased or lightly greased frying pan, pouring off fat as it accumulates. Sometimes pan is salted or rubbed with a piece of fat from the meat.

Pan-fry: To cook in a frying pan in a small amount of fat.

Parboil: To boil until partially cooked; remainder of cooking is done by another method.

Pare: To remove outer skin.

Peel: To strip, cut off, or pull away skin or rind.

Pit: To remove seed from whole fruits such as apricots, avocados, or cherries.

Poach: To cook gently in a simmering liquid, so that food retains its shape.

Pot roast: To cook a large piece of meat by braising; also, meat cooked by this method.

Precook: To cook food partially or completely before final cooking or reheating.

Preheat: To heat oven or griddle to desired temperature before beginning to cook (done when temperature is critical or cooking time is short).

Punch down: To deflate a risen yeast dough by pushing it down with fist to expel air.

Purée: To sieve in a food mill or whirl in a food processor or blender into a smooth, thick mixture.

Reduce: To decrease quantity and concentrate the flavor of a liquid by rapid boiling in an uncovered pan.

Refresh: To plunge a food that is hot from cooking into cold water, halting the cooking process.

Render: To free fat from animal tissue by heating.

Roast: To cook meat or poultry, uncovered, by dry heat (usually in an oven); also, a cut of meat cooked by this method.

Roux: Mixture of melted fat and flour, cooked until bubbly to remove the raw starch taste of flour; used to thicken soups and sauces.

Salad oil: Vegetable oil.

Scald: To heat milk to just below the boiling point (bubbles form slowly and burst before reaching the surface).

Score: To cut shallow grooves or slits through outer layer of food to increase tenderness, to prevent edge fat of meat from curling, or to make a decorative top before roasting certain meats.

Sear: To brown meat briefly over high heat to seal in juices.

Shortening, solid vegetable: A white, solid fat made from refined vegetable oil that has been partially hydrogenated, chilled, and whipped.

Shred: To cut or grate into thin strips.

Simmer: To cook in liquid over low heat just below the boiling point (bubbles form slowly and burst before reaching the surface).

Skim: To remove fat or foam from the surface of a liquid with a spoon or bulb baster.

Steam: To cook in steam, on a rack or in a steaming basket, in a covered pan above boiling water.

Stew: To cook food slowly in simmering liquid in a covered pot.

Stir: To mix ingredients (without beating), using a spoon or whisk in a broad, circular motion.

Stir-fry: To cook food quickly in a small amount of fat over high heat, stirring constantly.

Tart: A shallow open-faced pie with a filling.

Tent: To cover meat or poultry loosely with a piece of foil.

Texture: The structural quality of a food—roughness, smoothness, graininess, or creaminess.

Toss: To mix lightly and rapidly by lifting and turning ingredients with 2 forks or spoons.

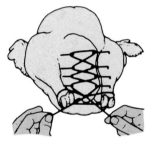

Truss: To secure poultry or meat with skewers or string so it will retain its shape during cooking.

Whip: To beat rapidly with a wire whisk or electric mixer, incorporating air to lighten a mixture and increase its volume.

Whisk: To beat with a wire whisk until blended and smooth.

Zest: Thin, colored outer layer of citrus peel.

Meats & Poultry

Many a chef has built a reputation on succulent, perfectly cooked meats and poultry. Knowledgeable shopping and skillful cooking can give the home cook results that earn high accolades, too. And not only are meats and poultry highly regarded for flavor, but they offer the added advantage of being supremely nutritious. Meat is very high in protein and also contains significant quantities of vitamins and minerals. Poultry boasts these qualities, too, and it's lower in cost and considerably lower in fat than most meats. When you plan meals, remember that for good food value and natural richness of flavor, meats and poultry come up winners every time.

BUYING & STORING MEAT

The first step toward success in meat cookery is knowing how to buy and store various types of meat. Familiarity with the basic cuts, knowledge of how much to buy and how to store it before you're ready to cook it—as well as an insistence on quality and freshness—will stand you in good stead.

CUTS OF MEAT

Some days confusion seems to reign at the meat counter. The only clear label is the price tag, and it's not always easy to know what you're actually buying. Names and cuts vary from region to region and even from store to store.

Simply put, meats fall into two categories—naturally tender cuts and those that are fibrous and tougher. The least exercised parts of any animal—in the middle of the back, called the *loin*—are the most tender. The parts adjacent to the loin get more exercise, so they're less tender. In fact, meat becomes increasingly tougher as its distance from the loin increases. Really hard-working muscles, such as the shoulder (or chuck) and neck, produce the toughest meat.

Obviously, it helps to become familiar with basic animal anatomy (see pages 34 to 36). Note that the loin portion of a steer that yields tender porterhouse and T-bone steaks is the same portion of the lamb, pig, or calf that produces lamb chops, pork chops, and veal loin chops.

COOKING METHODS

The anatomical origin of a cut of meat determines its tenderness, and the tenderness determines the cooking method. Tender cuts (from the loin or rib) should be cooked with dry heat—by roasting, broiling, grilling, pan-broiling, or frying. Tougher cuts (from the shoulder or shank) require moist heat—stewing or braising—in which the long, slow cooking in liquid breaks down the connective tissue that causes the meat's toughness.

Another option with less tender cuts of meat is to tenderize them before cooking; this will allow you to use one of the dry-heat methods. One method of tenderizing, often used in the market, involves mechanically breaking down the muscle fibers by pounding the meat with a cleated mallet or a tenderizing machine.

You can also tenderize raw meat in a marinade of wine, vinegar, or citrus juice. Or you can buy packaged chemical tenderizers (usually papaya derivatives) to apply to the meat. When using these tenderizers, be sure to follow the manufacturer's directions—if the tenderizer is applied too liberally or left to stand on the meat too long before cooking, the meat may go beyond tenderness to mush.

HOW MUCH TO BUY

Appetites vary, but usually it's enough to allow ¼ to ⅓ pound per serving of lean, boneless meat with little or no fat—such as ground meat, fillets, or boned, rolled roasts. For meat with a medium amount of bone and some edge fat—loin, rib, and shoulder roasts; steaks and chops; and bone-in ham—allow about ½ pound per serving. For very bony cuts— shank, spareribs, short ribs, and breast of veal or lamb—buy 1 full pound per serving.

STORAGE TIPS

Uncooked meat should be kept in the refrigerator for short-term storage; the length of time it will remain fresh depends on the type of meat as well as on the storage temperature and state of freshness when purchased. Ground meats, stew meat, and variety meats (organ meats) are more perishable than other types and should be used within 1 or 2 days; chops, cutlets, roasts, and steaks may be kept 3 to 5 days. If you wish to keep prepackaged meat in the refrigerator for more than 2 days, discard the original package and store the meat loosely wrapped (but not so loosely that it dries out).

For longer storage, meat should be frozen. Package the meat in moisture-proof freezer wrap and wrap tightly, eliminating all air if possible. Place a double thickness of wax paper between chops, steaks, and ground meat patties so they won't stick together. Remember to label the packages with the cut of meat, the weight or number of servings, and the date. The chart below lists suggested storage time for meats at 0°F.

Ground meat Stew meat	2 to 3 months
Variety meats Chops Cutlets	4 months
Roasts & steaks (pork or veal)	8 months
Roasts & steaks (beef or lamb)	12 months

For maximum retention of juices and least chance of bacterial growth, it's best to thaw all types of meat, well wrapped, in the refrigerator rather than at room temperature. It's safe to refreeze meat that has been partially thawed in the refrigerator, but you can expect some loss of quality.

BEEF CUTS

PRIMAL CUTS

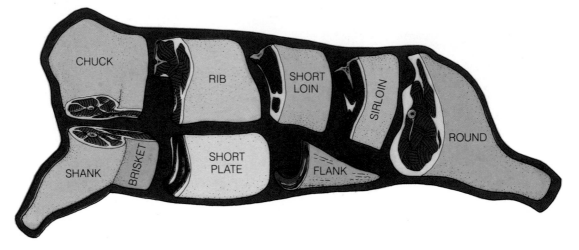

RETAIL CUTS—AND HOW TO COOK THEM

7-bone Chuck Steak
(from the chuck)
*Braise • Cook in
    liquid*

Blade Steak
(from the chuck)
*Braise • Cook in
    liquid*

Arm Roast
(from the chuck)
*Braise • Cook in
    liquid*

Rib Roast
(from the rib)
Roast

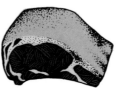...

Rolled Rump Roast
(from the round)
*Braise • Cook in
    liquid*

**Bottom Round
    Roast**
(from the round)
*Braise • Cook in
    liquid*

Porterhouse Steak
(from the short loin)
*Broil • Pan-broil •
    Grill*

T-bone Steak
(from the short loin)
*Broil • Pan-broil •
    Grill*

**Club (Top Loin
    Steak)**
(from the short loin)
*Broil • Pan-broil •
    Grill*

**Full-cut Round
    Steak**
(from the round)
*Braise • Cook in
    liquid*

Shank Cross Cuts
(from the shank)
*Braise • Cook in
    liquid*

Short Ribs
(from the short plate)
*Braise • Cook in
    liquid*

Corned Brisket
(from the brisket)
*Braise • Cook in
    liquid*

Flank Steak
(from the flank)
Broil • Braise • Grill

Tip Roast
(from the round)
*Braise • Cook in
    liquid*

LAMB CUTS

PRIMAL CUTS

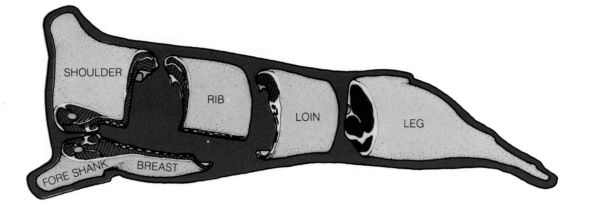

SHOULDER

RIB

LOIN

LEG

FORE SHANK

BREAST

RETAIL CUTS—AND HOW TO COOK THEM

Square Shoulder
(from the shoulder)
Roast

Blade Chop
(from the shoulder)
*Broil • Pan-broil •
Pan-fry*

Arm Chop
(from the shoulder)
*Broil • Pan-broil •
Pan-fry*

Crown Roast
(from the rib)
Roast

8-rib Rack
(from the rib)
Roast

Loin Chops
(from the loin)
*Broil • Pan-broil •
Pan-fry*

Leg (Sirloin Half)
(from the leg)
Roast

Leg (Shank Half)
(from the leg)
Roast

Lamb Shank
(from the fore
shank)
Braise

Breast
(from the breast)
Roast • Braise

PORK CUTS

PRIMAL CUTS

RETAIL CUTS—AND HOW TO COOK THEM

Blade Steak
(from the Boston
  shoulder)
Pan-fry • Braise

Center Loin Roast
(from the loin)
Roast

Rib Chop
(from the loin)
*Pan-broil • Pan-fry •
  Braise*

Smoked Arm Picnic
(from the picnic
  shoulder)
*Roast • Cook in
  liquid*

Fresh Hock
(from the picnic
  shoulder)
*Braise • Cook in
  liquid*

Spareribs
(from the side pork)
*Bake • Braise •
  Cook in liquid*

Slab Bacon
(from the side pork)
Broil • Pan-broil

Rump Butt Portion
(from the leg)
*Roast • Cook in
  liquid*

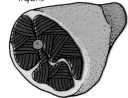

Shank Portion
(from the leg)
*Roast • Cook in
  liquid*

Center Ham Slice
(from the leg)
Broil • Pan-broil

COOKING MEAT

A beautifully broiled lamb chop, a succulent beef roast, a platter of aromatic barbecued pork spare-ribs—what could be a better main dish than hearty, simply cooked meat? Here we give basic instructions for some of the simplest ways to cook meat: broiling, roasting, barbecuing, and microwaving. In easy-to-follow chart form, you'll find all the information you need to obtain perfect results every time. First, however, a brief definition of the techniques involved.

Broiling. Broiling means cooking below direct heat in the broiler of an electric or gas range. It is a quick, high-heat method of cooking and is therefore most suitable for naturally tender cuts of meat (see suggestions below).

Roasting. Roasting is the technique by which meat or poultry is cooked, uncovered, by dry heat, usually in an oven.

Barbecuing. Barbecuing is outdoor cooking, in which the meat is cooked on a grill over hot coals. There are many different barbecue techniques and many types of equipment for barbecuing; be sure to read the manufacturer's instructions for your equipment before starting to cook.

Microwaving. Microwaved food is quickly cooked by the heat generated by high-frequency microwaves. Microwave ovens vary considerably depending on the manufacturer; don't cook in a microwave oven until you have thoroughly read the manufacturer's instructions.

BROILING MEAT

No matter which cut of beef or lamb you choose, the procedure for broiling is the same. The suggested cooking times in the chart below are for meat cooked rare or medium-rare (with the exception of ground lamb patties); for more well-done meat, continue to cook, checking at 1- to 2-minute intervals, until meat is done to your liking (cut to test). Serve broiled meats plain, or top them with a seasoned butter.

CUTS OF MEAT

Best beef candidates for the broiler are tender steaks such as porterhouse, T-bone, club, rib, and top sirloin.

Less tender steaks, such as flank and top round, also broil well if you marinate them first and cook just to rare or medium-rare.

Several lamb cuts are suitable for broiling; your selection will probably depend on the occasion and your budget. For special occasions, choose tender cuts such as lamb steaks cut from the leg, small loin chops, or rib chops. For everyday meals, buy round bone or blade shoulder chops. If you need lamb cubes, use boneless lamb from the leg or shoulder.

Because pork must be cooked until no longer pink, we do not consider it a good candidate for broiling; the high heat of the broiler would dry out the meat before it cooked completely. Better results are obtained cooking pork chops, cubes, and patties in a frying pan.

TECHNIQUE

Select a large, shallow pan with a rack and place the meat on the rack. Position the pan below the heat source in your broiler, adjusting the pan (or the rack on which it rests) until the top of the meat is the recommended distance below the heat source.

Remove the meat from the broiler, leaving the pan and rack inside. Preheat the broiler for 5 to 7 minutes. Meanwhile, if the meat has a border of fat, slash through the fat at 2- to 3-inch intervals, cutting just to the lean meat, to prevent curling. Remove the pan from the broiler and lightly grease the hot rack.

Place the meat on the rack and broil, turning as needed, for the time specified in the chart below or until browned on all sides and done to your liking (cut to center of thickest part to test).

CUT	THICKNESS	DISTANCE BELOW HEAT	APPROXIMATE TOTAL COOKING TIME (in minutes)
BEEF Steaks	¾ inch	3 inches	6–8 (R) 8–10 (MR)
	1 inch	3 inches	9–11 (R) 11–12 (MR)
	1½ inches	3 inches	10–12 (R) 12–14 (MR)
	2–2¼ inches	3 inches	20–22 (R) 22–25 (MR)
Ground patties	¾–1 inch	3–4 inches	8–10 (MR)
LAMB Chops, steaks	¾ inch	3 inches	8–10 (MR)
	1 inch	3 inches	9–11 (MR)
	1½ inches	3 inches	11–13 (MR)
Cubes	1½ inches	2½–3 inches	10–15 (MR)
Ground patties	¾–1 inch	4–6 inches	8–12 (MW)

(R) Rare   (MR) Medium-rare   (MW) Medium-well

ROASTING MEAT

The cooking times given below are merely a guide—the only *accurate* measure for doneness is a meat thermometer. First, estimate total cooking time by multiplying minutes per pound (for doneness you prefer) by weight of roast.

Then insert a meat thermometer in meat's thickest part (not touching bone); roast until thermometer registers degree specified for preferred doneness. Remove roast from oven and let stand for 10 to 20 minutes before carving.

NOTE: All testing was done with meat taken directly from the refrigerator and roasted on a rack in a shallow pan, in a conventional electric or gas oven; unless otherwise indicated, oven temperature is 325°F.

CUT	Approximate Weight (lbs.)	Approximate Cooking Time (minutes per lb.)	Meat Thermometer Reading (°F)	CUT	Approximate Weight (lbs.)	Approximate Cooking Time (minutes per lb.)	Meat Thermometer Reading (°F)

BEEF
Standing rib
	4–6	26–32
		34–38
		40–42
			135°–140° (R)
			150° (M)
			160° (W)
				FRESH PORK
				Loin roasts
				  Center, bone-in
				  Half, bone-in
				  Half, boneless, rolled
				  End, bone-in
				  Top, boneless
					
					3–5
					5–7
					3–5
					
					3–4
					2–4
						
						30–35
						35–40
						35–40
						
						35–40
						30–35
							
							170°
							170°
							170°
							
							170°
							170°

Standing rib	6–8	23–25 27–30 32–35	135°–140° (R) 150° (M) 160° (W)	**Crown**	4–6	35–40	170°

Rib eye
(Delmonico)
(use 350° oven)
	4–6	18–20
		20–22
		22–24
			135°–140° (R)
			150° (M)
			160°(W)
				Picnic shoulder
				  Bone-in
				  Boneless
					
					5–8
					3–5
						
						30–35
						35–40
							
							170°
							170°

Tenderloin (use 425° oven)	4–6	45–60 (total cooking time)	135°–140°(R)	**Boston shoulder** (butt)	4–6	40–45	170°

Boneless rolled rump	4–6	25–30	150°–170°	**Leg (fresh ham)**
				  Whole, bone-in
				  Whole, boneless
				  Half, bone-in
					
					12–16
					10–14
					5–8
						
						22–26
						24–28
						35–40
							
							170°
							170°
							170°

Sirloin tip	3½–4	32–40	135°–155°	**Tenderloin**	½–1	45–60 (total cooking time)	170°
VEAL **Leg**	5–8	22–32	165°–170°	**LAMB** **Leg, bone-in** Whole	 5–9	 20–22 22–25 25–30	 135°–140° (R) 150° (M) 160° (W)
Loin	4–6	22–28	165°–170°				
Shoulder, boneless	4–6	35–45	165°–170°	Shank half	3–4	25–28 28–30 30–35	135°–140° (R) 150° (M) 160° (W)

SMOKED PORK
Ham
(cook-before-eating)
  Whole
  Half
  Shank portion
  Butt portion
	
	10–14
	5–7
	3–4
	3–4
		
		18–20
		22–25
		35–40
		35–40
			
			160°
			160°
			160°
			160°
				Sirloin half	3–4	20–22
						22–25
						25–30
							135°–140° (R)
							150° (M)
							160° (W)

				Leg, boneless	4–7	25–28 28–30 30–35	135°–140° (R) 150° (M) 160° (W)
Ham (fully cooked) Half	5–7	18–22	140°	**Crown**	2½–4	30–32 32–35 35–40	135°–140° (R) 150° (M) 160° (W)
Loin	3–5	25–30	160°	**Shoulder** Square cut	 4–6	 20–25 25–30	 150° (M) 160° (W)
Picnic shoulder (cook-before-eating)	5–8	30–35	170°	Boneless	3½–5	30–32 32–35 35–40	135°–140° (R) 150° 160° (W)
Picnic shoulder (fully cooked)	5–8	25–30	140°	Cushion	3½–5	25–30	160° (W)
Shoulder roll (butt)	2–4	35–40	170°	**Rib** (use 375° oven)	2–3	25–28 28–30 30–35	135°–140° (R) 150° (M) 160° (W)

(R) Rare   (M) Medium   (W) Well-done

BARBECUE BASICS FOR MEAT

Barbecuing is one culinary art that even a novice back-yard chef can master with ease. Of course, there are a few essentials for success. Knowing how to start and maintain a fire is one key; understanding the different temperatures and techniques of barbecue cookery is another. Armed with this knowledge, you'll be able to produce a tempting array of barbecued dishes to delight family and friends.

STARTING THE FIRE

Every outdoor chef has a favorite method for firing up the barbecue. Six of the most popular starters are described below.

Fire chimney. Stack briquets inside the chimney on top of a few wadded sheets of newspaper, then light. When the coals are hot (about 30 minutes), remove the chimney and spread out the coals.

Solid starter. These small (about 1 by 2 inches), compressed, woodlike blocks or sticks light easily with a match. They're ideal for portable barbecues used on a boat, in the park, or at the beach. To use solid starter, place several blocks in with the charcoal, then light the starter; the coals will be hot in 30 to 40 minutes.

Liquid starter. If you use a liquid starter, be sure it's a product intended for charcoal. Pour the starter on the briquets and wait until it's absorbed, then light. Or soak a few briquets in a jar filled with liquid starter; then place the pretreated briquets on the bottom of the firebed, add the remaining briquets, and light. *Don't pour liquid starter on hot coals* —the coals could suddenly flare up.

Coals started with liquid starter will be hot in about 30 minutes.

Self-starting briquets. These briquets are easily ignited with a match and can be used in the same way as solid starter. They'll be hot just 15 minutes after lighting. Self-starting briquets are more expensive than regular briquets; and because they're impregnated with fuel that takes a while to burn off completely, you can't add more coals as the fire burns down. (The fuel in the fresh briquets would flavor the food.)

Electric starter. Set the starter on a few briquets in the firebed. Pile the remaining briquets on top, then plug in the starter. Remove the starter after 10 minutes. The coals should be hot in about 30 minutes.

FIRE TEMPERATURE

Three different terms are commonly used to indicate desired fire temperature at the start of cooking.

Hot describes coals that are just covered with gray ash. You can't hold your hand near the grill for more than 2 to 3 seconds.

Medium describes coals that glow through a layer of gray ash. You can't hold your hand near the grill for more than 4 to 5 seconds.

Low describes coals covered with a thick layer of gray ash. You should be able to hold your hand near the grill for 6 to 7 seconds.

BARBECUING BY DIRECT HEAT

Open the bottom dampers if your barbecue has them. Spread briquets on the fire grate in a solid layer that's 1 to 2 inches bigger all around than the grill area required for the food. Then mound the charcoal and ignite it. When the coals have reached the fire temperature specified, spread them out into a single layer again.

Set the grill in place at the recommended height above the coals. Grease the grill lightly, then arrange the food on the grill. Watch carefully and turn as needed to ensure even cooking. If you're using a baste that contains sugar or ingredients high in sugar (such as catsup or fruit), apply it during the last part of cooking and turn the food frequently to prevent scorching. Also keep a water-filled spray bottle handy to extinguish any flare-ups.

BARBECUING BY INDIRECT HEAT

Open or remove the lid from a covered barbecue, then open the bottom dampers. Pile about 50 long-burning briquets on the fire grate and ignite them. Let the briquets burn until they're hot (usually about 30 minutes). Using long-handled tongs, bank about half the briquets on each side of the fire grate; then place a metal drip pan in the center.

Set the cooking grill in place 4 to 6 inches above the pan; lightly grease the grill. Set the food on the grill directly above the drip pan.

(Continued on next page)

Place meat fat side up; if the meat has been marinated, drain it briefly before placing it on the grill. Cook as directed. Add 5 or 6 briquets to each side of the fire grate at 30- to 40-minute intervals if necessary to keep the fire temperature constant during cooking.

SPECIAL TIPS

When using the following charts, keep these tips in mind.

■ Our testing was done with the cooking grill 4 to 6 inches above the coals. If your grill is closer (2 to 3 inches), the cooking time will be shorter.

■ We used regular pressed charcoal briquets in our testing. If you use wood, cooking times will differ.

■ Always use potholders or mitts and long-handled cooking tools.

■ Use a water-filled spray bottle to extinguish flare-ups.

■ Turn food with tongs or a spatula—a fork pierces foods and allows juices to escape.

■ Salt food *after* cooking (salt draws the juices out of meat).

■ To prevent steaks and chops from curling, slash the edge fat at 2- to 3-inch intervals, cutting *just to the meat*.

■ To test roasts or thick steaks for doneness, insert a meat thermometer in the thickest part (not touching bone). To ensure accuracy, repeat the test in several places (if possible).

BARBECUING MEAT

CUT OF MEAT	WEIGHT OR THICKNESS	GRILL- ING METHOD	FIRE TEMPER- ATURE	TEST FOR DONENESS & APPROXIMATE COOKING TIME
BEEF **Standing rib roast**	3½–5 lbs.	Indirect	Hot, banked	Meat thermometer registers 135°–140°F (R), 150°F (M), 160°F (W). 24–26 minutes/lb. (R).
	6–8 lbs.	Indirect	Hot, banked	Meat thermometer registers 135°–140°F (R), 150°F (M), 160°F (W). 18–22 minutes/lb. (R).
Boned & tied roasts (rib, sirloin tip, crossrib)	3–5 lbs.	Indirect	Hot, banked	Meat thermometer registers 135°–140°F (R), 150°F (M), 160°F (W). 24–26 minutes/lb. (R).
Steaks (T-bone, New York, Porterhouse, top round, sirloin; chuck steak if marinated or tenderized)	1 inch	Direct	Hot	Cut meat to test. 5–6 minutes/side (R).
	1½ inches	Direct	Medium	Meat thermometer registers 135°–140°F (R), 150°F(M), 160°F (W). 8–9 minutes/side (R).
	2–2½ inches	Direct	Medium	Meat thermometer registers 135°–140°F (R), 150°F (M), 160°F (W). 12–15 minutes/side (R).
Flank steak	1–1½ lbs.	Direct	Hot	Cut meat to test. 5–7 minutes/side (MR).
Skirt steak (cut into serving-size pieces)	⅛–¼ inch	Direct	Hot	Cut meat to test. 1½–2 minutes/side (R).
	½ inch	Direct	Hot	Cut meat to test. 2½–3 minutes/side (R).
Boneless cubes	¾ inch	Direct	Hot	Cut meat to test. 5–6 minutes *total* (MR).
	1 inch	Direct	Hot	Cut meat to test. 8–10 minutes *total* (MR).
	1½ inches	Direct	Hot	Cut meat to test. 15 minutes *total* (MR).
Ground beef patties	1 inch	Direct	Hot	Cut meat to test. 4–5 minutes/side (R), 5–6 minutes/side (M), 6–7 minutes/side (W).
VEAL **Leg, bone-in**	8–9 lbs.	Indirect	Hot, banked	Meat thermometer registers 165°–170°F. 20–22 minutes/lb.
Leg, boned & tied	3–4 lbs.	Indirect	Hot, banked	Meat thermometer registers 165°–170°F. 32–34 minutes/lb.
Shoulder roast, bone-in	7–8 lbs.	Indirect	Hot, banked	Meat thermometer registers 165°–170°F. 18–20 minutes/lb.
Shoulder roast, boned & tied	3–4 lbs.	Indirect	Hot, banked	Meat thermometer registers 165°–170°F. 32–34 minutes/lb.
Chops (loin)	¾ inch	Direct	Hot	Cut near bone to test. 5–6 minutes/side (M).
	1 inch	Direct	Hot	Cut near bone to test. 6–7 minutes/side (M).
	1½ inches	Direct	Hot	Cut near bone to test. 8–9 minutes/side (M).

(R) Rare   (M) Medium   (W) Well-done

CUT OF MEAT	WEIGHT OR THICKNESS	GRILLING METHOD	FIRE TEMPERATURE	TEST FOR DONENESS & APPROXIMATE COOKING TIME
LAMB **Leg, bone-in**	5–7 lbs.	Indirect	Hot, banked	Meat thermometer registers 135°–140°F (R), 150°F (M), 160°F (W). 18–20 minutes/lb. (R).
Leg, boned & tied	4–5 lbs.	Indirect	Hot, banked	Meat thermometer registers 135°–140°F (R), 150°F (M), 160°F (W). 25–27 minutes/lb. (R).
Leg, boned & butterflied	4–5 lbs.	Indirect	Hot, banked	Meat thermometer registers 135°–140°F (R), 150°F (M), 160°F (W). 15–17 minutes/lb. (R).
Shoulder, bone-in	5–7 lbs.	Indirect	Hot, banked	Meat thermometer registers 135°–140°F (R), 150°F (M), 160°F (W). 18–20 minutes/lb. (R).
Shoulder, boned & tied	4–6 lbs.	Indirect	Hot, banked	Meat thermometer registers 135°–140°F (R), 150°F (M), 160°F (W). 25–27 minutes/lb. (R).
Rack	2–3 lbs.	Indirect	Hot, banked	Meat thermometer registers 140°–145°F (MR). 19–21 minutes/lb.
Chops (loin, rib, shoulder); **leg steaks**	¾ inch 1 inch 1½ inches	Direct Direct Direct	Hot Hot Hot	Cut near bone to test. 4–5 minutes/side (MR). Cut near bone to test. 5–6 minutes/side (MR). Cut near bone to test. 6–7 minutes/side (MR).
Boneless cubes	¾ inch 1 inch 1½ inches	Direct Direct Direct	Hot Hot Hot	Cut meat to test. 5 minutes *total* (R), 6–8 minutes *total* (M), 8–10 minutes *total* (W). Cut meat to test. 6 minutes *total* (R), 8 minutes *total* (M), 12 minutes *total* (W). Cut meat to test. 12 minutes *total* (R), 15 minutes *total* (M), 18–20 minutes *total* (W).
Ground lamb patties	¾ inch 1 inch	Direct Direct	Hot Hot	Cut meat to test. 4–5 minutes/side (MR). Cut meat to test. 5–6 minutes/side (MR).
PORK **Half leg** (shank or butt), **bone-in**	6–8 lbs.	Indirect	Hot, banked	Meat thermometer registers 170°F. 27–30 minutes/lb.
Loin roast, half, bone-in	4½–6 lbs.	Indirect	Hot, banked	Meat thermometer registers 170°F. 24–26 minutes/lb.
Loin roast, half, boned & tied	3–5 lbs.	Indirect	Hot, banked	Meat thermometer registers 170°F. 21–24 minutes/lb.
Loin roast, rib or sirloin end, bone-in	3–4 lbs.	Indirect	Hot, banked	Meat thermometer registers 170°F. 30–32 minutes/lb.
Shoulder roast (picnic or butt), **bone-in**	4–6 lbs.	Indirect	Hot, banked	Meat thermometer registers 170°F. 27–30 minutes/lb.
Shoulder roast (picnic or butt), **boned & tied**	3–5 lbs.	Indirect	Hot, banked	Meat thermometer registers 170°F. 33–35 minutes/lb.
Tenderloin Fold & tie thin end underneath for even thickness	½–1 lb.	Indirect	Hot, banked	Meat thermometer registers 170°F. 20–22 minutes *total*.
Chops (loin, rib, shoulder); **leg steaks**	¾ inch 1 inch 1½ inches	Direct Direct Direct	Medium Medium Medium	Meat near bone is no longer pink; cut to test. 4–5 minutes/side. Meat near bone is no longer pink; cut to test. 5–7 minutes/side. Meat near bone is no longer pink; cut to test. 8–10 minutes/side.
Spareribs	2½–3 lbs. whole slab	Indirect	Hot, banked	Meat near bone is no longer pink; cut to test. 1 to 1¼ hours *total*.
Spareribs, country-style	3–4 lbs., cut into serving-size pieces	Indirect	Hot, banked	Meat near bone is no longer pink; cut to test. 1 to 1¼ hours *total*.
Boneless cubes	¾ inch 1 inch	Direct Direct	Hot Hot	Meat is no longer pink; cut to test. About 8 minutes *total*. Meat is no longer pink; cut to test. 12–14 minutes *total*.

MICROWAVING MEAT

Caution: To prevent overcooking, use shortest cooking time. Allow food to stand for recommended time. On standing, internal temperature will rise 10 to 15 degrees. If necessary, microwave longer, checking for doneness at 1-minute intervals.

CUT OF MEAT	PREPARATION	COOKING TIME (CT) STANDING TIME (ST)
BEEF **Beef roast, boneless** (sirloin tip, rolled rib, crossrib) **3½–4 lbs.**	Place roast, fat side down, on a nonmetallic rack in a 7- by 11-inch baking dish.	**CT:** 9–11 minutes/lb. (rare); 10–13 minutes/lb. (medium) Determine total cooking time. Microwave on HIGH (100%) for 5 minutes, then on MEDIUM (50%) for remaining time, rotating dish ¼ turn every 10 minutes. Turn roast over halfway through cooking and baste with juices. Meat thermometer inserted in center of roast should register 125°–130°F (rare) or 135°F (medium). **ST:** 10–15 minutes, covered.
Ground beef patties **¼ lb. *each***	Season to taste with salt, pepper, Worcestershire, finely chopped onion. Shape into patties about ¾ inch thick. To add color, if desired, brush patties with a mixture of 2 tablespoons water and 2 tablespoons bottled brown gravy sauce.	**CT:** Microwave a browning skillet or dish on HIGH (100%) for 4 minutes. Carefully remove skillet from oven and place on a heatproof surface. Add patties to dish and microwave for time given below, turning over after 1 minute to brown other side. For medium doneness, microwave, uncovered, on HIGH (100%). 1 patty 2–3 minutes; 2 patties 3–4 minutes; 3 patties 4–4½ minutes; 4 patties 4½–5 minutes **ST:** 1 minute, uncovered; juices should run clear when slashed.
PORK **Pork loin roast, bone-in or boneless** **3½–4 lbs.**	Place roast, fat side down, on a nonmetallic rack in a 7- by 11-inch baking dish.	**CT:** 14–16 minutes/lb. Determine total cooking time. Microwave, uncovered, on MEDIUM-HIGH (70%), rotating dish ½ turn every 10 minutes. Turn roast over halfway through cooking and baste with pan juices. Meat thermometer inserted in thickest part (not touching bone) should register 160°F. **ST:** 10–15 minutes, loosely covered.
Spareribs, country-style **3 lbs.**	In a 7- by 11-inch baking dish, arrange ribs with meaty portions to outside of dish. Top with onion slices, if desired. Pour in ¼ cup water. Cover with heavy-duty plastic wrap.	**CT:** 18–20 minutes/lb. Determine total cooking time. Microwave, covered, on HIGH (100%) for 10 minutes. Pour off juices and turn ribs over. Microwave on MEDIUM (50%) for remaining time, discarding accumulated juices and bringing cooked portion to inside of dish halfway through cooking. If desired, uncover and baste with a barbecue sauce during last 10 minutes. **ST:** 5 minutes, covered (uncovered, if basted). Meat in thickest part should no longer be pink; cut to test.
Spareribs, one medium-size side **2½–3 lbs.**	Cut ribs into 2-rib pieces. In an 8- by 12- or a 9- by 13-inch baking dish, arrange ribs with meaty portions toward outside of dish. Thinner portions may overlap. Pour in ¼ cup water. Cover with heavy-duty plastic wrap.	**CT:** 13–16 minutes/lb. Determine total cooking time. Microwave on HIGH (100%) for 7 minutes. Pour off liquid and turn ribs over. Microwave on MEDIUM (50%) for remaining time, discarding accumulated juices and bringing cooked portion to inside of dish every 7 minutes. If desired, uncover and baste with a barbecue sauce during last 10 minutes. **ST:** 5 minutes, covered (uncovered, if basted). Meat in thickest part should no longer be pink; cut to test.
Bacon **1–8 strips** (For even cooking, microwave no more than 8 strips at a time.)	Arrange bacon strips in a single layer on a nonmetallic rack or on 2 thicknesses of paper towels in a 7- by 11-inch baking dish. Cover with a paper towel and top with another layer of bacon, if desired. Cover with a paper towel.	**CT:** About 1 minute per strip Microwave on HIGH (100%). Cooking time varies depending on thickness, starting temperature, curing process, amount of fat, and crispness desired. If towels absorb a lot of fat and bacon is not cooked, replace bottom towels with fresh ones. **ST:** 2–3 minutes, covered. Bacon should be crisp.
LAMB **Leg of lamb, shank half** **5–5½ lbs.**	If desired, sliver 1 or 2 cloves garlic and insert into a few small slashes in flesh. Place leg, fat side down, on a nonmetallic rack in an 8- by 12- or a 9- by 13-inch baking dish. Shield shank end with a 2-inch strip of foil.	**CT:** 8½–10 minutes/lb. (medium); 10–12 minutes/lb. (well-done) Determine total cooking time. Microwave on HIGH (100%) for 5 minutes. Microwave on MEDIUM (50%) for remaining time, turning meat over and rotating dish ¼ turn every 10 minutes. Remove foil shield halfway through cooking and baste with pan juices. Meat thermometer inserted in thickest part (not touching bone) should register 135°F (medium) or 150°F (well-done). **ST:** 15 minutes, covered.
VEAL **Leg of veal, boned & tied** **4 lbs.**	If desired, rub meat with garlic powder, paprika, and pepper. Place roast, fat side down, on a nonmetallic rack in a 7- by 11-inch baking dish.	**CT:** 10 minutes/lb. Determine total cooking time. Microwave on HIGH (100%), rotating dish ¼ turn every 10 minutes. Turn roast over halfway through cooking and baste with pan juices. Meat thermometer inserted in thickest part should register 155°F. **ST:** 10 minutes, covered loosely.

BUYING & STORING POULTRY

Following is a handy reference guide to the various forms of poultry, as well as tips for purchasing, storing, and thawing these birds.

TYPES OF POULTRY

The kind of poultry you buy will depend on the occasion. For a family dinner, you might want a roasting chicken, while for company fare it's nice to try something more festive—perhaps duckling, or specialty birds such as squab or quail. Here are the options to consider when shopping for poultry.

Frying chickens. Also called broilers and broiler-fryers, these are the perfect all-purpose birds—suitable not only for broiling and frying, but for roasting, baking, simmering, steaming, poaching, and barbecuing as well. Frying chickens are sold whole, cut up, and in parts—drumsticks, thighs, whole legs, breasts (boned or bone-in), and wings.

Frying chickens average 3 to 4 pounds, though weights may run as low as 2½ pounds or as high as 4½ pounds. By definition, these birds are 7 weeks old.

Roasting chickens. Roasting chickens—also known as young roasters—typically weigh 5 to 6 pounds, though some are as heavy as 8 pounds. Because of their size, these birds look almost as impressive as a turkey. They're a good choice when you're serving dinner for six. Roasters are usually about 9 weeks old.

Stewing hens. Older and less tender than frying and roasting chickens, 3- to 5-pound stewing hens (or "heavy hens") are also much less available in retail markets. These birds are best used in slow-cooked soups and stews—long, slow simmering tenderizes them and brings out their rich flavor.

Rock Cornish game hens. These small (1 to 1½ lbs.), delicately flavored birds are a hybrid developed from the Cornish breed of chicken. Smaller game hens can be served one to a diner; larger ones make two servings. Game hens are usually 4 to 5 weeks old.

Turkeys. Choose between hen turkeys, averaging 8 to 15 pounds, and tom turkeys, averaging 16 to 24 pounds. During holiday time, you can find even larger toms, some as heavy as 30 pounds. Size has no bearing on tenderness or flavor, but it does affect the ratio of meat to bone. As a general rule, heavier birds have a higher proportion of meat to bone (and are thus a more economical purchase).

In addition to whole turkeys, most markets offer a variety of turkey parts. You'll find drumsticks, thighs, wings, and various cuts of breast meat—half or whole breasts, fillets, and boneless "steaks."

Ducks. Many varieties of duck are raised domestically; the most common one, Pekin, is what you'll find in grocery stores. These ducks are usually labeled simply "duckling" and weigh 4 to 5 pounds. They're readily available frozen; some stores also offer them fresh.

Geese. Like ducks, domestic geese are generally sold frozen, though you may be able to buy fresh birds during the holiday season. Fresh or frozen, geese are often a special-order item—so unless you live near a supplier carrying frozen birds in stock all year round, you'll need to plan in advance whenever you want to serve goose.

Geese are usually marketed in three basic sizes. The smallest birds weigh 8 to 10 pounds, medium-size birds weigh 10 to 12 pounds, and large ones average 12 to 14 pounds.

Specialty birds. The availability of farm-raised specialty birds is increasing, since they're now being produced in greater numbers. You'll find them fresh and frozen, in specialty food stores and even in some grocery stores. In certain parts of the country, though, you'll need to order the birds through service meat markets or directly from game farms. Check listings under "Poultry" or "Game" in the Yellow Pages of the telephone directory; some game farms also advertise in cooking magazines.

Quail, weighing just 3 to 6 ounces each, are perhaps the most widely available specialty bird. **Squab** (young pigeons) are fairly available; they weigh ¾ to 1 pound each. **Pheasant** (1½ to 3 lbs. each) and **chukar** (partridge, ¾ to 1 lb. each) are very seasonal; they're marketed primarily from late summer through autumn.

PURCHASING GUIDELINES

When you buy fresh poultry, make sure it has been kept refrigerated, not held at room temperature. If you're purchasing prepackaged poultry (either whole or cut up), choose packages with little or no liquid in the bottom.

Good-quality whole chickens and turkeys have smooth, tight skin and plump breasts and drumsticks. Turkey should have cream-colored skin, but a chicken's skin color is no real indication of quality; color ranges from yellow to bluish white, depending on what the bird was fed.

In choosing frozen poultry, avoid torn packages—if the bird hasn't been kept airtight, it has probably lost moisture. Also steer clear of packages containing frozen liquid. This indicates that the meat was partially thawed, then refrozen, and may have deteriorated in quality.

(Continued on next page)

How much to buy. In general, you can figure the number of servings by a bird's weight (bone-in). For very small birds, just allow a certain number of birds for each serving. **Chickens** and **Rock Cornish game hens:** about 1 pound per serving. **Turkey:** ¾ to 1 pound per serving. **Goose:** 1¼ to 1½ pounds per serving. **Duck:** 2 or 3 servings for a 4- to 5-pound bird. **Quail:** 1 serving for every 2 or 3 birds (3 to 4 oz. *each*). **Squab** and **chukar:** 1 serving for a ¾- to 1-pound bird. **Pheasant:** 1 serving for a 1½-pound bird; about 3 servings for a 3-pound bird.

STORAGE TIPS

Fresh poultry is perishable and should be cooked within 3 days of purchase; if you won't use it within that time, freeze it. Securely wrap poultry to be refrigerated in plastic wrap or butcher paper and store in the coldest part of the refrigerator. You can freeze poultry just as it comes from the market, but to prevent any chance of freezer burn, add an extra layer of insulation by enclosing the wrapped poultry in foil, heavy-duty plastic wrap, a plastic bag, or moisture-proof freezer wrap. Squeeze out as much air as possible before sealing, then mark the package with the type of bird, its weight, and the date. For best results, use frozen poultry within 6 months.

If you buy poultry complete with neck and giblets but don't want to cook them with the bird, freeze them for later use. Freeze necks, hearts, and gizzards in one container, collecting them until you have enough for stock or other purposes. Freeze livers in another container, saving them for recipes such as pâté. All frozen giblets should be used within 3 months.

THAWING FROZEN POULTRY

For maximum retention of juices and least chance of bacterial growth, it's best to thaw all types of poultry, well wrapped, in the refrigerator. Allow 12 to 16 hours for a whole chicken and 4 to 9 hours for chicken parts, depending on weight. Whole turkeys take 2 to 3 days.

If you decide to cook poultry on the spur of the moment, though, there won't be time for thawing in the refrigerator. In that case, you'll need to use another safe thawing method. You can easily defrost chicken in the microwave (see chart below) or in cold water.

Microwave method. Begin by unwrapping chicken and placing it on a microwave-safe platter; then cover with heavy-duty plastic wrap or wax paper. Microwave as directed below, using MEDIUM (50%) power. Halfway through each microwaving period, turn chicken over and rotate platter a quarter turn. As soon as possible, separate pieces, arranging them with meatiest portions to outside. If some pieces thaw before others, remove them from the microwave. Wing-tips and drumstick ends of whole birds may thaw before the rest of the bird; shield them with small pieces of foil while center continues to thaw.

Thawed meat should be flexible, but still very cold.

Cold water method. To defrost chicken quickly without a microwave oven, you can use the cold water method. Completely seal chicken or other small bird in a plastic bag, then submerge the bag in cold water. (The outside of the bird thaws first, and the cold water keeps the skin cool while the inside continues to thaw.) Change the water frequently so it won't get *too* cold and slow down thawing.

The cold water method also works well for turkey; except for very large birds, whole turkeys usually thaw in 5 to 8 hours. Another good method is to enclose the turkey, still in its store wrappings, in a double thickness of paper bags. Seal the bags tightly and leave the turkey at room temperature for about 8 hours. Like cold water, the bags serve as insulation, keeping the thawed parts cool until the entire bird has thawed.

Refreezing. It's safe to refreeze poultry (though it may lose moisture) if it has thawed only partially and ice crystals remain in the meat. But if it has thawed beyond this point, don't refreeze it; cook as soon as possible.

THAWING POULTRY IN THE MICROWAVE

TYPE OF CHICKEN/ WEIGHT	DEFROSTING INSTRUCTIONS
WHOLE, 3½ lbs.	Microwave for 10 minutes; let stand for 10 minutes. Repeat. Microwave for 5 minutes; let stand for 5 minutes. Set aside neck and giblets for other uses. Microwave for 2 minutes.
CUT UP, 3½ lbs.	Microwave for 10 minutes; let stand for 10 minutes. Repeat. Reserve neck and giblets for other uses; set aside wings (they should be thawed). Arrange remaining pieces in a single layer. Microwave for 5 minutes; let stand for 5 minutes. Microwave for 2 minutes.
WHOLE LEGS (2), THIGHS ATTACHED (1 lb. *total*)	Microwave for 5 minutes; let stand for 5 minutes. Microwave for 4 minutes; let stand for 4 minutes. Microwave for 1 more minute, if necessary.
WHOLE BREAST (1), SPLIT (1 lb.)	Microwave for 5 minutes; let stand for 5 minutes. Microwave for 3 minutes; let stand for 3 minutes. Microwave for 1 more minute, if necessary.

COOKING POULTRY

One of the most versatile types of food, poultry can take on myriad personalities depending on the type of bird and how it's cooked. The following pages offer instruction in the simplest ways to prepare poultry.

We begin with a lesson in how to cut a whole bird into serving-size pieces. Buying poultry whole and cutting it yourself is much more economical than buying precut pieces, and you can save the back, neck, and giblets for making soup later. On page 49, you'll also learn how to bone a chicken breast.

Starting on page 46, we present some of the most basic cooking methods for poultry: roasting, microwaving, barbecuing, and broiling. Using these techniques with different birds and different seasonings, you can come up with a great variety of tempting poultry dishes.

CUTTING UP A WHOLE BIRD

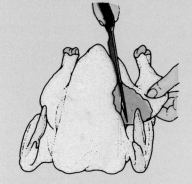

1 To remove drumstick and thigh, grasp drumstick and pull away from body. Cut through skin and meat, exposing joint. Bend thigh back from body; cut close to body through hip joint. Repeat with other leg.

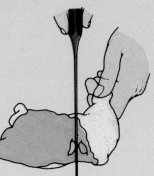

2 To separate drumstick from thigh, cut through skin at joint. Then bend drumstick back from thigh to expose joint; cut through joint and bottom skin.

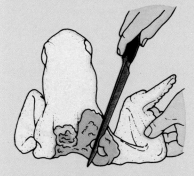

3 To remove wing, pull away from body. Cut through skin to expose shoulder joint; sever at joint. To remove wingtip, cut at joint. Repeat with other wing.

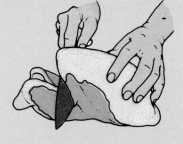

4 To remove lower back, cut along bottom ribs on each side of breast to backbone. Bend back in half; cut to separate.

5 With breast down, cut to shoulder joints along sides of upper back. Bend breast and back apart to expose joints; sever.

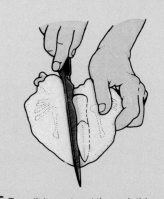

6 To split breast, cut through thin membrane to keel bone; then cut through skin and meat along one side of bone and cartilage.

ROASTING POULTRY

What's the best way to roast poultry? How long will it take? How do I know when the bird is done? If you're unsure of the answers to these questions, you'll find the following guidelines helpful.

PREPARING & ROASTING THE BIRD

Remove neck and giblets from body cavity; rinse bird inside and out, then pat dry. Stuff chicken, game hens, or turkey, if you wish; then truss. If you're roasting goose or duck, prick skin all over to allow fat to escape during cooking.

Estimate total cooking time by multiplying the bird's weight by the minutes per pound indicated in the chart. If the bird is stuffed, add a few minutes to the total. Place bird, breast down, on a rack in a shallow roasting pan; rub skin generously with butter or margarine (or follow recipe directions). About halfway through estimated cooking time, turn bird breast up. Large turkeys can be awkward to turn by yourself, so enlist some help. Protecting hands with paper towels, firmly hold turkey legs and neck end; then turn.

CHECKING DONENESS

For a whole chicken or turkey, insert a meat thermometer in thickest part of thigh (not touching bone) after turning bird breast up. (For a turkey breast, insert in thickest part, not touching bone.) Begin checking thermometer three-quarters of the way through cooking; when it registers the correct temperature (see below), the bird is done.

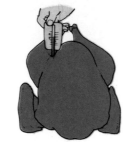

Geese and ducks are fairly bony, so it's hard to insert a thermometer in the thigh without hitting bone. Game hens are too small for a thermometer to work correctly. To check doneness of these birds, slash meat near thighbone; it should no longer look pink.

If the bird finishes browning before it's completely cooked, cover it loosely with foil.

After taking the bird from the oven, let it stand, loosely covered, for 10 to 20 minutes so the juices will settle back into the meat. Then carve. To slice meat off breast, make a horizontal cut under ribs near neck, cutting through to bone. Slice meat down at a right angle to cut.

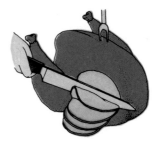

BIRD	APPROXI-MATE WEIGHT (lbs.)	APPROXI-MATE COOKING TIME (minutes/lb.)	OVEN TEMPER-ATURE (°F)	MEAT THER-MOMETER READING (°F)
FRYING CHICKEN	3–4	17–20	375°	185°
ROASTING CHICKEN	5–6	20–25	350°	185°
ROCK CORNISH GAME HEN	1–1½	30–45	425°	—
DUCK	4–5	20–25	375°	—
GOOSE	8–14	10–12*	400°/325°*	—
HEN TURKEY	8–15	15	325°	185°
TOM TURKEY	16–30	12	325°	185°
TURKEY BREAST Half, bone-in Half, boneless	2–4 2–4	15–20 20–25	350° 350°	170° 170°
TURKEY THIGH	½–1½	60	350°	185°

*Roast goose at 400° for 1 hour, then reduce heat to 325°. Continue roasting for an additional 10 to 12 minutes per pound.

MICROWAVING POULTRY

Caution: To prevent overcooking, use shortest cooking time. Allow food to stand for recommended time. On standing, internal temperature of poultry will rise 10 to 15 degrees. If necessary, microwave longer, checking for doneness at 1-minute intervals.

TYPE OF POULTRY	PREPARATION	COOKING TIME (CT) STANDING TIME (ST)
Frying chicken, whole 3–3½ lbs.	If frozen, thaw completely. Remove giblets and neck; rinse inside and out and pat dry. Stuff, if desired. Secure neck skin to back with a non-metallic skewer. If stuffed, hold stuffing in body cavity with a heel of bread. With string, tie legs together and wings to breast. Rub skin with butter or margarine and paprika. Place, breast side down, on a nonmetallic rack in a 7- by 11-inch baking dish. Cover with wax paper.	**CT:** 6–7 minutes/lb. Determine total cooking time. Microwave on HIGH (100%). Turn breast up halfway through cooking. **ST:** 5 minutes, loosely covered. Meat near thighbone should no longer be pink; cut to test.
Frying chicken, cut up 3–3½ lbs.	Rinse; pat dry. In a 7- by 11-inch baking dish, arrange pieces, skin side down, with meaty portions to outside of dish. Cover with wax paper.	**CT:** 6–7 minutes/lb. Determine total cooking time. Microwave on HIGH (100%), turning pieces skin side up halfway through cooking. If desired, uncover, discard accumulated liquid, and baste with a barbecue sauce during last 10 minutes. **ST:** 5 minutes, covered (uncovered, if basted). Meat near thighbone should no longer be pink; cut to test.
Chicken breast, split 1–1¼ lbs.	Remove bone and skin, if desired. Place in a 9-inch square baking dish. Cover with wax paper.	**CT:** 4–5 minutes/lb. Determine total cooking time. Microwave on HIGH (100%), turning over halfway through cooking. **ST:** 5 minutes, covered. Meat in thickest part should no longer be pink; cut to test.
Whole chicken legs, thighs attached 6–8 oz. *each*	Rinse; pat dry. In a 7- by 11-inch baking dish, arrange pieces, skin side down, with thighs to outside of dish and drumstick ends to center. Cover with wax paper.	**CT:** 7 minutes/lb. Determine total cooking time. Microwave on HIGH (100%), turning over halfway through cooking. **ST:** 5 minutes, covered. Meat near thighbone should no longer be pink; cut to test.
Rock Cornish game hens 1–1½ lbs. *each*	Same as whole chicken, except leave legs free; secure wings akimbo-style. Place, breast down, on a nonmetallic rack in a 7- by 11-inch baking dish. Cover with wax paper.	**CT:** 6 minutes/lb. Determine total cooking time. Microwave on HIGH (100%), turning breast up halfway through cooking. **ST:** 5 minutes, loosely covered. Meat near thighbone should no longer be pink; cut to test.
Turkey, whole 10–14 lbs. (We do not recommend microwaving a bird over 14 lbs.)	If frozen, thaw completely. Rinse inside and out; pat dry. Stuff neck and body cavities, if desired. Secure neck skin to back with a non-metallic skewer. If stuffed, hold stuffing in body cavity with a heel of bread. With string, tie legs together and wings to breast. Rub skin with butter or margarine and paprika. Place bird, breast down, in a 9- by 13-inch baking dish.	**CT:** 7–8 minutes/lb. Microwave on HIGH (100%). Determine total cooking time; divide into 4 equal cooking periods. Position bird as follows: first period, breast down; second period, right wing down; third period, left wing down; fourth period, breast up. Discard accumulated juices each time bird is turned. A meat thermometer inserted in thickest part of thigh (not touching bone) should register 170°F. **ST:** 15 minutes, loosely covered.
Turkey breast, half 3–3½ lbs.	Remove bone and skin, if desired. Place in a 7- by 11-inch baking dish. Cover with heavy-duty plastic wrap.	**CT:** 4–5 minutes/lb. Determine total cooking time. Microwave on HIGH (100%), turning over halfway through cooking. **ST:** 5–7 minutes, covered. Meat in thickest part should no longer be pink; cut to test.
Turkey drumsticks 1–1¼ lbs. *each*	Rinse; pat dry. In a 7- by 11-inch baking dish, arrange turkey legs with meaty portions to outside of dish. Brush with melted butter or margarine. Cover with heavy-duty plastic wrap.	**CT:** 20 minutes/lb. Determine total cooking time. Microwave on HIGH (100%) for 10 minutes. Turn legs over; microwave on MEDIUM-LOW (30%) for remaining time, turning legs over halfway through cooking. Discard juices as they accumulate in dish. **ST:** 15 minutes, covered. Meat near bone should no longer be pink; cut to test.
Duck 4–5 lbs.	Same as whole turkey, except leave legs free; secure wings akimbo-style. With a fork, prick skin in several places.	**CT:** 8–9 minutes/lb. Determine total cooking time. Microwave on HIGH (100%), turning breast up halfway through cooking. Discard juices as they accumulate in dish. **ST:** 5–10 minutes, loosely covered. Meat near bone at hip socket should no longer be pink; cut to test.

BARBECUING POULTRY

For general information on barbecuing methods, see "Barbecuing Basics for Meat," pages 39 to 40.

TYPE OF POULTRY	WEIGHT OR THICKNESS	GRILLING METHOD	FIRE TEMPERATURE	TEST FOR DONENESS & APPROXIMATE COOKING TIME
CHICKEN Whole	3–4 lbs.	Indirect	Hot, banked	Meat thermometer inserted in thigh registers 185°F.* 1–1¼ hours.
	6–7 lbs.	Indirect	Hot, banked	Meat thermometer inserted in thigh registers 185°F.* 1½–1¾ hours.
Halved	3–4 lbs. *total*	Direct	Medium	Meat near bone is no longer pink; cut to test. 40–50 minutes.
Quartered	3–4 lbs. *total*	Direct	Medium	Meat near bone is no longer pink; cut to test. 40–50 minutes.
Cut up	3–4 lbs. *total*	Direct	Medium	Meat near bone is no longer pink; cut to test. Dark meat 35–40 minutes; white meat 15–20 minutes.
Breast halves, bone-in	½–¾ lb. *each*	Direct	Medium	Meat near bone is no longer pink; cut to test. 15–20 minutes.
Breast halves, boned	5–7 oz. *each*	Direct	Medium	Meat is no longer pink; cut to test. 10–12 minutes.
Whole legs, thighs attached	8–10 oz. *each*	Direct	Medium	Meat near bone is no longer pink; cut to test. 35–45 minutes.
Drumsticks or thighs	4–6 oz. *each*	Direct	Medium	Meat near bone is no longer pink; cut to test. 30–35 minutes.
Wings	3–4 oz. *each*	Direct	Medium	Meat near bone is no longer pink; cut to test. About 30 minutes.
Boneless cubes	¾–1 inch	Direct	Low	Meat is no longer pink in center; cut to test. 10–12 minutes.
ROCK CORNISH GAME HEN Whole	1–1½ lbs.	Indirect	Hot, banked	Meat near thighbone is no longer pink; cut to test. 45–60 minutes.
Halved	1–1½ lbs. *total*	Direct	Medium	Meat near bone is no longer pink; cut to test. 30–40 minutes.
TURKEY Whole	9–15 lbs.	Indirect	Hot, banked	Meat thermometer inserted in thigh registers 185°F.* 15 minutes/lb.
	16–22 lbs.	Indirect	Hot, banked	Meat thermometer inserted in thigh registers 185°F.* 12 minutes/lb.
Halved	10–12 lbs. *total*	Indirect	Hot, banked	Meat thermometer inserted in thigh registers 185°F.* 1½–2 hours.
Breast halves, bone-in	2½–3 lbs. *each*	Indirect	Hot, banked	Meat near bone is no longer pink; cut to test. 1–1½ hours.
Drumsticks or thighs	1–2 lbs. *each*	Direct, covered	Medium	Meat near bone is no longer pink; cut to test. 55–65 minutes.
Wings	1 lb. *each*	Direct, covered	Medium	Meat near bone is no longer pink; cut to test. 40–50 minutes.
Boneless cubes	1 inch	Direct	Medium	Meat is no longer pink in center; cut to test. 12–15 minutes.
Breast steaks	½ inch	Direct	Medium	Meat is no longer pink; cut to test. 7–9 minutes.
DUCK Whole	4–5 lbs.	Indirect	Hot, banked	Meat near bone at hip socket is no longer pink; cut to test. 2–2½ hours.

*Insert meat thermometer in thickest part of thigh (not touching bone).

BROILING POULTRY

If you're looking for a way to cook poultry that's especially quick, choose broiling. The broiler's intense heat seals in juices in minutes, keeping meat moist while the skin turns deliciously brown and crisp.

BROILING TECHNIQUE

Select a large, shallow pan with a rack and place the poultry on the rack. Position the pan below the heat source in your broiler, adjusting the pan (or the oven rack on which the pan is resting) until the top of the poultry is the recommended distance below the heat source.

Remove the poultry from the broiler, leaving the pan and rack inside. Preheat the broiler for 5 to 7 minutes. Meanwhile, rub poultry with butter, margarine, or oil, and season with herbs as desired. Remove the pan from the broiler and lightly grease the hot rack.

Place pieces of poultry slightly apart on the rack, skin side down, and broil for the time specified below. Turn over and continue to broil, basting occasionally with more butter, margarine, or oil if desired, for the time specified or until meat near thighbone is no longer pink; cut to test.

TYPE OF POULTRY*	DISTANCE BELOW HEAT	COOKING TIME, SKIN SIDE DOWN	COOKING TIME, SKIN SIDE UP
CHICKEN HALVES OR QUARTERS	6–8 inches	15 minutes	15–20 minutes
CHICKEN WINGS	6 inches	15 minutes	8–10 minutes
ROCK CORNISH GAME HENS, HALVED	2 inches	12 minutes	5–7 minutes

*Birds larger than chickens are not appropriate for broiling.

BONING A CHICKEN BREAST

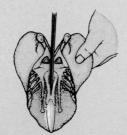

1 Lay breast skin side down; run a sharp knife down center to sever thin membrane and expose keel bone (dark spoon-shaped bone) and thick white cartilage.

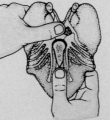

2 Placing one thumb on tip end of keel bone and other at base of rib cage, grasp breast firmly in both hands. Bend breast back with both hands until keel bone breaks through.

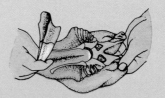

3 Run finger under edge of keel bone and thick cartilage, then pull out and discard bone and cartilage.

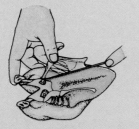

4 Insert knife under long first rib. Resting knife against ribs, scrape meat away. Sever shoulder joint; remove ribs and attached bone. Repeat with other side of breast.

5 With fingers, locate wishbone. Cutting close to bone, remove wishbone.

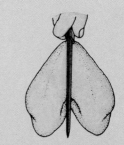

6 Lay breast flat on a cutting board and cut breast in half; remove white tendon from bottom side of each half. Pull off skin, if suggested in recipe.

Fish & Shellfish

Fish and shellfish are wondrous foods; their multiple advantages have long been known and cultivated among the world's cuisines, and today their appeal is as great as ever. They're remarkably adaptable, accommodating a wide variety of cooking methods and seasonings. They're quick-cooking, saving precious time and energy. They're generally low in fat and high in other nutrients. And when fresh and properly prepared, they're undeniably delicious!

Familiarize yourself with the various kinds of fish and shellfish in your market, their available forms, and the basic cooking methods that suit them. You'll be surprised how easy it is to master the fine art of fish cookery.

BUYING & STORING FISH

Unlike meats, which are sold in a bewildering array of cuts, the forms of fish available in most markets are quite simple and straightforward. But as with meats, it's important to choose the right cut of fish—the one that suits your recipe and makes preparation easiest.

Whole or round. This form is the fish as it comes from the water, scales and all. To cook it, you must at least eviscerate, scale, and dress it yourself. Fish tends to be least expensive in whole form, but remember that, on average, only 45 percent of it is edible meat.

Drawn. It is possible to buy whole fish that are already eviscerated or "drawn." These are about 48 percent edible. However, you must still scale, dress, and, if necessary, cut up the fish yourself.

Dressed or pan-dressed. A dressed fish is a whole fish that has been drawn and scaled; usually, it has also had its fins and often its head and tail removed. Dressed fish are ready to cook; they contain about 67 percent edible meat.

Chunks & steaks. These pieces are cross-section slices of a dressed large fish. A chunk is usually 4 to 6 inches thick; a steak is ¾ to 1 inch thick. Because the only bone is a piece of backbone, these cuts are about 84 percent edible. They're ready to cook as purchased.

Fillets. The most common form of fish available, fresh or frozen, fillets are the fleshy sides of the fish, cut away from the backbone and ribs.

They're practically boneless. A "butterfly fillet" is a double fillet formed by both sides of the fish, still joined by the uncut flesh and skin of the belly. A single fillet is just one side of the fish and is generally skinless. Both butterfly and single fillets are almost 100 percent edible.

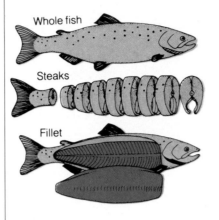

Whole fish

Steaks

Fillet

Portions & fish sticks. Frozen fish is available in uniform, ready-to-cook rectangles cut from boneless frozen fish blocks and breaded. These may be raw or partially cooked; in either case, they require no preparation for cooking.

PURCHASING GUIDELINES

In a fresh fish, the flesh is firm and springs back when pressed gently; it hasn't begun separating from the bones. Fresh fillets and steaks are moist and firm, and look freshly cut; they show no traces of drying or browning at the edges. The odor should be fresh and mild. Never buy fish whose odor is disagreeably strong—it won't taste any better than it smells.

The eyes of a really fresh whole fish are clear, full, and often protruding; cloudy, sunken eyes indicate an old fish that's starting to spoil. The gills should be pinkish red and free of slime; as the fish ages, the gills turn gray, then brownish or greenish. Finally, the skin of a whole fish should be shiny, with unfaded color and pronounced markings.

Like fresh fish, frozen fish should be checked for spoilage—if it hasn't been frozen correctly, it probably will have had ample opportunity to spoil before you buy it. The flesh should be solidly frozen. There should be no discoloration, no brownish tinge, and no white, cottony appearance. The odor, if any, should be very slight. Packaging should be airtight and undamaged. The best-protected frozen fish is that which has been covered completely in a glazing of ice, so that it is totally shielded from contact with the air.

HOW MUCH TO BUY

If you're buying fish pieces (chunks, steaks, or fillets), reckon on 4 to 6 servings for every 1½ to 2½ pounds of fish. For whole fish, use this guideline: one 4-pound fish yields 6 to 8 servings.

STORAGE TIPS

Fresh fish are known for their perishability. Refrigerate them in a leakproof wrapper as soon as possible after purchase (eviscerate first, if necessary); cook them within 2 days. Fish can also be frozen for extended periods of time, though they're most delicious when eaten fresh. To freeze fish, wrap airtight in moisture-proof freezer wrap and seal securely. Stored at 0°F or lower, fish of moderate fat content will keep for 3 months; leaner fish may remain frozen for up to 6 months. (For information on fat content, see the charts on pages 52 to 55.)

It's best to thaw frozen fish in the refrigerator, allowing 18 to 24 hours for a 1-pound package. If quicker thawing is desired, place the package, unopened, in *cold* water; let it stand for 1 to 2 hours. Cook thawed frozen fish as soon as possible; never store thawed fish for more than a day, and never refreeze partially or completely thawed fish.

A PROFILE OF COMMON FISH

NAMES & ALTERNATE NAMES	FLAVOR & TEXTURE	FAT CONTENT*	SIZE RANGE
ALBACORE, PACIFIC **Longfin tuna**	Rich flavor; soft flesh becomes firm and meaty when cooked	Moderate	10–25 lbs.
BLUEFISH **Blue snapper, skipjack, tailor, fatback, snapping mackerel**	Mild flavor; tender flesh	Low	1–7 lbs.
BUTTERFISH **Harvestfish, silver dollar, dollarfish, pumpkin seed**	Mild, delicate flavor; soft, melting flesh	Moderate	¼–1¼ lbs.
CARP **German carp, summer carp**	Mild flavor; firm flesh	Low to moderate	2–8 lbs.
CATFISH **Channel catfish, flathead catfish, yaqui, headwater catfish, blue catfish, white catfish, madtom, widemouth and toothless blindcats, stonecats, gafftopsail catfish**	Mild flavor; tender flesh	Low	1–40 lbs.
COD, ATLANTIC OR PACIFIC **Codfish**	Mild flavor; tender-firm flesh that flakes easily when cooked	Very low	1½–20 lbs.
CROAKER **Crocus, hardhead, Texas croaker, chut, golden croaker, corvina, roncadina, drum**	Mild flavor; tender flesh	Low	½–2 lbs.
DRUM, BLACK **Oyster cracker, oyster drum, sea drum, gray drum, channel bass, barbed drum, big drum, striped drum, drumfish, sheepshead**	Mild flavor; tender-firm flesh	Low	1–40 lbs.
EEL, COMMON **American eel, silver eel**	Mild flavor; tender-firm flesh	Moderate	1–5 lbs.
FINNAN HADDIE **Smoked haddock, smoked cod**	Rich, smoky flavor; tender texture	Low	½–3 lbs. per fillet
FLOUNDER OR SOLE **Blackback flounder, winter flounder, fluke, summer flounder, dab, sea dab, lemon sole, gray sole, southern flounder, yellowtail flounder; petrale sole, rex sole, sand dab, sand sole, Dover sole, English sole**	Mild, delicate, distinctive flavor; tender, flaky flesh	Low	¾–12 lbs.
GROUPER **Sea bass**	Mild flavor; tender-firm flesh	Low	5–12 lbs.
HADDOCK **Scrod**	Mild flavor; tender-chewy, flaky flesh	Low	1½–7 lbs.
HALIBUT, PACIFIC **Northern halibut; if 6–10 lbs., chicken halibut**	Mild flavor; tender-firm flesh	Very low	6–100 lbs.
HERRING, ATLANTIC **Sea herring**	Pronounced flavor; tender flesh	Moderate	⅛–¼ lb.
KINGFISH **King mackerel, cero**	Pronounced flavor; firm flesh	Moderate	5–20 lbs.
LINGCOD **Cultus cod, blue cod, buffalo cod (not a true cod)**	Delicate flavor; tender flesh	Very low	5–10 lbs.
MACKEREL **Boston mackerel, Atlantic mackerel, Spanish mackerel, Pacific mackerel, blue mackerel, American mackerel**	Rich, pronounced flavor; firm flesh	High	1–4 lbs.
MULLET **Jumping mullet, striped mullet, silver mullet, black mullet, liza, sand mullet, white mullet**	Mild flavor; tender flesh	Moderate	½–3 lbs.

*Very low: less than 2 percent fat; Low: 2–5 percent fat; Moderate: 6–10 percent fat; High: more than 10 percent fat

FORMS AVAILABLE	WHERE AVAILABLE	WHEN AVAILABLE	HOW TO COOK**
Whole (sometimes steaks, chunks)	Western coast (on request from market)	Summer (in Northwest, midsummer through October)	Steaks: butter-saute, pan-fry, oven-fry, broil, barbecue Chunks: poach or bake
Whole, drawn	Eastern, Gulf coasts	All year	Oven-fry, broil, bake
Whole, drawn	Eastern coast	Spring to late autumn	Butter-sauté, pan-fry, oven-fry, broil
Whole, dressed, steaks, fillets	Great Lakes, other U.S. lakes, inland rivers	All year (best from October to March)	Oven-fry, broil, poach, bake
Whole, dressed, dressed and skinned, fillets	Great Lakes, other U.S. lakes, inland rivers, western states	All year	Pan-fry, oven-fry, broil, barbecue
Drawn, dressed, steaks, fillets, dried and salted	Northeastern, mideastern, western coasts (available frozen in rest of U.S.)	All year	Poach, or cook in soups, stews, casseroles, fish cakes
Whole, drawn, fillets	Mideastern and southeastern coasts	March to October (especially summer and autumn)	Butter-sauté, pan-fry, oven-fry, broil
Whole, drawn, steaks	Mideastern, southeastern, Gulf coasts	October through February	Oven-fry, poach, bake
Whole, dressed, dressed and skinned	Eastern coast	All year (less in winter)	Butter-sauté, pan-fry, poach; or cook in soups, stews, or casseroles
Fillets	Eastern coast	All year	Oven-fry, broil, poach, bake in casseroles
Whole, dressed, fillets	Northeastern, mideastern, western coasts	All year	Butter-sauté, pan-fry, oven-fry, broil, poach
Drawn, dressed, steaks, fillets	Southeastern coast	November to May	Pan-fry, deep-fry, oven-fry, broil, poach, bake
Drawn, fillets	Northeastern coast (available frozen in rest of U.S.)	All year	Butter-sauté, pan-fry, deep-fry, oven-fry, broil, poach, bake
Steaks, fillets (chicken halibut available whole, on request from market)	Western coast (available frozen in rest of U.S.)	May to September (available frozen the rest of the year)	Butter-sauté, pan-fry, oven-fry, broil, poach, barbecue
Whole, drawn, packed in brine	Northeastern, mideastern, western coasts	All year	Pan-fry, oven-fry
Drawn, fillets, steaks	Southeastern, Gulf coasts	November to March	Oven-fry, broil, barbecue, poach
Whole, fillets, steaks	Western coast	All year (best April to October on California coast, October to May in Northwest)	Butter-sauté, pan-fry, deep-fry, oven-fry, broil, poach
Whole, fillets	Northeastern, mideastern, western coasts	All year (spring and summer in East)	Broil, barbecue, bake
Whole	Southeastern, Gulf coasts	April to November	Pan-fry, oven-fry, broil, barbecue, bake

**Basic methods described on pages 56–60

(Continued on next page)

A PROFILE OF COMMON FISH

NAMES & ALTERNATE NAMES	FLAVOR & TEXTURE	FAT CONTENT*	SIZE RANGE
OCEAN PERCH, ATLANTIC **Redfish, red perch, rosefish**	Mild flavor; tender, flaky flesh	Very low	½–2 lbs.
PIKE **Common pike, pickerel, muskellunge, yellow pike perch, walleyed pike, blue pike perch, sauger, sand pike**	Mild flavor; firm flesh	Low	1–30 lbs.
POMPANO **Great pompano, permit, golden pompano, Carolina permi, cobblerfish, butterfish, palmenta**	Rich, distinctive flavor; firm flesh	Moderate	½–3½ lbs.
PORGY/SCUP **Fair maid, northern porgy, paugy, porgee, white snapper**	Mild flavor; tender, flaky flesh	Low	½–1½ lbs.
ROCKFISH **Rock cod, sea bass, rosefish, grouper, red snapper, Pacific ocean perch**	Mild flavor; firm flesh	Very low	2–5 lbs.
SABLEFISH **Black cod, Alaska cod, butterfish**	Buttery, mild flavor; very soft, melting flesh	Moderate to high	4–20 lbs.
SALMON, PACIFIC **King (chinook, spring) and coho (silver, silverside); also sockeye or red salmon, pink or humpback salmon, chum or keta or calico salmon**	Rich, distinctive flavor; firm flesh of a light pink to bright red	Moderate	6–30 lbs.
SEA BASS **Black sea bass (black jewfish, giant seabass, grouper bass, California black seabass), white sea bass**	Mild flavor; tender flesh	Very low	Black: 50–600 lbs. White: up to 50 lbs.
SEA BASS, COMMON **Blackfish, black sea bass**	Mild flavor; tender flesh	Low	½–4 lbs.
SEA TROUT, GRAY OR SPOTTED **Weakfish, gray trout, squeteague, speckled trout, spotted sea trout, spotted trout, sand sea trout**	Mild flavor; tender-firm flesh	Low	1–6 lbs.
SHAD & ROE **American shad, white shad (roe are the eggs of the shad)**	Mild flavor; firm, meatlike flesh, quite bony	High	1½–7 lbs.
SHARK **Greyfish, grayfish, dogfish, pinback, soupfin, thresher, leopard, tiger, bull, mako**	Pronounced flavor (like swordfish); firm, meatlike flesh	Low	Western variety: 12–30 lbs. (except dogfish, 12–18 lbs.); Southeastern and Gulf variety: up to 200 lbs.
SMELT **Whitebait, icefish, frostfish, candlelight fish**	Rich flavor; tender-firm flesh	Low to moderate	8–12 lbs.
SNAPPER, RED **Snapper**	Mild, distinctive flavor; tender-firm flesh	Low	2–20 lbs.
SPOT	Mild flavor; tender flesh	Low	¼–1¼ lbs.
STRIPED BASS **Rockfish, striper**	Mild flavor; tender-firm flesh	Low	2–50 lbs.
SWORDFISH **Broadbill**	Rich, distinctive flavor; firm, meatlike flesh	Moderate	200–600 lbs.
TROUT **Rainbow trout, brook trout, brown trout**	Mild, distinctive flavor; firm flesh	Moderate to high	⅓–2 lbs.
TURBOT, GREENLAND	Mild flavor; tender, soft, flaky flesh	Low	5–15 lbs.
WHITEFISH **Cisco, lake whitefish, chub**	Delicate flavor; tender flesh	Moderate	2–6 lbs.
WHITING **Silver hake**	Mild, delicate flavor; tender, flaky flesh	Low	¾–3 lbs.

*Very low: less than 2 percent fat; Low: 2–5 percent fat; Moderate: 6–10 percent fat; High: more than 10 percent fat

FORMS AVAILABLE	WHERE AVAILABLE	WHEN AVAILABLE	HOW TO COOK**
Whole, fillets	Northeastern coast (available frozen in rest of U.S.)	All year	Butter-sauté, pan-fry, oven-fry, broil, poach
Whole, drawn, fillets	Great Lakes, other U.S. lakes	All year	Butter-sauté, pan-fry, deep-fry, oven-fry, broil, barbecue, poach, bake
Whole, drawn	Gulf coast	All year (especially March through May)	Butter-sauté, pan-fry, oven-fry, broil, barbecue, bake
Whole, drawn	Eastern coast	September to May (especially January to April)	Pan-fry, oven-fry, broil, barbecue
Whole, fillets	Western coast	All year	Butter-sauté, pan-fry, deep-fry, oven-fry, broil, barbecue, poach, bake
Whole, fillets, steaks	Western coast	All year (best in summer on California coast; August to November in Northwest)	Oven-fry, broil, barbecue, poach
Whole, drawn, steaks, fillets	Western coast (available frozen in rest of U.S.)	Varies by area (available frozen all year)	Butter-sauté, pan-fry, deep-fry, oven-fry, broil, barbecue, poach
Steaks, chunks, fillets	Western coast	All year	Butter-sauté, pan-fry, oven-fry, broil, poach
Whole, drawn, dressed, fillets	Eastern coast	All year	Butter-sauté, pan-fry, oven-fry, broil, poach
Whole, drawn, fillets	Mideastern, southeastern coasts	April to November	Butter-sauté, pan-fry, oven-fry, broil, barbecue, bake
Whole, drawn	Eastern, northwestern coasts	March through May	Oven-fry, barbecue, poach
Steaks, chunks, fillets	Western, southeastern, Gulf coasts	All year (especially in summer)	Oven-fry, broil, barbecue, poach
Whole, drawn	Northeastern, western coasts	All year	Butter-sauté, pan-fry, deep-fry, oven-fry, broil
Whole, drawn, steaks, fillets	Gulf coast	All year	Butter-sauté, pan-fry, oven-fry, broil, poach
Whole, drawn	Mideastern, southeastern coasts	All year	Butter-sauté, pan-fry, oven-fry, broil
Whole, drawn, steaks, fillets	Mideastern, southeastern coasts	All year	Butter-sauté, pan-fry, oven-fry, broil, barbecue, poach, bake
Steaks, chunks	Northeastern, mideastern, western coasts	August through October (frozen the rest of the year)	Oven-fry, broil, barbecue
Drawn, dressed	Inland rivers and fish farms	All year	Butter-sauté, pan-fry, deep-fry, oven-fry, broil, barbecue, poach
Fillets	Imported (available frozen throughout the U.S.)	All year	Butter-sauté, pan-fry, oven-fry, poach
Whole, drawn, fillets, smoked	Great Lakes, other U.S. lakes	April to December	Butter-sauté, pan-fry, deep-fry, oven-fry, broil, barbecue, poach, bake
Drawn, dressed, steaks, fillets	Northeastern, mideastern coasts	All year (especially in summer)	Butter-sauté, pan-fry, deep-fry, oven-fry, broil, poach

**Basic methods described on pages 56–60

COOKING FISH

All fish cookery rests on a foundation of eight simple preparation methods—baking, broiling, butter-sautéing, pan-frying, deep-frying, oven-frying, barbecuing, and poaching. Once you've mastered these basic techniques, you can master any fish dish. On the following pages, we offer simple instructions for cooking fish by these eight methods—plus a chart giving instructions for cooking fish in a microwave oven. (*Note:* Here we discuss cooking only fillets, steaks and small whole fish, since these are the most commonly available forms. For help in cooking a large whole fish, consult the *Sunset Seafood Cook Book.*)

Judging doneness. Recognizing when a fish is done is the essential step in learning to cook it well. Most recipes tell you to cook fish "until it flakes when prodded." This is because the fish flakes at the precise moment of doneness, when the heat has broken down the connective fibers just enough to permit the tender flesh to slide apart along its natural divisions at the gentle probing of a fork, but not so much that the flavor and moisture have escaped. Another moment or two and the fish will be overcooked. When a fish is badly overcooked, it will, of its own accord, fall into pieces along its natural divisions, and the flesh will be very tough and tasteless.

Be sure you probe with your fork into the center of the thickest portion of the fish or piece of fish, because the thinner parts may appear done when the thicker part is still raw inside. If this is the case, the inside of the thicker portion will feel resistant to the fork and appear translucent, while the thinner portion will be opaque and tender.

BAKING

On days when both time and energy are in short supply, you'll find baking an appealingly quick, no-nonsense approach to fish cookery. Unlike oven-fried fish, baked fish needs no coating; nor must it be immersed in liquid, as for poaching. And baking adapts to any size, shape, or kind of fish.

We recommend baking plain fish at a high temperature (though not as high as for oven-frying). The high heat decreases the cooking time and locks in the fish's juicy freshness.

How to bake. Preheat oven to 425°. Place a large, shallow baking pan in oven to preheat. Use **fish fillets or steaks (up to 1½ inches thick) or small whole fish (up to 3 lbs.), cleaned and scaled;** wipe fish with a damp paper towel. Cut into serving-size pieces (about 3 by 5 inches), if desired.

Remove pan from oven. Put equal amounts of **butter** or margarine and **salad oil** in pan; swirl until butter is melted (fat should be about ⅛ inch deep).

Place a piece of fish in pan; turn to coat with butter and oil. Repeat with remaining fish, arranging as many pieces in pan as will fit without crowding. (If using thin—½-inch-thick or less—fillets, you can layer them 2 deep. Drizzle top layer with a little butter and oil and adjust cooking time accordingly.)

Drizzle **seasoning liquid** (suggestions follow) over fish, if desired; liquid should be about ¼ inch deep. Sprinkle with **herbs** (suggestions follow), if desired.

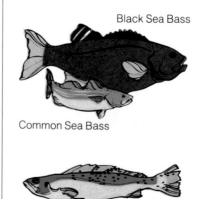

Black Sea Bass

Common Sea Bass

Spotted Sea Trout

Bake, uncovered, just until fish flakes readily when prodded in thickest part. Total cooking time depends on thickness of fish (measured in thickest part). For every inch of thickness, allow 8 to 10 minutes. (If fish fillets are layered, measure total thickness of both layers.)

When fish is done, transfer to a warm platter. Sprinkle with **salt** and **pepper** and serve immediately, garnished with **lemon wedges,** if desired. Spoon any remaining seasoning liquid over individual servings.

Seasoning liquid. Use **regular-strength chicken broth,** dry white wine, or dry sherry. For 4 to 6 servings (1½ to 2½ lbs. fish pieces), you'll need about ½ cup.

Herbs. Select 1 or 2 of the following: chopped **parsley; dry basil; dry tarragon; savory, thyme, or marjoram leaves;** or finely chopped **green onion** (including top).

BROILING

A platter of fish grilled briefly under the broiler is simplicity itself. Broiling is a quick method of cooking that's a good choice for calorie-counters—the only fat involved is a brush-on baste. And it can be done without even coating the fish.

Thick fish pieces seem to fare better under the broiler than very thin ones (under ¼ inch), particularly if no coating is used. A thicker piece of fish has plenty of time to develop a golden surface before the inside is cooked, but the high heat penetrates and cooks a thin, uncoated piece before it has a chance to brown. However, any fish fillet, steak, or small whole fish can be broiled; just make sure that you baste thinner fish pieces with plenty of butter or oil to keep them from drying out.

How to broil. Use **fish fillets, fish steaks, or small whole fish (up to 1½ inches thick), cleaned and scaled;** wipe fish with a damp paper towel. Cut into serving-size pieces (about 3 by 5 inches), if desired.

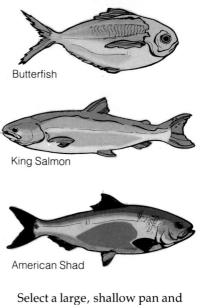

Butterfish

King Salmon

American Shad

Select a large, shallow pan and place one piece of fish in pan. Position pan below heat source in your broiler, adjusting pan (or oven rack on which it rests) until top of fish is recommended distance below heat source: 2 inches for pieces up to ¼ inch thick; 3 inches for pieces ¼ to ¾ inch thick; 4 inches for pieces ¾ to 1½ inches thick; 6 inches for thicker pieces.

Remove fish from broiler, leaving pan inside. Preheat broiler for 5 to 7 minutes. Meanwhile, prepare a **baste** (suggestions follow). Remove pan from broiler and grease lightly. Arrange as many fish pieces in pan as will fit without crowding. Brush with baste. Broil, basting once or twice, until fish is lightly browned and flakes readily when prodded in thickest part. Pieces thicker than ¼ inch will need to be turned once to brown evenly. Total cooking time depends on thickness of fish (measured in thickest part). For every inch of thickness, allow 8 to 10 minutes—4 to 5 minutes per side.

When fish is done, transfer to a warm platter. Keep warm if more fish is to be cooked; otherwise, sprinkle fish with **salt** and **pepper** and serve immediately, garnished with **lemon wedges,** if desired.

Basting suggestions. To make the simplest baste for 4 to 6 servings of fish (1½ to 2½ lbs. fish pieces), use ¼ cup melted **butter** or margarine; or use ¼ cup **olive oil** or salad oil.

For a seasoned baste, combine ¼ cup melted **butter** or margarine and ¼ cup **lemon juice,** dry sherry, or dry vermouth.

Rex Sole

BUTTER-SAUTÉING

In French cuisine, there's a quick and easy method of cooking fish that has elegantly appealing results: crisp, golden pieces of fish with meltingly tender flesh. The French call it *à la meunière;* we call it *butter-sautéing.* Steaks, fillets, and even small whole fish such as trout, smelt, or butterfish go into a pan of foaming hot butter to be quickly sautéed to doneness.

The term *butter-sautéing* suggests that this style of cooking uses high heat, but in fact this is true only for thin fish pieces (no more than ⅝ inch thick) that must brown quickly before they cook through. Thicker pieces should be cooked over medium heat, allowing time for the heat to penetrate the interior of the fish without overcooking the surface. Whatever thickness of fish you butter-sauté, you'll need a frying pan that distributes heat evenly.

Though butter is the preferred fat for reasons of flavor, it burns easily at the temperatures required for butter-sautéing. We recommend using a combination of half butter, half salad oil—you'll avoid the risk of burning but still get a marvelously buttery flavor.

How to butter-sauté. Use **fish fillets, fish steaks, or small whole fish (up to 1½ inches thick), cleaned and scaled;** wipe fish with a damp paper towel. Cut into serving-size pieces (about 3 by 5 inches), if desired. Coat fish with **all-purpose flour;** shake off excess. Arrange fish in a single layer on wax paper within reaching distance of range.

COOKING FISH IN THE MICROWAVE

Caution: To prevent overcooking, use shortest cooking time. Allow food to stand for recommended time. On standing, fish will continue to cook. If necessary, microwave longer, checking for doneness at 1-minute intervals.

FISH	PREPARATION	COOKING TIME (CT) STANDING TIME (ST)
FISH STEAKS OR FILLETS Red snapper or other rockfish, Greenland turbot, sole, halibut, sea bass, salmon, ½–¾ inch thick **1 lb.**	If frozen, thaw completely. Wipe with a damp paper towel. In a greased 7- by 11-inch baking dish, arrange fish in an even layer, with thicker portions to outside of dish. Brush with melted butter or margarine. If desired, sprinkle with paprika, dill weed, grated lemon peel, or lemon juice. Cover with heavy-duty plastic wrap.	**CT:** 3–5 minutes/lb. Microwave on HIGH (100%), turning fish over after 2 minutes. **ST:** 3 minutes, covered. Fish should flake readily when prodded in thickest part.
TROUT, WHOLE (CLEANED AND DRESSED) **1 or 2** **(8–10 oz.** *each***)**	If frozen, thaw completely. Wipe with a damp paper towel. Stuff with lemon or onion slices, if desired. In a greased 7- by 11-inch baking dish, arrange fish lengthwise, with backbones to outside edge of dish. Brush with melted butter or margarine. Cover with heavy-duty plastic wrap.	**CT:** 1 trout: 2½–3½ minutes 2 trout: 5–7 minutes Microwave on HIGH (100%), turning fish over and bringing cooked portion to inside of dish halfway through cooking. **ST:** 3 minutes, covered. Fish should flake readily when prodded in thickest part.

(Continued on next page)

In a wide frying pan, heat equal amounts of **butter** or margarine and **salad oil** (fat should be about ⅛ inch deep) until foamy but not browned. Promptly add as many fish pieces as will fit without crowding. Cook until lightly browned on bottom, using medium-high heat if pieces are ⅝ inch thick or less, medium heat if pieces are thicker than ⅝ inch. Then turn each piece carefully with a wide spatula; cook just until fish is browned on other side and flakes readily when prodded in thickest part. Total cooking time depends on thickness of fish (measured in thickest part). For every inch of thickness, allow 8 to 10 minutes —4 to 5 minutes per side.

Remove each piece of fish from pan as soon as it is done; arrange on a warm platter and keep warm until all fish is cooked. Sprinkle with **salt, pepper,** and chopped **parsley;** serve immediately, garnished with **lemon wedges.**

PAN-FRYING

A pan-fried fish is any fish that has been coated, then cooked in a small amount of fat in a wide frying pan on top of the range. You can pan-fry any fish fillets, steaks, or small whole fish; the results will be most successful if you have a frying pan that distributes heat evenly.

How to pan-fry. Use **fish fillets, fish steaks, or small whole fish (up to 1½ inches thick), cleaned and scaled;** wipe fish with a damp paper towel. Cut into serving-size pieces (about 3 by 5 inches), if desired. For 4 to 6 servings (1½ to 2½ lbs. fish pieces), combine 2 **eggs** and 2 tablespoons **milk** in a shallow dish; beat lightly. Spread 1 cup **coating** (suggestions follow) in another shallow dish or on a piece of wax paper.

Dip each piece of fish in egg mixture; drain briefly. Then roll in coating to cover all sides evenly; arrange in a single layer on wax paper within reaching distance of range.

In a wide frying pan, heat equal amounts of **butter** or margarine and **salad oil** (fat should be about ⅛ inch deep) until foamy but not browned. (Or use only salad oil and heat until oil ripples when pan is tilted.) Promptly add as many fish pieces as will fit without crowding. Cook until lightly browned on bottom, using medium-high heat if pieces are ⅝ inch thick or less, medium heat if pieces are thicker than ⅝ inch. Turn each piece carefully with a wide spatula; cook just until fish is browned on other side and flakes readily when prodded in thickest part. Total cooking time depends on thickness of fish (measured in thickest part). For every inch of thickness, allow 8 to 10 minutes —4 to 5 minutes per side.

Remove each piece of fish from pan as soon as it is done; arrange on a warm platter and keep warm until all fish is cooked. Sprinkle with **salt, pepper,** and chopped **parsley;** serve immediately, garnished with **lemon wedges.**

Coating. Choose one of the following: **fine dry bread crumbs, cracker crumbs, wheat germ, all-purpose flour, cornmeal,** or finely ground **walnuts,** hazelnuts (filberts), or almonds. (To grind nuts, whirl ¾ cup nuts in a food processor until finely ground.)

Atlantic Ocean Perch

DEEP-FRYING

For this method of cooking, you can use a deep-fryer, a large, heavy pan, a deep frying pan, or a wok. (Because it's round-bottomed, a wok requires less oil for deep-frying than the other pans mentioned.) You'll also need a deep-frying thermometer to check the oil temperature before frying.

Catfish

How to deep-fry. Into a pan (see suggestions preceding), pour **salad oil** to a depth of 1½ to 2 inches; do not fill pan more than half-full. Heat oil to 375°F on a deep-frying thermometer.

Use **fish fillets, fish steaks, or small or large whole fish, cleaned and scaled;** wipe fish with a damp paper towel. Cut into serving-size pieces (about 3 inches wide, 5 inches long, and ½ to ¾ inch thick). Prepare **coating** (directions follow).

When oil has reached 375°F, coat pieces of fish, one at a time, and gently lower into hot oil. Cook several pieces at a time, but be careful not to add too much fish at once. If pan is crowded, oil temperature will drop, and fish won't brown on the outside before cooking through; it's also likely to absorb oil and become greasy.

Cook, turning occasionally, just until fish pieces are golden brown on outside and flake readily when prodded in thickest part. As you cook, frequently skim and discard any bits of coating from oil. Remove fish with a slotted spoon, tongs, or chopsticks; drain briefly. Keep warm until all fish is cooked. Or, if you prefer, serve each batch of fish immediately, accompanied with a garnish or sauce, if desired. Then repeat with more fish.

Coating. To coat fish for deep-frying, you can use either a crumb coating or a batter. Use your favorite recipe, or try this basic crumb coating (it makes enough to coat 4 to 6 servings of fish—1½ to 2½ lbs. fish pieces).

Basic crumb coating. In a shallow dish, combine 2 **eggs** and 2 tablespoons **milk;** beat lightly. Spread about 1 cup **fine dry bread crumbs,** cracker crumbs, or wheat germ in another shallow dish or on a piece of wax paper. Dip each piece of fish in egg mixture; drain briefly, then roll in crumbs to coat all sides.

OVEN-FRYING

Pop a panful of fish into a superhot oven, and in a very short time the fish toasts to a buttery doneness, golden brown on the outside, moist and tender inside. The high temperature of the oven in oven-frying produces results that are similar to those of pan-frying, but the oven technique requires less attention during cooking.

How to oven-fry. Preheat oven to 500°. Use **fish fillets, fish steaks, or small whole fish (up to 1½ inches thick), cleaned and scaled;** wipe fish with a damp paper towel. Cut into serving-size pieces (about 3 by 5 inches), if desired.

Place a large, shallow baking pan in oven to preheat. Meanwhile, for 4 to 6 servings (1½ to 2½ lbs. fish pieces), combine 2 **eggs** and 2 tablespoons **milk** in a shallow dish; beat lightly. Spread 1 cup **coating** (suggestions follow) in another shallow dish or on a piece of wax paper. Dip each piece of fish in egg mixture and drain briefly; then roll in coating to cover all sides. Arrange in a single layer on wax paper within reaching distance of range.

Remove baking pan from oven. Place equal amounts of **butter** or margarine and **salad oil** in pan and swirl until butter is melted (fat should be about ⅛ inch deep).

Place a piece of fish in pan; turn to coat with butter and oil. Repeat with remaining fish, arranging as many pieces in pan as will fit without crowding.

Bake, uncovered, turning halfway through cooking, just until fish is browned and flakes readily when prodded in thickest part. Total cooking time depends on thickness of fish (measured in thickest part). For every inch of thickness, allow 8 to 10 minutes —4 to 5 minutes per side.

When fish is done, transfer to a warm platter. Keep warm if more fish is to be cooked; otherwise, sprinkle fish with **salt, pepper,** and chopped **parsley** and serve at once, garnished with **lemon wedges.**

Coating. Choose **fine dry bread crumbs, cracker crumbs, wheat germ,** or other coating mixture of your choice.

BARBECUING

When you barbecue fish, the tantalizing aroma of sizzling fish and smoky charcoal is all you need as an appetizer. Moderately fat and full-flavored fish, such as salmon, mackerel, and swordfish, are the best choices for the barbecue. Smoke enhances the flavor of these fish but sometimes overpowers more delicate-flavored types such as sole.

Fillets and steaks that are ¾ inch thick or thicker can cook directly on the greased grill of your barbecue, as can small whole fish. But thinner fish pieces are easier to handle and turn if held inside a hinged wire barbecue basket. To prevent drying, every form and variety of fish must be brushed with a butter-baste or a marinade while barbecuing.

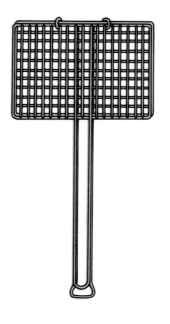

How to barbecue. For a discussion of basic barbecue techniques, see pages 39 to 40. And always read the manufacturer's directions for your barbecue carefully before you start to grill.

Use **fish fillets, fish steaks, or small whole fish (up to 1½ inches thick), cleaned and scaled;** wipe fish with a damp paper towel. Cut fish into serving-size pieces (about 3 by 5 inches), if desired. Refrigerate until ready to cook. Or prepare your favorite marinade and pour over fish; cover and refrigerate for at least 30 minutes (some marinades require several hours).

Prepare barbecue for grilling over direct heat (see page 39). Remove fish from refrigerator; if it's marinated, reserve marinade for use as a baste. If using a plain baste (suggestions follow), prepare baste and have ready near barbecue.

Arrange fish pieces, without crowding, on a lightly greased grill 4 to 6 inches above a solid bed of medium coals. (If pieces are less than ¾ inch thick, arrange them in a hinged wire barbecue basket and place basket on grill.) Generously brush fish with baste or marinade. Continue to cook, basting frequently and turning once halfway through cooking, just until fish is browned on outside and flakes readily when prodded in thickest part. Total cooking time depends on thickness of fish (measured in thickest part). For every inch of thickness, allow 8 to 10 minutes —4 to 5 minutes per side. (*Note:* Length of cooking time can be affected by varying barbecue conditions, such as air temperature or exact heat of coals.)

When fish is done, transfer it to a warm platter. Keep warm if more fish is to be cooked; otherwise, sprinkle fish with **salt** and **pepper** and serve immediately, garnished with **lemon wedges,** if desired.

Basting suggestions. For the simplest baste for 4 to 6 servings of fish (1½ to 2½ lbs. fish pieces), use ¼ cup melted **butter** or margarine.

For a seasoned baste, combine ¼ cup melted **butter** or margarine with ¼ cup **lemon juice,** dry sherry, or dry vermouth; then season (if desired) with ¼ teaspoon *each* **dry rosemary** and **thyme leaves** or ½ teaspoon dry tarragon. If you have rosemary growing in your garden, you might tie a few sprigs together to make an aromatic basting brush.

(Continued on next page)

POACHING

Poaching is unmatched as a versatile method of preparing fish. Just as an egg poaches in water, whole fish and fish pieces simmer to firmness in a gently bubbling, savory liquid that delicately flavors the fish as it cooks.

To poach serving-size fish pieces, you need only a wide spatula and a wide frying pan or other pan just deep enough to immerse the pieces in simmering liquid. You can poach on top of the range or in the oven.

How to poach. Prepare **poaching liquid** (recipe follows). If fish is to be oven-poached, preheat oven to 425°.

Use **fish fillets, fish steaks, or small whole fish, cleaned and scaled;** wipe fish with a damp paper towel. Cut into serving-size pieces (about 3 by 5 inches), if de-

sired. If using pieces much larger than the surface area of your spatula, wrap in cheesecloth, folding edges together on top of fish to make handling easier after cooking.

For oven-poaching, arrange fish in a single layer in a greased wide baking pan. Bring poaching liquid to a boil and pour over fish. There should be just enough liquid to cover fish; if not, add equal parts water and dry white wine (or all water) just to cover fish. Cover pan and place in preheated oven.

For poaching on top of range, bring poaching liquid to a boil in poaching pan. Lower fish into simmering liquid. There should be just enough liquid to cover fish; if not, add equal parts water and dry white wine (or all water) just to cover fish. Reduce heat, cover, and simmer gently (water should never be allowed to boil).

Cook, either in oven or on top of range, just until fish flakes readily when prodded in thickest part. Total cooking time depends on thickness of fish (measured in thickest part); for every inch of thickness, allow 8 to 10 minutes, starting from the moment simmering resumes after fish is added to poaching liquid.

When fish is done, lift it from liquid with a wide spatula, supporting it with cheesecloth (if used). Drain well; then open cheesecloth (if used) and gently remove from beneath fish. Fish may break easily after cooking, so be very careful.

Arrange fish on a warm platter and serve with a sauce, if desired; or let cool, then cover and refrigerate for use in salads or cold entrées.

Basic poaching liquid. In a 3-quart pan (or in poaching pan, if you like), combine 1 medium **onion** (sliced), 6 **whole black peppercorns,** 2 **whole allspice,** 3 tablespoons **lemon juice** or white wine vinegar, 1 **bay leaf,** 1 teaspoon **salt,** about ½ cup **dry white wine** (or water), and about 4 cups **water** (you will need just enough liquid to cover fish pieces, so amount of water and wine may be varied accordingly). Cover and simmer for at least 20 minutes.

Recipe may be doubled or tripled if larger amounts are needed (if so, simmer for 30 minutes to 1 hour). Poaching liquid may be reused several times—it will simply acquire more flavor with every use. However, liquid should not be stored in the refrigerator longer than 2 days after using; freeze in an airtight container if longer storage is necessary.

WRAPPING FISH FOR POACHING

1 Wrap whole fish snugly in cheesecloth, folding edges together on top of fish.

2 When fish is done, lift out with wide spatulas, supporting whole fish with cheesecloth.

BUYING & STORING SHELLFISH

Modern methods of storage and transportation have made fresh shellfish more readily available than ever before. Here are some selection tips.

PURCHASING GUIDELINES

The availability of certain shellfish depends on weather, tides, and angler's luck; your dealer can tell you which kinds are the best buys each day.

The freshness of shellfish depends on how well they're handled. If they're alive, you know they're fresh. Shellfish that have died naturally won't necessarily make you sick, but their meat spoils so rapidly it's wise to discard them.

In the case of *hard-shell clams, oysters, and mussels,* a tightly closed shell is the best indication of a live shellfish; if the shell is slightly open, it should close when gently tapped. Touch the neck of a *soft-shell clam* to see if it twitches.

Live crabs, lobsters, and crayfish move their legs. A live lobster's tail curls under the body rather than hanging down when the lobster is picked up. If you purchase *fresh-cooked crabs or lobsters,* they should have bright red shells and be free of any odor of ammonia. It's best to use them the day of purchase.

Shucked oysters and clams should be plump and free of any sour aroma. The liquid inside a jar of oysters should be clear, not cloudy or pink. *Fresh scallops* should have a slightly sweet aroma and be practically free of liquid when bought in packages. The meat's color is no indication of quality; it varies from creamy white to tan to orange.

Fresh shrimp are firm and have a mild, faintly sweet smell (as they deteriorate, you'll notice an ammonia-like odor). Signs of mishandling are black legs and shells that are slippery, patched with dry-looking areas, or spotted with brown or black.

In buying *frozen shrimp, crab, or lobster tail,* make sure any exposed meat is well glazed and not dried out; the meat should be white with no yellowing.

STORAGE TIPS

After you leave the fish market, keep your shellfish purchases as cool as possible. Refrigerate as soon as you can.

Store oysters with cup side down, so the juices won't leak out. Keep live oysters, clams, and mussels covered with damp paper towels; never store them in water or in an airtight container, or they'll suffocate. They should stay alive 7 to 10 days from harvest. Shucked oysters kept in the original container should stay fresh for a week in the refrigerator.

Shrimp are often shipped to market in frozen blocks, which are thawed before being displayed or packaged; they should be cooked the day you buy them. After arriving home from the market, unwrap shrimp and refrigerate, covered with damp paper towels. Store scallops the same way.

Store live crab, lobster, or crayfish in the refrigerator, covered with damp paper towels; use within 12 hours. It's best to eat fresh-cooked crab or lobster the day you buy it, but in any case, you shouldn't keep it more than 2 days.

Crab and lobster can be frozen at 0°F or lower for up to 3 months. Other shellfish (shells removed) may remain frozen for up to 6 months. To freeze any shellfish, wrap it airtight in freezer wrap.

A PROFILE OF COMMON SHELLFISH

NAMES & ALTERNATE NAMES	FORMS AVAILABLE	SIZE RANGE	WHERE AVAILABLE
ABALONE	Steaks (pounded to tenderize)	3–8/lb.	Western coast
CLAM **Butter clam**	Live in shell Shucked, whole	100/sack, live 25–30/quart	Western coast
Geoduck clam **(king clam, gooey-duck, gweduc)**	Live, fresh on request from market Frozen steaks, minced meat, chunks	Each clam: 3 lbs. (yields 1½ lbs. meat)	Northwestern coast
Hard clam **(quahog, sharp clam, hard-shell clam, littleneck clam, cherrystone clam)**	Live in shell Shucked, whole Shucked, minced	80 lbs./ bushel 25–30/quart	Eastern coast
Razor clam	Live in shell Shucked, whole Shucked, minced	80/box	Western coast
Soft-shell clam **(manninose clam)**	Live in shell Shucked, whole	45 lbs./bushel 50–75/quart	Eastern coast

(Continued on next page)

A PROFILE OF COMMON SHELLFISH

NAMES & ALTERNATE NAMES	FORMS AVAILABLE	SIZE RANGE	WHERE AVAILABLE
Surf clam (skimmer clam, beach clam, giant clam, sea clam, hen clam, bar clam)	Shucked, whole	25–75/quart	Eastern coast
CRAB **Blue crab** (hard-shell crab, soft-shell crab)	Live in shell Steamed and picked from shell; sold in ½- or 1-lb. cans as lump meat, flake meat (from body), or claw meat	*Hard-shell:* ¼–1 lb. *Soft-shell:* ⅐–⅓ lb.	Mideastern, southeastern, Gulf coasts
Dungeness crab	Live in shell Cooked in shell, fresh or frozen Cooked and picked from body, claws	1¼–2½ lbs.	Western coast
Alaska king crab	Cooked in shell, frozen Legs cooked in shell, frozen	6–20 lbs.	Eastern, western coasts
Rock crab	Live in shell	⅓ lb.	Northeastern coast
CRAYFISH **Crawfish, crawdad, ecrevisse, mudbug**	*From western coast:* Live in shell Cooked in shell Frozen in shell *From rivers of Louisiana and Mississippi:* Live in shell Cooked in shell Tail meat in 5-lb. cans	*Western variety:* 4–7 inches long *Southern variety:* less than 3 inches long	Western rivers, southern rivers, particularly in Louisiana and Mississippi
LANGOSTINO	Frozen in shell Cooked and shelled, frozen	6–15/lbs.	Available frozen throughout U.S. (most imported from Chile)
LOBSTER **Northeastern lobster**	Live in shell Cooked, shelled	¾–4 lbs.	Eastern, western coasts
Spiny Pacific lobster	Live in shell Frozen raw in shell	1–4 lbs.	Southwestern coast
MUSSEL	Live in shell	55 lbs./bushel	Northeastern, mideastern coasts
OCTOPUS **Polpi, pulpi, devilfish**	Whole on request from market	*Imported:* frozen 1–4 lbs. *Western:* fresh or frozen 3–5 lbs.	Western coast, imported
OYSTER **Eastern oyster** (cove oyster)	Live in shell Shucked, whole	80 lbs./bushel 40–50/quart	Eastern, Gulf coasts
Olympia oyster (western oyster)	Live in shell Shucked, whole	120 lbs./sack 300–400/quart	Northwestern coast
Pacific oyster (Japanese oyster)	Live in shell Shucked, whole	80 lbs./sack 12–60/quart	Western coast
SCALLOP **Bay scallop** (cape scallop)	Shucked, whole	62–85/quart	Eastern, Gulf coasts
Sea scallop	Shucked, whole	25–30/quart	Eastern coast (available frozen in rest of U.S.)
SHRIMP **Prawn, ocean shrimp, bay shrimp, northern shrimp, Alaska shrimp**	Raw in shell Cooked in shell Cooked, shelled; fresh or frozen	*Ocean shrimp:* 150–180/lb. *Small:* 45–65/lb. *Medium:* 30–32/lb. *Large* (or jumbo or prawn): 6–15/lb.	Northeastern, southeastern, Gulf coasts Ocean shrimp: western coast (available frozen in rest of U.S.)
SQUID **Inkfish, calamari**	Whole Cleaned, frozen	10–12 inches long	Northeastern, mideastern, and western coasts

COOKING SHELLFISH

Simmering and steaming are easy ways to cook many shellfish. Directions are on page 64; the chart below gives preparation and serving details and approximate cooking times for the basic kinds, both mollusks and crustaceans. Shellfish may also be cooked in a microwave oven; for directions, see page 65.

Judging doneness. Shellfish overcook quickly, so watch carefully as you cook them and remove them from the heat just as soon as they're done. Add cooked shellfish to hot dishes at the last minute, just to heat through.

The flesh of shrimp, crabs, and lobsters turns from translucent to opaque when cooked. To test, cut a shrimp in half, or cut into the center of a lobster tail.

Remove mollusks such as oysters and clams from the heat as soon as the shells barely open. Shucked oysters are done when the edges curl.

(Continued on next page)

TYPE OF SHELLFISH	AMOUNT PER SERVING	DO AHEAD	APPROXIMATE COOKING TIME	TO SERVE & EAT
CLAMS, HARDSHELL, live	About 1½ lbs.	Rinse in cold running water	5–10 minutes (until shells open)	Serve warm in wide bowls. Strain cooking liquid and serve in small bowls as a dip. Offer melted butter and lemon wedges, if desired.
CRAB, DUNGENESS (1½–2 lbs.), live	1–1¼ lbs.	Rinse in cold water	20–25 minutes	Clean (see page 66). Twist off legs, claws; use mallet to strike each section on thin ridge. Break body into sections. Offer melted butter or mayonnaise, if desired.
CRAYFISH, live	10–12 crayfish	Rinse in cold water	5–7 minutes	Twist off tail where it joins body; remove shell segments from tail. Twist off claws; pull small claw section back and off. Crack claws. Offer melted butter, if desired.
LANGOSTINO, frozen tails	¼–½ lb.	Cook frozen; or thaw in cold running water	Simmer only. *Frozen:* 1–1¼ minutes *Thawed:* ¾–1 minute	Grasp edges of shell with both hands and bend back to remove meat in one piece. Offer melted butter, if desired.
LOBSTER, NORTHEASTERN, small (¾–1¼ lbs.) or large (1½–2½ lbs.), live	½–1 lobster	Rinse in cold water	*Small:* 10–15 minutes *Large:* 15–20 minutes	Twist off claws; crack with nutcracker. Twist off tail; remove meat as for spiny lobster, below. Remove legs; suck out meat as if using straw. Serve with melted butter or mayonnaise, if desired.
LOBSTER, SPINY, live and whole (1–2 lbs.) or frozen tails	1 small or ½ large whole lobster; 6–8 oz. frozen tails	Rinse live lobsters in cold water; thaw frozen tails in refrigerator or cold water	*Whole:* 1–1½ lbs., 12–15 minutes; 1½–2 lbs., 15–18 minutes *Tails:* 2–4 oz., 3–5 minutes; 4–6 oz., 5–7 minutes; 6–8 oz., 7–9 minutes	Twist off tail of whole lobster where it joins body; twist off and discard tail flippers. Push fork deep into big end of tail; gently pull out meat in one piece. Or cut away undershell with scissors to remove meat. Serve with melted butter or mayonnaise, if desired.
MUSSELS, live	About 1 lb.	Pull off beard. Scrub if needed; rinse in cold running water	4–8 minutes (until shells open)	Serve warm in soup bowls with melted butter and lemon wedges, or with pan juices (see "To steam mussels in seasoned liquid," page 64).
OYSTERS (small to medium), live	6–9 oysters	Scrub with stiff brush in cold running water; rinse	8–20 minutes (remove when shells open enough to insert knife)	Serve as soon as cool enough to handle. Offer lemon wedges and liquid hot pepper seasoning; or serve with garlic butter (see "To steam oysters in seasoned liquid," page 64).
SHRIMP, large or jumbo (6–15/lb.) or medium (30–32/lb.)	¼–⅓ lb.	Thaw if frozen; shell and devein before or after cooking (see page 66)	*Large:* shelled, 4–5 minutes; unshelled, 5–6 minutes *Medium:* shelled, 3–4 minutes; unshelled, 4–5 minutes	Shell (if not done before). Serve warm with melted butter or serve cold with prepared seafood cocktail sauce or mayonnaise, if desired.

How to simmer crustaceans. For up to 5 pounds crab or lobster or 2 pounds shrimp or crayfish, pour enough **water** into a pan to generously cover shellfish. If desired, add 2 teaspoons **salt** for each quart of water. Bring to a boil over high heat. Add shellfish (plunge live shellfish head first into water; tuck lobster tails under to prevent muscle reflex, which could splash boiling water). Cover pan. When water returns to a boil, reduce heat and simmer for the time suggested on the chart or until the shellfish tests done (see "Judging doneness," page 63). Remove shellfish at once and immerse briefly in cold water to stop cooking.

How to steam crustaceans. You'll need a steamer or a large pan with an inside rack that sits at least 2 inches above pan bottom. Pour 1 inch **water** into pan and bring to a boil over high heat. Set **shellfish** (up to 5 pounds crab or lobster or 2 pounds shrimp or crayfish) on rack and tightly cover pan. When steam begins to escape from under lid, reduce heat to medium and cook for the time suggested on the chart or until meat tests done (see "Judging doneness," page 63). Remove shellfish immediately and immerse briefly in cold water to stop cooking.

How to steam live oysters, mussels, or clams. For up to 3 dozen oysters or 5 pounds mussels or clams, pour about ¼ inch **water** into a 5- to 7-quart pan. Add shellfish (oysters with cup side down), cover, and boil over medium-high heat just until shells open (see chart on page 63 for times). Serve as suggested in chart.

To steam oysters in seasoned liquid: Substitute **beer** for water, if desired; add 1 clove **garlic** (crushed) and 1 **bay leaf** to cooking liquid. Serve with melted **garlic butter.**

To steam mussels or clams in seasoned liquid: Instead of water, use 1½ cups **dry white wine** (or 1 cup water and ¼ cup lemon juice); add 6 **green onions** (including tops), chopped, and ¼ teaspoon **thyme leaves.** After mussels or clams are cooked, transfer them to serving bowls. Boil liquid in pan until reduced to 1½ cups. Blend 6 tablespoons **butter** or margarine, softened, with 1½ teaspoons **cornstarch;** add to liquid and cook, stirring, until it boils and thickens slightly. Pour over mussels or clams in bowls.

SHUCKING OYSTERS

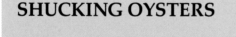

1 To shuck live oysters safely, you'll need an oyster knife. Place oyster on a firm surface with cup side down and hinge at your left. Using a heavy potholder or glove to protect your left hand, grasp oyster firmly at hinge end. Work knife into shell on front right edge. Angling knife blade downward, insert it 1 to 2 inches into shell and scrape blade across bottom shell to cut muscle free (you'll feel it relax).

2 Lift off top shell with oyster attached; cut meat free and place in cupped shell with juices. Serve within 5 to 10 minutes.

COOKING SHELLFISH IN THE MICROWAVE

Caution: To prevent overcooking, use shortest cooking time. Allow food to stand for recommended time. On standing, shellfish will continue to cook. If necessary, microwave longer, checking for doneness at 1-minute intervals.

SHELLFISH	AMOUNT	PREPARATION	COOKING TIME (CT) STANDING TIME (ST)
CLAMS IN SHELL	1 dozen	Scrub well. On a 10-inch glass pie dish or serving plate, arrange clams in a circle, hinge side to outside edge of plate. Cover with heavy-duty plastic wrap, allowing room for expansion.	**CT:** 3–4 minutes Microwave on HIGH (100%) until shells pop open. Remove opened clams from oven; continue cooking remaining clams, checking at 30-second intervals. **ST:** 1 minute, covered.
CRAB IN SHELL (cleaned, cooked, and cracked)	1 large (about 2 lbs.)	In a 7- by 11-inch baking dish, arrange crab pieces with meaty portions to outside of dish. Brush with melted butter or margarine. Cover with heavy-duty plastic wrap.	**CT:** 2–3 minutes Microwave on HIGH (100%). **ST:** 1–2 minutes, covered. Meat in shells should be heated through.
LOBSTER TAILS	8–9 oz. *each*	If frozen, thaw completely. Use scissors to cut off soft undershell and fins along outer edges; discard. Bend shell back, cracking some joints to prevent curling. With your fingers, start at thickest end and pull meat free in 1 piece. Place meat, rounded side up, in a 7- by 11-inch baking dish. Brush with melted butter or margarine and drizzle with lemon juice. Cover with heavy-duty plastic wrap.	**CT:** 2 tails: 5–6 minutes 4 tails: 9–11 minutes Microwave on HIGH (100%), turning meat over and basting generously with melted butter halfway through cooking. **ST:** 3–5 minutes, covered. Meat should be tender and opaque throughout; cut to test.
MUSSELS IN SHELL	1 dozen	Scrub well. On a 10-inch glass pie dish or serving plate, arrange mussels in a circle, hinge side to outside edge of plate. Cover with heavy-duty plastic wrap, allowing room for expansion.	**CT:** 3–4 minutes Microwave on HIGH (100%) until shells pop open. Flesh of mussels should turn bright orange. **ST:** 1 minute, covered.
OYSTERS IN SHELL **Eastern** **Pacific, medium-size**	10–12 8	Same as mussels in the shell.	**CT:** 4–5 minutes Microwave on HIGH (100%) until shells pop open. Edges of oysters should be curled. **ST:** 2 minutes, covered.
OYSTERS, SHUCKED **Eastern** **Pacific, small**	8–10 1 jar (10 oz.)	On a 10-inch glass pie dish or serving plate, arrange oysters in a circle. Drizzle with their juices and melted butter or margarine. Cover with heavy-duty plastic wrap.	**CT:** 4–5 minutes Microwave on HIGH (100%), turning over after 2 minutes. Oysters should be heated through and edges curled. **ST:** 1–2 minutes, covered.
SCALLOPS	1 lb.	Rinse well; if large, cut in half. Place in a 1½-quart casserole. Drizzle with melted butter or margarine and dry white wine or lemon juice. Cover with a lid or heavy-duty plastic wrap.	**CT:** 2½–3½ minutes Microwave on HIGH (100%), stirring after 1½ minutes. **ST:** 2–3 minutes, covered. Meat should be tender and opaque throughout; cut to test.
SHRIMP, **medium-size (30–32/lb.)**	1 lb.	Rinse well. Shell and devein, if desired (see page 66). On a flat 12-inch plate, arrange shrimp in a single layer with meaty portion to outside edge of plate. Cover with heavy-duty plastic wrap.	**CT:** 4–5 minutes Microwave on HIGH (100%), bringing cooked portion to inside of plate after 2 minutes. **ST:** 3–5 minutes, covered. Shrimp should be pink and meat tender and opaque throughout; cut to test.

CRACKING & CLEANING COOKED CRAB

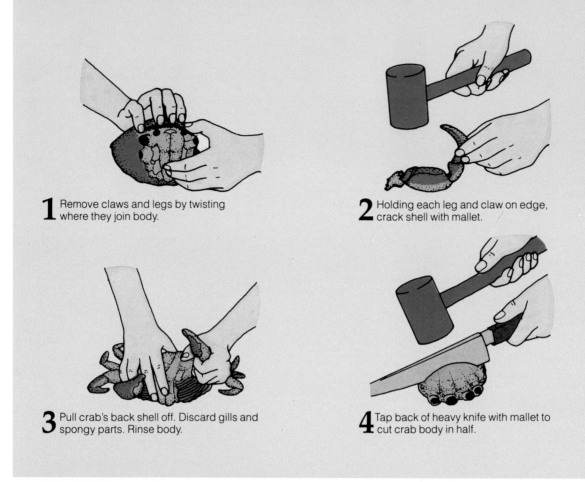

1 Remove claws and legs by twisting where they join body.

2 Holding each leg and claw on edge, crack shell with mallet.

3 Pull crab's back shell off. Discard gills and spongy parts. Rinse body.

4 Tap back of heavy knife with mallet to cut crab body in half.

SHELLING & DEVEINING SHRIMP

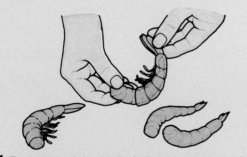

1 To shell raw shrimp, split shell open down belly of shrimp, then gently tug tip of tail-shell free and pull shell away from body.

2 To remove sand vein, make a shallow cut down back of shrimp, then rinse out sand vein. To devein unshelled shrimp, cut along back with scissors and remove vein.

CLEANING & PREPARING SQUID

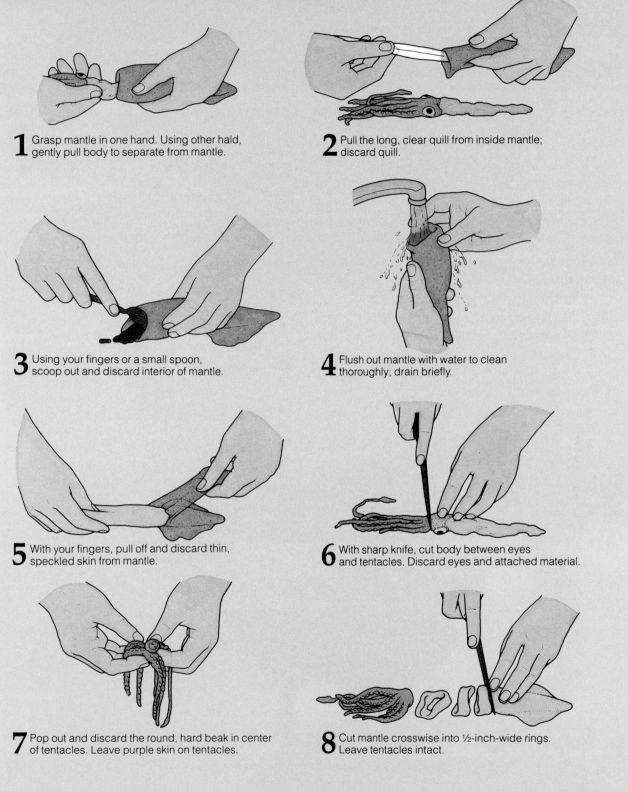

1 Grasp mantle in one hand. Using other hald, gently pull body to separate from mantle.

2 Pull the long, clear quill from inside mantle; discard quill.

3 Using your fingers or a small spoon, scoop out and discard interior of mantle.

4 Flush out mantle with water to clean thoroughly; drain briefly.

5 With your fingers, pull off and discard thin, speckled skin from mantle.

6 With sharp knife, cut body between eyes and tentacles. Discard eyes and attached material.

7 Pop out and discard the round, hard beak in center of tentacles. Leave purple skin on tentacles.

8 Cut mantle crosswise into ½-inch-wide rings. Leave tentacles intact.

Eggs & Cheese

Individually or in tandem, eggs and cheese form the basis of some of the world's most celebrated dishes. From omelets to fondues, soufflés to Welsh rarebits, eggs and cheese have proven time and again to be favorite menu choices for both entertaining and informal family meals.

One doesn't have to look far to see why these foods are popular in nearly every cuisine around the globe. Eggs and cheese are rich in protein and amazingly versatile, giving the cook plenty of options for exercising kitchen creativity. On the following pages, you'll find information to help you take advantage of all that these culinary treasures have to offer.

ABOUT EGGS

Be choosy when you shop for eggs. Buy only the freshest refrigerated eggs, and make sure that none are cracked. Grade AA eggs are the freshest and most widely available. Eggs are also graded by size—small, medium, large, extra-large, and jumbo. In many cook books, recipes are based on large eggs; if you use another size instead, the recipe may not turn out as it should.

Shell color has no effect on an egg's flavor or nutritional value. The one difference you will notice is price—brown-shelled eggs are usually more expensive than white ones.

Generally speaking, eggs maintain good quality for up to a month if stored in the refrigerator (keep them covered—they can absorb odors through the shells). The sign of a fresh egg is a plump yolk that sits up a bit higher than the surrounding white, which—in a very fresh egg—is thick and dense. Freshness matters most when you're frying or poaching, or separating the egg for a more elaborate concoction. Save slightly less fresh eggs for hard-cooking or for well-mixed creations like omelets, scrambled eggs, or sauces.

If you crack an egg and see a fleck of blood, don't be alarmed. Just remove it with a spoon. It won't affect the egg's flavor or quality.

Eggs are delicate; even slight shifts of temperature can affect them appreciably in cooking. When a recipe calls for eggs at room temperature, take the advice seriously; don't expect chilly subjects to perform as energetically as the recipe promises. You can bring refrigerated eggs to room temperature quickly by covering them for a minute or two with very warm tap water.

When you cook eggs, always use medium or low heat. High heat and overcooking produce disappointingly rubbery results.

SCRAMBLED EGGS

A little liquid beaten into eggs before cooking produces the tender, velvety-textured golden mass known as scrambled eggs. We suggest adding 1 to 3 teaspoons milk or cream for each egg, and ¼ teaspoon salt for every 2 or 3 eggs.

Break **eggs** into a bowl, add **milk** or cream and **salt,** and beat with a fork until thoroughly blended but not frothy. Choose a frying pan to fit the amount of egg mixture to be cooked—an 8-inch pan for 2 to 4 eggs, a 10- to 12-inch pan for a larger quantity (but not more than a dozen). Place pan over medium-low heat and add about ½ tablespoon **butter,** margarine, bacon fat, or salad oil per egg. When fat is hot, pour in egg mixture. Cook, gently lifting cooked portion to allow uncooked portion to flow underneath, until eggs are softly set. Use a wide spatula to lift the eggs. Keep the temperature constant during cooking and don't try to hurry things along—overheating makes scrambled eggs rubbery. Remove pan from heat when eggs are still creamy; they'll finish cooking in their own heat.

FRIED EGGS

You can fry eggs in a nonstick pan as the manufacturer directs, but you'll probably enjoy the flavor more if you use a little fat. Butter, margarine, bacon fat, or salad oil—the choice is yours.

For tender, evenly cooked eggs, always fry in a preheated pan over medium heat. If the pan isn't preheated, the eggs will cook unevenly. If the heat is too high or the pan too hot, the eggs will cook on the bottom before they're set on the top, resulting in crisp, brown, leathery whites.

Melt **fat** (1 to 2 teaspoons per egg) in a wide frying pan over medium heat. (Use 2 pans to cook more than 6 eggs at one time.) For well-shaped eggs, break each **egg** directly into pan, holding shell almost against pan surface; lift shell away carefully to avoid stretching or tearing egg. Over medium heat,

eggs begin to set as soon as they touch the pan surface.

For over-easy style, just fry eggs on one side, then turn over and fry briefly on the other. For opaquely covered yolks, sprinkle 1 to 2 teaspoons water over each egg in pan (or baste eggs with the melted fat in pan), cover, and cook for about 2 minutes.

SOFT- OR HARD-COOKED EGGS

Though the expression "hard-boiled eggs" is familiar to us all, in fact you should *never* boil eggs. If you do, you may end up with cracked, leaking shells and water-logged, rubbery whites. Eggs need only a gentle simmer.

A perfect soft-cooked egg has a tender white, solidified to the consistency you prefer, and a hot, liquid to semiliquid yolk. In an excellent hard-cooked egg, the white is completely firm, yet tender; the yolk is firm and dry throughout, with the same color on the outside as in the center. (A greenish or bluish cast on the outside of the yolk is a sure sign of overcooking.)

When cooking eggs in their shells, it's best to use eggs at room temperature to prevent the shells from cracking. If you use eggs directly from the refrigerator, follow the directions below but increase the total cooking time by 2 minutes.

Place **eggs,** without crowding, in a single layer in a straight-sided pan. Add enough **cold water** to cover. Set pan, uncovered, over high heat and bring to a simmer (bubbles will form slowly and burst before reaching the surface). This takes 8 to 10 minutes.

For soft-cooked eggs, reduce heat and continue to simmer for 3 to 5 minutes; drain and serve immediately.

For hard-cooked eggs, reduce heat and simmer for 15 to 18 minutes. Then drain eggs and immediately cover with cold water.

To shell hard-cooked eggs, tap each egg gently all over with the back of a spoon (or tap lightly on a flat surface). Under cold running water, roll the egg between your palms to loosen the shell.

POACHED EGGS

A beautifully poached egg has a well-centered yolk snugly surrounded by the white, cooked just to the firmness you like.

To make good-looking poached eggs, pour **water** into a greased wide frying pan to a depth of 1½ inches. Heat until bubbles form on the pan bottom. Add 1 tablespoon **distilled white or cider vinegar.** Break each **egg** into the water, keeping eggs separate. (Cook no more than 6 at a time in a 10-inch pan.) Cook, with water barely simmering, until eggs are done to your liking (touch yolk gently to check firmness). For soft yolks and firm whites, allow 3 to 5 minutes.

With a slotted spoon, lift eggs from hot water. Drain well on paper towels, then serve.

To make poaching easier for entertaining, and to eliminate a lot of last-minute work, you can poach your eggs a day ahead, then reheat them at serving time. To do this, immerse poached eggs in cold water as soon as you lift them from the hot water. Cover and refrigerate for up to 24 hours. To reheat, transfer eggs to a bowl of very hot tap water; cover and let stand until hot to the touch (5 to 10 minutes). Lift out with a slotted spoon, drain on paper towels, and serve.

SOUFFLÉS

Soufflés have always had a reputation for being complicated—yet once you've mastered a few techniques, they're really remarkably easy to make. The ingredients for a main-dish soufflé are simply a thick white sauce, eggs, and your choice of vegetables, fish, poultry, meat, or cheese. Make your white sauce first, then beat the egg yolks into it and let the mixture cool while you prepare the whites.

To achieve the greatest volume in your soufflé, start with eggs at room temperature. Separate the eggs carefully. If a bit of yolk falls

into the whites, remove it before beating; if you can't remove all traces of yolk, use the eggs for another purpose. The slightest amount of fat from the yolk—or, for that matter, an oily bowl or beaters—will decrease the volume of beaten whites. Beat the whites only until they hold stiff, moist peaks. If the whites are overbeaten and become dry, they'll be difficult to fold into the sauce-yolk mixture.

To maintain the volume of the beaten whites, lighten the heavy white sauce by gently folding in a portion of the beaten whites. Then gently fold the lightened sauce into remaining whites.

To bake the soufflé, you don't need a traditional soufflé dish; any deep, straight-sided baking dish will do, as long as the volume is correct. Be sure to grease the dish well.

Always preheat the oven before baking a soufflé; the soufflé bakes from the bottom up, so it needs quick bottom heat to achieve height. For a moist soufflé, bake until the top is golden brown and the center jiggles slightly when the dish is gently shaken. For a firmer soufflé, bake until the center feels firm when lightly touched.

Ideally, a soufflé should be served as soon as it's baked—but if necessary, it can remain in the turned-off oven for about 10 minutes before it begins to collapse. It will continue to cook slightly during this time, becoming more firm.

OMELETS

A plain omelet (also called a French omelet) has just two basic components—eggs and seasoning. To dress up your omelet a bit, you need only add a simple filling, such as diced vegetables, shredded cheese, or crumbled crisp bacon. All plain omelets, filled or not, are speedy to prepare, going from kitchen to table quickly.

For a 2- or 3-egg omelet (one generous serving), use a 7- to 8-inch omelet pan with a nonstick finish. Beat together **eggs,** 1 tablespoon **water,** and ¼ teaspoon **salt.** Heat frying

pan over medium-high heat. Add 1 tablespoon **butter** or margarine and tilt pan to coat bottom and sides. Pour egg mixture into pan and cook, gently lifting cooked portion around edges to allow uncooked portion to flow underneath. Shake pan frequently to keep egg moving freely. Omelet is done when egg is set but top still looks liquid and creamy. Remove from heat; omelet will continue to cook slightly in its own heat.

Omelets, especially with a filling, are often folded—either in half or in thirds.

To fold an omelet in half, spoon filling over half of omelet; run a spatula around edge of omelet, then tip pan and slide spatula under omelet to loosen it from pan. Fold omelet in half and slide out onto a warm serving plate.

To fold an omelet in thirds, first spoon 2 to 3 tablespoons filling down center of omelet, in line with pan handle. Holding pan in your left hand, slide spatula under right edge of omelet, lift edge, and fold about ⅓ of omelet over filling. Switch pan to your right hand and, tilting right end up and holding pan over a warm serving plate, gently shake pan to slide unfolded edge of omelet just onto plate. Flick your right wrist downward so that previously folded edge of omelet (guided by your spatula) falls neatly over omelet edge on plate.

ABOUT CHEESE

A connoisseur once observed that cheese was milk's leap into immortality. One of our oldest and most satisfying foods, cheese comes in a glorious and bountiful array.

Today's market displays reflect the influence of Europe, where cheese has long been an everyday food in many forms and flavors. You can find both European and domestic versions of many cheeses; others are unique to a single region.

Natural cheeses (those without additives) are derived directly from milk—most often cow's milk, occasionally milk from sheep or goats. These cheeses differ considerably in flavor and texture, depending on how they're made and how long they've been "ripened" (aged) to develop a characteristic flavor.

Cheese families. Cheeses fall into several basic families, according to the method of production; sharpness and texture may vary within a family, but flavors are similar. Also classified by consistency, cheeses come in soft or firm unripened varieties and in several ripened varieties—soft, semisoft, firm, and hard.

Fresh soft cheeses (cottage cheese, Neufchâtel, ricotta) are not ripened at all at the dairy and are meant to be consumed immediately.

Brie, Camembert, and several related cheeses are *soft ripened* cheeses, which means the curd is heated little or not at all and is unpressed. Such cheeses ripen for only a week or so before being marketed; from that time, they ripen fully and then become overripe within 2 to 3 months. Their flavors grow steadily stronger with age. Subgroups of soft ripened cheeses

are the double and triple creams, such as Explorateur and Crema Danica. For these cheeses, cream is added to whole milk, increasing the butterfat content from about 50 percent to 60 percent for doubles and 75 percent for triples.

Blue-veined cheeses—Gorgonzola, Roquefort, Stilton, and others—vary in texture from semisoft to soft. All are flavored by a blue mold which sometimes grows spontaneously in the curd but is more usually inoculated into it by the cheese maker. Blues ripen steadily, becoming stronger flavored as they age.

Washed-rind cheeses are semisoft. Though most are mild (U.S. Münster), the group also includes fairly strong (Port Salut, Pont l'Évêque) to outright stinky types (Limburger, European Münster, beer cheese). The surfaces of these cheeses are kept moist during their brief aging period to encourage the development of flavoring bacteria. Flavors rapidly grow stronger with age.

Pasta filatas (mozzarella, Provolone, string) are made by kneading the curd, a technique that leaves the cheese stringy—especially when melted. Most are semisoft or soft, with a mild to bland flavor.

Cheddars are the most familiar cheese family in the United States. Their firm texture results from warming ("cooking" in the trade, though temperatures stay at 105°F or lower), the dense matting ("cheddaring") of the curd as it forms, and firm pressing. These cheeses ripen far more slowly than any others except the grating cheeses, becoming sharper with age.

Swiss is perhaps the largest cheese family of all, including the original Switzerland Swiss cheeses (Emmentaler, Gruyère) and many followers, such as American Swiss and all of the Danish "bo" cheeses—Tybo, Fynbo, and so forth. The fontinas and Norway's Jarlsberg are made in very similar ways. Aged more briefly and pressed less than Cheddars, firm Swiss-style cheeses are also softer in texture and milder in flavor. They last well.

Grating cheeses (*granas,* in Italian—Asiago, Parmesan, Romano, dry jack) are the hard cheeses. Started much like Swiss cheeses, but cooked longer and pressed harder, they ripen the most slowly of all cheeses.

Storing cheese. Grating cheese can successfully be stored either in or out of the refrigerator. All others can be hurried toward ripeness at room temperature or slowed in ripening by refrigeration. Refrigerated cheese should be tightly wrapped in freezer or plastic wrap. Don't use foil; it may interact with milk acids. Strong cheese—especially blues and washed-rind cheeses—should be wrapped and stored separately from others, since they will taint the flavor of milder types.

You can freeze most kinds of cheese (except ricotta and cottage cheese), but changes in texture are likely, and it's by far the best idea to enjoy cheese while it's fresh. To use cheese from the freezer, thaw it, unopened, in the refrigerator and use as soon as possible.

Cooking with cheese. Use low temperatures—325° to 350°F—and short cooking times when cooking with cheese. Excessive heat and overcooking cause cheese to become tough and stringy, and fat may separate. If possible, add cheese at the last minute; it melts quickly and blends in easily if it is first shredded or grated. In general, 4 ounces of cheese yield 1 cup of shredded cheese. For hard cheeses like Parmesan and Romano, the proportions are a bit different. If you grate hard cheese in the food processor, you'll need about 5 ounces for 1 cup grated; if you grate it by hand, you'll get a cup of grated cheese for every 3 ounces or so.

Serving cheese. Serve ripened cheeses at room temperature to enjoy their fullest aroma, flavor, and texture. Unripened cheeses taste best when they're chilled. Light and fruity wines enhance the milder ripened cheeses; a full-bodied red wine complements stronger, tangier cheese varieties.

A CHEESE SAMPLER

CHEESE/Country of Origin	PERSONALITY PROFILE	SERVING SUGGESTIONS
BLUE France	Semisoft ripened cheese; pasty, sometimes crumbly texture; white interior marbled with blue-green veins. Pungent, tangy flavor.	Use in appetizers or dips, crumbled into salads or salad dressings, in cooking, with pears or apples for dessert.
BRIE France	Soft cheese with edible thin white crust; creamy yellow interior becomes satiny and spreadable when fully ripened. Mild to pungent flavor.	Present as an appetizer with crackers, French bread, or raw vegetables; or serve for dessert with grapes, pears, or other fresh fruit.
CAMEMBERT France	Soft cheese with edible thin white crust; smooth creamy yellow interior when fully ripened. Mild to pungent flavor grows stronger with age.	Serve small wheels or wedges as an appetizer paired with crackers or French bread; or serve as dessert with grapes, melon, or pears.
CHEDDAR England	Firm ripened cheese with smooth body; ivory to medium yellow-orange in color. Mild to very sharp flavor grows stronger with age. Domestic forms include Colby, Coon, Longhorn, Tillamook.	Enjoy as an appetizer, in sandwiches, or with fresh fruit for dessert. Shred to use in omelets, cheese sauce, or other cooked dishes, or as a casserole topping.
CHÈVRE France	Soft ripened cheese made from goat's milk; flaky texture, tangy flavor. Many shapes; some coated with vegetable ash, others wrapped in leaves or coated with pepper or herbs. Common types include Bûcheron, Banon, Montrachet, Pyramide.	Serve as an appetizer, paired with crackers or French bread; use in pasta sauces; bake briefly and serve warm, over dressed salad greens.
COTTAGE CHEESE Unknown	Soft unripened white cheese; lumpy large or small curds. Mild, slightly acid flavor. Less moist than ricotta.	Eat as a snack or use in appetizers and dips, in salads with fruit, in cooking and baking, in cheesecake.
CREAM CHEESE U.S.	Soft unripened white cheese with smooth, buttery texture. Mild flavor, slightly acid.	Use in appetizers, dips and spreads, sandwiches, salads, cheesecake, frostings.
EDAM Netherlands	Firm ripened cheese; creamy yellow interior has small holes. Sold in cannonball shape with wax coating. Mild, nutlike flavor.	Good table cheese served with crackers or fresh fruit; also use in sandwiches or salads.
EMMENTALER Switzerland	Firm ripened cheese; light yellow wheels have large holes, natural rind. Sweet, nutlike flavor, slightly salty tang. The original Swiss cheese, it has been widely copied.	Perfect for sandwiches, as a snack, in salads, with fruit for dessert. A good cooking cheese, often used in fondue, it shreds well and melts readily.
FETA Greece	Soft ripened white cheese, made from sheep's or goat's milk and "pickled" in brine; flaky texture. Sharp, tangy flavor, usually very salty.	Serve with Greek olives as an appetizer; use in salads and cooking.
FONTINA Italy	Semisoft to firm ripened cheese; yellow interior; may have wax coating. Bland to nutty flavor. European kinds more full-flavored than domestic.	Use in appetizers and sandwiches, in cooking, for dessert with fruit.
GORGONZOLA Italy	Semisoft ripened cheese; pasty, sometimes crumbly texture; creamy white interior marbled with blue-green veins; light tan surface. Piquant, tangy flavor; most pungent of the blues.	Classic dessert cheese served with pears and crackers or dark breads; also use in salads and salad dressings, and in cooking.
GOUDA Netherlands	Semisoft to firm ripened cheese; compact texture with a few holes. Flattened balls of yellow cheese may have wax coating. Mild to mellow flavor.	Favorite for snacks or appetizers, in sandwiches and salads, in cooking, for dessert served with crackers and fresh fruit.
GRUYÈRE Switzerland	Firm ripened cheese; light yellow with texture similar to Emmentaler but with smaller and fewer holes. Buttery, slightly nutty flavor.	Classic cooking cheese used in fondue, quiche, and other dishes; also enjoy as an appetizer or with fruit for dessert.
JACK (MONTEREY) U.S.	Semisoft ripened cheese produced in creamy white wheels; smooth open texture. Mild flavor.	All-purpose cheese: good for snacks, in sandwiches, in cooking.
JARLSBERG Norway	Firm ripened, buttery cheese similar to Swiss in appearance but less nutty in flavor.	Serve for snacks, in sandwiches and salads, on cheese board. Good melting cheese.
LIMBURGER Belgium	Semisoft cheese, smooth when fully ripened; creamy white interior usually contains small, irregular holes; yellow-orange rind. Robust flavor and aroma. Made extensively in Germany.	Use in sandwiches, as a snack with crackers or dark breads. Keep separate from other cheeses, since Limburger's strong aroma can affect their flavor.
MOZZARELLA Italy	Slightly firm unripened cheese; creamy white; supple texture. Mild, delicate flavor. Italian imports are more tender, less rubbery than domestic types.	Use as an appetizer, in sandwiches and salads, and in cooking—especially Italian dishes. Serve mellow Italian mozzarella (bufalo) as a dessert cheese.

CHEESE/Country of Origin	PERSONALITY PROFILE	SERVING SUGGESTIONS
MÜNSTER France, Germany	Semisoft ripened cheese has creamy white interior with many small holes; yellow-tan surface. Mild to pungent flavor.	Serve in sandwiches, on cheese boards, with fruit for dessert.
NEUFCHÂTEL France	Soft unripened white cheese; smooth and creamy texture. Mild flavor. Similar to cream cheese.	Use for snacks, in dips and spreads, in salads, in cheesecake, for dessert with fruit.
PARMESAN Italy	Hard ripened grating cheese; granular, brittle texture; creamy white or light yellow with brown or black coating. Sharp, piquant flavor. Pregrated version much less flavorful.	Grate or shred for cooking; use in Italian dishes, especially pasta; for garnishing soups or casseroles; on toasted bread or croutons. Serve wedges for dessert with fresh fruit.
PROVOLONE Italy	Firm ripened cheese; compact, flaky texture; creamy interior with light golden brown surface; firm, smooth shapes bound with cord. Mild to sharp flavor, depending on age; smoky, salty.	Use for snacks and appetizers, in sandwiches and salads, with fruit for dessert. Good for cooking, especially in Italian dishes. Suitable for grating when fully cured and dried.
RICOTTA Italy	Soft unripened white whey cheese; moist and grainy texture. Bland but semisweet flavor.	Use in cooking, especially Italian dishes; also for appetizers, in salads, for dessert.
ROMANO Italy	Hard ripened grating cheese; hard granular texture; yellow-white interior with greenish-black surface. Sharp, piquant flavor.	Grate or shred for seasoning or garnishing soups, salads, or cooked dishes, especially pasta, or for use in sauces.
ROQUEFORT France	Semisoft cheese made from sheep's milk and ripened in limestone caves; pasty and sometimes crumbly texture; creamy white interior marbled with blue-green veins. Sharp, pungent flavor.	Enjoy with crackers or crusty bread as an appetizer, or with pears or apples for dessert. Crumble in salads or salad dressings, or use in cooking.
SWISS U.S.	Firm ripened, light yellow cheese resembles Emmentaler; smooth texture with large round holes. Sweet, nutlike flavor.	Serve in sandwiches, as a snack, in salads. Shred to use in cooking sauces, fondue; grate to sprinkle atop soup.

SERVING IDEAS FOR CHEESE

Cheese and fruit make a refreshing appetizer or a sophisticated dessert. They are, in fact, a welcome combination at almost any time of day. A more unusual but equally enjoyable match-up is cheese and vegetables.

Following are but a few of the cheese-with-fruit and cheese-with-vegetable pairings that naturally enhance each other. You might also like to experiment and put together your own favorite combinations.

To serve, cut cheese and fruit or vegetables into bite-size pieces (drizzle cut fruit with lemon juice to prevent darkening). Or set up a large wooden tray with wedges of cheese and a basket of whole fruits or vegetables; provide cheese cutters and small sharp knives for do-it-yourself service.

Allow about ⅛ pound of cheese and about ½ to ¾ cup of fruits or vegetables for each appetizer serving.

CHEESE	FRUITS	VEGETABLES
BLUE, GORGONZOLA, ROQUEFORT	Apples, pears, grapes	Fennel, cauliflowerets, carrot sticks
BRIE	Berries, pears, grapes	Cucumber, mushrooms
CAMEMBERT	Grapes, melon, berries, pears	Mushrooms, green beans
CHEDDAR	Red-skinned apples, pears	Zucchini slices, cauliflowerets
CREAM CHEESE, NEUFCHÂTEL	Nectarines, peaches, apricots	Green onions, edible-pod peas
EDAM, GOUDA	Apples, pears, apricots	Green bell peppers, tomatoes, mushrooms
FETA	Grapes, melon	Tomatoes, cucumber, green bell pepper strips
FONTINA	Muscat grapes, Golden Delicious apples	Broccoli flowerets, green beans
JACK	Apricots, melon	Cucumber slices
MÜNSTER	Apples, pears	Red and green bell pepper strips, tomatoes
PROVOLONE	Pineapple	Edible-pod peas, celery
SWISS, EMMENTALER, GRUYÈRE, JARLSBERG	Pears	Asparagus spears, green beans

Pasta & Grains

Pasta and grains usually take a supporting role in meal planning, providing a satisfying accompaniment to the main dish. Consider a hearty sauerbraten without buttered noodles beside it, or a poached salmon steak without a mound of tender rice, and you'll see how valuable a flavor contribution these foods can make. Sometimes they even take the spotlight as part of a main dish—as in spaghetti or the Spanish rice extravaganza known as paella.

In this chapter, you'll learn all about the various types of pasta, grains, flours, and legumes—what they're like and how to cook them. You'll discover how these nourishing carbohydrates can add pizzazz to even the simplest meal.

ABOUT GRAINS

Grains play a multiple role in menu planning. With richly sauced entrées, rice or wheat acts as a neutral background and provides a base to soak up flavors. But with simpler, plainer dishes, well-seasoned grains can stand on their own—maybe even steal the show.

Cooking grains. Following are general guidelines for preparing the grains described in the chart below.

- *Yield:* 1 cup uncooked grain will yield about 3 cups cooked grain.

- *Salt:* For each cup of uncooked grain, add about ¼ teaspoon salt to the cooking water.

- *Cooking option:* For some grains—bulgur, buckwheat, millet, and, of course, rice—one alternative to simple boiling is to cook the grain like a pilaf. Sauté the dry grain first in butter, margarine, or salad oil (about 1 tablespoon per cup); then, instead of water, add boiling chicken broth. Cover and simmer until grain is done.

- *Doneness:* The doneness test for grains is like that for pasta: *al dente.* At this point, each grain is tender but has a slightly resilient core. Taste all grains after the minimum cooking time; if you prefer a softer texture, continue to cook, tasting often, until grain is done to your liking.

A MEDLEY OF GRAINS

NAME	DESCRIPTION	HOW TO COOK
BARLEY	*Pearl variety:* mild, starchy flavor. *Hulled variety:* nutty flavor. Use both in soups, stews, casseroles.	2 parts water to 1 part barley. Bring to a boil; reduce heat, cover, and simmer for 40–45 minutes. Let stand, covered, for 5–10 minutes.
BUCKWHEAT (kasha)	Not a true grain but a member of a herbaceous plant family. Available untoasted or toasted; strong, distinct flavor. Use in casseroles or serve with sauces.	Cook as directed for bulgur, but only for 10–12 minutes. Or, in an ungreased frying pan, mix 2 cups buckwheat and 1 beaten egg; cook over high heat, stirring, for 2 minutes. Then add boiling broth or water; reduce heat, cover, and simmer for 12–15 minutes.
BULGUR (bulgur wheat)	Wheat berries that have been steamed, dried, and cracked; delicate, nutty flavor. Use in casseroles, whole-grain breads, salads.	1½ parts water to 1 part bulgur. Bring to a boil; reduce heat, cover, and simmer for 12–15 minutes. Or see "Cooking option," above.
MILLET	Mild, nutty flavor. Use in stuffings, casseroles, whole-grain breads; serve with sauces.	2½ parts water to 1 part millet. Bring to a boil; reduce heat, cover, and simmer for 18–20 minutes. Or see "Cooking option," above.
OATS	Rolled, quick-cooking, or groats (steel-cut); mild flavor, creamy texture. Use as a cereal or in baked goods.	1 part boiling water to 1 part *rolled or quick-cooking oats* (or use up to 2 parts water for a creamier consistency). Reduce heat, cover, and simmer for 3–10 minutes. Soak 1 part *groats* in 2 parts water for 1 hour. Bring to a boil; reduce heat, cover, and simmer for 25–30 minutes.
RICE, BROWN	Unpolished; long or short grain; sweet, nutty flavor. Use in soups, stews, casseroles; serve with sauces.	2 parts water to 1 part brown rice. Bring to a boil; reduce heat, cover, and simmer for 35–40 minutes. Let stand, covered, for 5–10 minutes. Or see "Cooking option," above.
RICE, WHITE	Long, medium, or short grain, polished or preprocessed (parboiled to remove surface starch); mild, delicate flavor. Use in soups, salads, casseroles, puddings; serve with sauces.	2 parts water to 1 part white rice. Bring to a boil; reduce heat, cover, and simmer for 15–20 minutes. Let stand, covered, for 5–10 minutes. Or see "Cooking option," above. For preprocessed rice, follow package directions.
RICE, WILD	Not a true rice, but a grass seed. Nutty flavor, chewy texture. Use in salads or stuffings; serve with sauces.	Rinse in several changes of cold water. For cooking, use 4 parts water to 1 part wild rice. Bring to a boil; reduce heat, cover, and simmer for 40–45 minutes. If too moist, drain well.
RYE & TRITICALE	Both have earthy flavor; triticale (a wheat-rye hybrid containing more protein than either parent grain) is slightly milder than rye. Use in casseroles and whole-grain breads.	3 parts water to 1 part rye or triticale. Bring to a boil; reduce heat, cover, and simmer for 1–1¼ hours. If too dry, add water and continue to cook. If too moist, drain well.
WHEAT, CRACKED	Similar to bulgur, but not steamed before being cracked. Same uses as bulgur.	See directions for bulgur.
WHEAT, WHOLE KERNELS (wheat berries)	Nutty, mild flavor; chewy texture. Use in casseroles, stews, whole-grain breads; serve with sauces.	3 parts water to 1 part whole wheat. Bring to a boil; reduce heat, cover, and simmer for 2 hours. If too dry, add water and continue to cook. If too moist, drain well.

FLOURS & GRAINS FOR BAKING

In addition to being cooked for use as side dishes or in soups and casseroles (page 75), grains may be milled into flour or fine meal and used in baking. Here is a list of the more common flours and grains for baking; they add an interesting variety of flavors and textures to homemade baked goods.

All-purpose flour (regular white flour), available either bleached or unbleached, is a blend of refined wheat flours. As its name suggests, it's suitable for a variety of purposes. It consists mainly of the starchy interior (the "endosperm") of the wheat kernel, with the bran and germ removed and vitamins and minerals added. In bread baking, heavier whole-grain flours are often combined with all-purpose flour to improve texture.

Bran (unprocessed) & wheat germ are portions of the wheat kernel sometimes added in small quantities to breads or cookies for nutritional enrichment, heartiness, and flavor. Both are much coarser than flour. Bran contributes roughage; wheat germ is rich in food value (B and E vitamins, proteins, iron, and fat).

Bread flour is a high-gluten flour that has also been treated with potassium bromate—a conditioner that enhances gluten development and ensures a loaf with good volume and a fine grain.

Buckwheat flour is made from the seeds of a herbaceous (nonwoody) plant, *Fagopyrum esculentum*. This strong-flavored flour is most commonly used in small amounts in pancakes and some dark breads.

Cake flour is a low-gluten flour, especially appropriate for cake baking because of the tender texture it produces. It is generally bleached and enriched with vitamins and minerals.

Cornmeal & oatmeal come, respectively, from coarsely ground white or yellow corn and from rolled or steel-cut oats. In some recipes, one or the other is combined with wheat flour to create distinctive flavors and textures.

Cracked wheat, also much coarser than flour, is simply whole-wheat kernels cracked into angular fragments. In small additions (¼ to ½ cup per recipe), it gives whole-grain breads a nutty flavor and crunchy texture.

Gluten flour is wheat flour that has been treated to remove nearly all the starch, leaving a flour with a very high gluten content. Sometimes used in bread baking, it's sold in health food stores and some supermarkets.

Since gluten is the protein in wheat that makes dough elastic, you can successfully substitute a higher proportion of nonglutenous flours (such as soy flour) for gluten flour than you could for all-purpose flour.

Graham flour is practically indistinguishable from regular whole wheat flour. It is stone-ground, and it contains noticeable flecks of coarse bran.

Millet is a mildly nutty-flavored grain that is available, ground or whole, in most stores that sell bulk grain products. It has only a trace of gluten, so it can't replace a very high proportion of the wheat flour in breads; most recipes call for about 1 cup ground millet to 5 cups wheat flour.

Rye is available in most markets as dark or light flour and in some health food stores as meal. Because it is less glutenous than wheat, the two grains are often combined in bread baking.

Triticale is a high-protein grain—a cross between wheat and rye. It has a mild rye flavor. Because triticale is low in gluten, triticale flour must be combined with at least the same amount of wheat flour to make a bread that rises well. Triticale is available in stores carrying bulk grain products. It comes in two forms: flour and flakes (flattened kernels).

Whole wheat flour, ground from the entire wheat kernel, is heavier, richer in nutrients, and more perishable than all-purpose flour. Unless you use it up quickly, store it in the refrigerator to prevent the wheat germ it contains from becoming rancid. Many people prefer stone-ground whole wheat flour (or graham flour) to the regularly milled type, since it's slightly coarser and has a heartier flavor. Whole wheat flour is good in breads and some cookies and cakes, but is generally not the best choice for pastry or other delicate baked goods.

BAKING IN HIGH COUNTRY

It's hard to resist the lure of homemade baked goods—everyone seems to succumb to their tantalizing aromas, their fresh, homey flavors. But if you've ever tried baking in the mountains, you probably know that, at high elevations, many recipes just don't turn out the way they should. Above 3,000 feet, some recipes require adjustment for good results.

Why is baking in particular so greatly affected by altitude? The explanation lies in the effect of elevation on leavenings. At high altitudes, leavenings produce gases at a greatly accelerated rate. In the early stages of baking, this can create too great a volume; then the gas cells burst, causing your bread or cake to collapse. Whether you're using a chemical leavening such as baking powder or baking soda, a biological leavening such as yeast, or just eggs (as when making popovers), you'll need to follow the guidelines below if you wish to bake successfully at a high altitude.

For biscuits, muffins, and quick breads, specialists in high-elevation cooking suggest that the baking powder and baking soda in standard, sea-level recipes be decreased by one-fourth the amount specified.

Yeast breads are affected even more by high elevations. Yeast dough rises more rapidly in high country, so you must punch it down after the first rising and let it rise again until fully doubled in bulk before continuing with the recipe. Use slightly less yeast, too, unless you're in a hurry. Also you may need to use a little more liquid in the dough because liquid evaporates faster at high elevations and ingredients dry out more quickly.

Popovers pop even faster at high elevations, so use an extra egg in standard recipes—this will strengthen the popovers' hollow shells.

Pastry is not usually affected by altitude, though you may need to use slightly more liquid at high elevations because liquids evaporate so quickly there.

Cake, with its delicate structure, is more affected by high elevation than almost any other baked food. Above 3,000 feet, a cake is likely to fall and become coarse textured unless you alter the recipe. Because each cake recipe differs in the proportions of its ingredients, there can be no set rules for modifying sea-level cake recipes to suit high elevations. You'll have to experiment.

With angel food cakes, the trick is to beat egg whites just to the soft-peak stage and reduce the total amount of sugar by 1 tablespoon for each 1,000 feet of elevation above 3,000 feet.

For cakes that use shortening, increase the baking temperature by 25° and follow these general guidelines:

- *At 3,000 to 5,000 feet,* reduce each teaspoon of baking powder by ⅛ teaspoon, reduce each cup of sugar by up to 1 tablespoon, and increase each cup of liquid by up to 2 tablespoons.

- *At 5,000 to 7,000 feet,* reduce each teaspoon of baking powder by ⅛ to ¼ teaspoon, reduce each cup of sugar by up to 2 tablespoons, and increase each cup of liquid by 2 to 4 tablespoons.

- *At 7,000 to 10,000 feet,* reduce each teaspoon of baking powder by ¼ teaspoon, reduce each cup of sugar by 1 to 3 tablespoons, and increase each cup of liquid by 3 to 4 tablespoons.

- *Above 10,000 feet,* reduce each teaspoon of baking powder by ¼ to ½ teaspoon, reduce each cup of sugar by 2 to 3 tablespoons, increase each cup of liquid by 3 to 4 tablespoons, add an extra egg to the batter, and increase each cup of flour by 1 to 2 tablespoons.

Because cakes tend to stick to their baking pans at high elevations, be generous in greasing and flour-dusting pans (unless you're making a sponge-type cake).

ABOUT LEGUMES

Low in cost, high in nutrition, and rich in good, earthy flavors, legumes are one of the best food bargains going. To begin with, they pack in a powerhouse of protein—a navy bean, for example, is a full 20 percent protein. Legumes also contain plenty of iron, calcium, potassium, and B vitamins. They're high in fiber, low in sodium, and entirely innocent of cholesterol.

Ideal a food as they may sound, legumes do have a few small drawbacks. Some people find them hard to digest at first, though adequate soaking and cooking usually help solve that problem. The long soaking-cooking time is another drawback, but you can always speed things up by using the quick-soaking method described below. (Lentils and split peas, fastest of all legumes to prepare, require no soaking at all.)

SOAKING LEGUMES

Rinse and sort through legumes before soaking, discarding any debris.

Quick soaking. For each pound **dry legumes,** bring 8 cups **water** to a boil. Add washed and sorted legumes and boil for 2 minutes. Remove from heat, cover pan, and let stand for 1 hour. Drain and rinse legumes, discarding water.

Overnight soaking. For each pound **dry legumes,** dissolve 2 teaspoons **salt** in 6 cups **water.** Add washed and sorted legumes; soak until next day. Drain and rinse legumes, discarding water.

COOKING LEGUMES

Cooking times given on packaged legumes will vary and may differ from the times we list here. Always test for doneness after the minimum suggested time; legumes should be tender to the bite.

For each pound of dry legumes (weight before soaking), dissolve 2 teaspoons **salt** in 6 cups **water;** bring to a boil. Add **soaked legumes** and boil gently, with pan lid partially on, until tender (individual cooking times are listed in the chart below). Add more water if needed to keep legumes submerged. Drain cooked legumes; if desired, season to taste with salt. Each pound of dry legumes makes 6 to 7 cups cooked legumes.

A GUIDE TO LEGUMES

NAME	DESCRIPTION	SOAKING	COOKING TIME
BLACK BEANS	Robust flavor; popular in Caribbean, Central American, South American cooking.	Yes	1–1½ hours
BLACK-EYED PEAS	Smooth texture, pealike flavor; good mixed with other vegetables.	Yes	About 1 hour
GARBANZO BEANS (chick-peas, ceci beans)	Firm texture, nutlike flavor; popular in Middle East, Africa. Good in minestrone, salads.	Yes	2–2½ hours
GREAT NORTHERN BEANS (white beans)	Mild flavor; good in soups or combined with other vegetables.	Yes	1–1½ hours
KIDNEY BEANS	Firm texture, hearty flavor. Hold shape well in chili, casseroles.	Yes	1–1½ hours
LENTILS	Mild flavor blends well with many foods, spices. Popular in Middle East, India, Europe.	No	25–30 minutes
LIMAS, BABY	Mild flavor; use like other white beans in soups, casseroles.	Yes	¾–1¼ hours
PINK, PINTO & RED BEANS	Hearty flavor; good in soups, casseroles, barbecue-style beans. Popular in Mexican cooking.	Yes	1¼–1½ hours
SOYBEANS	Strong flavor; ancient crop of Asia.	Yes*	3–3½ hours
SPLIT PEAS, GREEN & YELLOW	Earthy flavor; good for soups, side dishes.	No	35–45 minutes
WHITE BEANS, SMALL (navy beans)	Mild flavor. Hold shape well; classic for baked beans.	Yes	About 1 hour

*Soak soybeans overnight in the refrigerator.

ABOUT PASTA

On these three pages, we offer an illustrated guide to some of the types of pasta available on today's market. The cooking time for pasta varies with the pasta's size and shape, but the doneness test is the same for all: *al dente* ("to the tooth")—tender but firm to the bite. That's the way pasta tastes best.

Cooking pasta. For each 8 ounces (½ lb.) **fresh or dried pasta**, bring 3 quarts **water** to a rapid boil. Add 1 tablespoon **salt**. (For a pound of pasta, double the water only.) Add pasta; stir only if pasta needs to be separated. Keep water boiling continuously. Cook dried pasta, uncovered, for the time suggested on the package. Cook fresh pasta, uncovered, for only about 2 minutes.

As soon as pasta is *al dente*, drain it and dress with sauce. Rinse pasta with cold water only if you want to use it in a salad or need to cool it for easier handling (as for lasagne).

To estimate pasta quantities, use this general guideline: 2 ounces dried pasta or about 3 ounces fresh pasta make about 1 cup cooked pasta (1 serving).

Acini di pepe. Tiny "peppercorn" pastas for soup. Just one among dozens of tiny soup pastas that come under the general name of *pastina*.

Agnolotti. "Fat little lambs"—plump semicircular or square ravioli. A holiday favorite of the Piedmont region of Italy.

Alphabets. Alphabet soup would be illiterate without tiny pasta letters.

Anelli. Little "rings" for your soup, not your finger; very tiny rings are called *anellini*.

Anolini. Round or ring-shaped ravioli. Serve with a sauce or in broth.

Ave Maria. So named because they're shaped like rosary beads. Put these short little tubular beads in soup.

Bows. Also called bow ties or, in Italian, *farfalle* ("butterflies"). They come in small, medium, and large; in yellow, red, and green. Can be made with eggs or just flour and water.

Bucatini. Thin spaghetti with a hole through the middle; use like spaghetti.

Cannelloni. "Large reeds," usually made from 4- to 6-inch pieces of fresh pasta. They're rolled around a filling, then sauced and baked. Also available as dried squares or tubes.

Capellini. "Fine hairs" to be used in soup or with sauce. Often sold coiled. Same as *fideo* or *fidelini*. Angel hairs, *capelli d'angeli*, are even finer.

Cappelletti. "Little hats" can be made with fresh dough and stuffed; or they can be bought dried as shown above. Dried cappelletti are not stuffed; use like macaroni.

Conchiglie. "Conch shells" (also called *marruze*) come in a variety of sizes, from minute shells for soup to giant shells for stuffing. They can be smooth or ridged.

Creste di galli. Handsome "cockscombs" can be used in place of medium-size elbow macaroni.

(Continued on next page)

Ditali rigati. Short "thimbles" with ridges. Can be sauced, used in salads, or baked. Tiny thimbles are called *ditalini.*

Elbow macaroni. Short, curved tubes of pasta, available in many colors and sizes.

Farfalle. *See* Bows.

Fettuccine. "Little ribbons," ¼ to ⅜ inch wide. Often made fresh, but also available dried, straight or in coils. Interchangeable with tagliatelle.

Fideo or fidelini. *See* Capellini.

Funghini. Intricate, baby-size "mushrooms" for soup.

Fusilli. Long strands of spaghetti-size pasta that appear to have been twisted on a spindle. (Some manufacturers use the name *fusilli* for rotelle.) Use in place of spaghetti.

Gemelli. "Twin" strands of spaghetti, about 3 inches long, twisted like embroidery thread. Sauce and serve as you would spaghetti.

Gnocchi. Homemade gnocchi (literally, "lumps") look like dumplings. Can be made with mashed potatoes, cornmeal, ricotta cheese, or semolina. Manufacturers make a dried gnocchi as shown above; use the dried version as you would medium-size elbow macaroni.

Lasagne. Wide ribbons, sometimes with curly edges, sometimes straight, used in baked dishes. Size varies from 1 to 2½ inches wide.

Linguine. Oval-shaped "little tongues" halfway between a flat ribbon and a cylindrical strand; can be used as you would spaghetti.

Lumache. "Snails" come in small and medium sizes for salads, baked dishes, and sauced entrées. Use as you would medium-size elbow macaroni.

Macaroni. This is the U.S. pasta industry's generic term for any dried wheat pasta product. More commonly, *macaroni* means dried pasta tubes of assorted sizes, like elbow macaroni.

Maccheroni alla chitarra. Noodles made on a noodle-cutting instrument that is strung with wires like a guitar.

Mafalde. Long noodles, about ¾ inch wide, rippled on both edges. A thinner version is called *mafaldine.* Sauce them as you would spaghetti or fettuccine.

Manicotti. "Little muffs" are actually one of the larger tubes of pasta available. You can find them ridged or smooth; stuff, sauce, and bake them.

Margherita. The name means "daisy," but the noodles don't look much like flowers. They're about as wide as fettuccine, with one curly edge.

Mostaccioli. Two-inch-long, ridged or smooth "mustaches" with diagonally cut ends. They look more like quill pens (*penne*), which is their other name. Good with a chunky meat sauce or robust tomato sauce.

Occhi di lupo. "Wolf's eyes" are thick, 1½-inch-long tubes. Good with robust sauces.

Occhi di pernice. Little "partridge eyes" that stare back at you from your soup.

Orzo. "Barley" for soup. Sometimes cooked like rice.

Pansotti. Triangular ravioli popular around Genoa. The name means "potbellied."

Pappardelle. Long, 1-inch-wide noodles (like thin lasagne), often homemade, with pinked edges. Served with hare in Tuscany.

Pastina. General term used for tiny pasta meant for soup.

Paternoster rigati. Small, ridged pastina for soup, named after beads on the rosary.

Penne. "Quill pens." *See* Mostaccioli.

Ravioli. Square, stuffed pasta, served with sauce or in soup. Best when homemade.

Ricci. Adjective indicating a curled edge on the pasta.

Riccini. "Little curls" about 1½ inches long. Use as you would medium-size macaroni, when you are in a baroque mood.

Rigati. Adjective indicating pasta has little ridges.

Rigatoni. Large, 1½-inch-long tubes with ridges. Good with assertive, chunky sauces.

Rotelle. Literally "little wheels," but they look more like corkscrews or spirals. Sometimes called *fusilli*. Use them as you would medium-size macaroni.

Ruote. "Wheels" that really look like wheels, complete with spokes. Use as you would medium-size macaroni.

Semi di melone. "Melon seeds" for your soup. Apple seeds are also available.

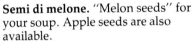

Spaghetti. "Little strands" are perhaps the best-known pasta. They come in many sizes, from fine spaghettine to thick spaghettoni.

Stellini. "Miniature stars"—pastina to star in your soup.

Tagliatelle. The verb *tagliare* means "to cut," and tagliatelle are little cut noodles. They are interchangeable with fettuccine. *Tagliarini* are narrow tagliatelle.

Tortellini. "Little twists" rumored to have been modeled after Venus's navel. A Bolognese specialty, they are filled like ravioli and served with sauce or in soup.

Tripolini. Named to honor Italy's conquest of Tripoli, these ½-inch pastas can go in soups or salads, or be served with a simple sauce.

Vermicelli. "Little worms"—an unappetizing name for fine strands of spaghetti. Slightly thicker than capellini, they come straight or in coils.

Wheels. *See* Ruote.

Ziti. These "bridegrooms" are tubular macaroni, sometimes sold long, then broken into pieces to cook. Use as you would mostaccioli.

Fruits & Vegetables

Fresh fruits and vegetables add color and variety to every culinary occasion, along with vitamins, minerals, plenty of fiber, and only a modest number of calories. Each time of year has its own fruit and vegetable specialties, so let the seasonal harvest be your guide when you shop. That way, you'll enjoy top quality as well as lower prices.

Today's improved growing methods have extended the seasons of many fruits and vegetables, increasing market variety and availability. Innovative cooks are taking advantage of this trend to experiment with new preparation techniques. As a result, an unprecedented abundance of fresh, creatively prepared produce is ours to enjoy.

BUYING & STORING FRUIT

Offering better nutrition than almost any other snack or dessert, fruit also presents a nearly endless variety. Brimming with vitamins and minerals, fruits contain very little fat, a minuscule amount of protein, and lots of water. Their carbohydrates come from natural sugars—a good source of energy.

Thanks to modern transportation and storage, perishable fruits now travel the year around to most parts of the country. But for best flavor and texture and lowest price, buy fruits when they're in season. At almost any time of year you'll find many varieties of apples and pears, as well as oranges, bananas, pineapple, papaya, and kiwi.

Summer, of course, brings the fruit cornucopia—apricots, cherries, Gravenstein apples, Bartlett pears, grapes, peaches, nectarines, and plums; watermelon and cantaloupe, as well as casaba, crenshaw, honeydew, and Persian melons; and a bounty of berries from blue to black, plus raspberries, gooseberries, and many others.

In autumn you'll see more melons and grapes and some continuing stone fruits, along with Bosc and Anjou pears, Delicious apples, and pomegranates.

With the winter months come tangerines, mandarins, navel oranges, and grapefruit. Then spring opens the show once again, as strawberries reappear among the apples, pears, and citrus fruits that kept us through the wintertime.

Fruit quality shows in degree of ripeness, color, firmness, and of course, freedom from decay. Exceptionally large fruits are a risky choice—they may lack flavor and juice. The least expensive varieties may not prove to be bargains after all, if they're priced low because of bruises, pithy texture, or bitter flavor.

Since fruit quality varies throughout a season and depends on the location of the harvest, only experience can guide you to wise choices. But a few general rules will help you select fruit of high quality. In all cases, buy loose fruit rather than fruit wrapped in cellophane, since stacked, tightly wrapped fruit may have bruises or blemishes you can't see. Check the chart below for selection tips for specific fruits; store your fruit purchases as the chart directs. In general, fruit to be refrigerated should be covered with plastic wrap or enclosed in plastic bags.

A MEDLEY OF FRUITS

FRUIT	SELECTION	MONTHS OF PEAK AVAILABILITY	STORAGE
APPLES	Select apples that are firm and well colored for their variety; avoid bruised or shriveled fruit.	All year, depending on variety	Keep at room temperature for a few days; or place unwashed apples in a plastic bag and refrigerate for longer storage. (Apples stay crisp longer if refrigerated.)
APRICOTS	Look for plump, juicy-looking apricots with as much golden color as possible. Avoid fruit that is pale yellow or greenish yellow, hard, shriveled, or bruised.	May–August	Keep at room temperature in a loosely closed paper bag until fully ripe; then place in a plastic bag and refrigerate.
BANANAS	Choose firm bananas free from bruises. Bananas may be purchased green; they ripen when kept at room temperature. Fruit is best for eating when fully yellow with some brown specks.	All year	Keep at room temperature until ripe; do not refrigerate (skins will turn black).
BLACKBERRIES	Select plump, well-colored blackberries; they should not have stem caps attached. Avoid berries showing any signs of decay.	May–August	Pick through berries and discard any that are bruised or decaying; cover with plastic wrap and refrigerate for up to 2 days. Do not wash until shortly before using.
BLUEBERRIES	Choose plump, well-colored blueberries; avoid those that look green, shriveled, or decayed.	May–September	Pick through berries and discard any that are bruised or decaying; cover with plastic wrap and refrigerate for up to 2 days. Do not wash until shortly before using.
CHERRIES	Select plump, bright cherries; mahogany or reddish-brown ones have the most flavor. Avoid any that are overly soft and shriveled.	May–August	Place in a plastic bag and refrigerate. Do not wash until shortly before using.

(Continued on next page)

A MEDLEY OF FRUITS

FRUIT	SELECTION	MONTHS OF PEAK AVAILABILITY	STORAGE
CRANBERRIES	Cranberries should appear well colored, plump, firm, and unbruised.	September–December	Place in a plastic bag and refrigerate for up to 1 month; freeze for longer storage. Shortly before using, wash cranberries; pick through them and discard any that are bruised or decaying.
DATES **Common varieties:** **Deglet Noor** (sold packaged) **Medjool** (sold loose)	Choose plump, fresh-looking dates with a deep amber color.	Deglet Noor: all year Medjool: November–May	Place in a plastic bag and keep at room temperature for several weeks; or refrigerate for up to a year.
FIGS	Figs should have deep, uniform color (according to variety) and yield slightly to pressure.	June–October	Place in a plastic bag and refrigerate for up to 4 days; do not wash until shortly before using.
GRAPEFRUIT	Choose smooth-skinned fruit that is compact, fairly round, and heavy for its size.	September–June	Keep in a cool place for up to 1 week; refrigerate for longer storage.
GRAPES	Look for plump grapes that are firmly attached to the stem. Red and purple varieties should be free of green coloration.	All year, depending on variety	Place in a plastic bag and refrigerate; do not wash until shortly before using.
KIWI FRUIT	Choose fruit that is plump and unbruised. When ripe, kiwi fruit yields to gentle pressure.	All year	Keep at room temperature until ripe; then place in a plastic bag and refrigerate.
LEMONS	Choose smooth-skinned fruit that is heavy for its size.	All year	Keep refrigerated.
LIMES	Select limes that are glossy, green, and heavy for their size.	All year	Keep refrigerated.
MANGOES	Look for smooth-skinned, unbruised fruit. When ripe, mangoes yield to gentle pressure; their green skin is colored with red or yellow.	May–August	Keep at room temperature until ripe, then place in a plastic bag and refrigerate.
MELONS **Common varieties:** **Cantaloupe** **Persian** **Honeydew** **Crenshaw** **Casaba**	**Cantaloupe.** Look for a dry, gray netting that stands out over green-gold rind. Also, check stem end for a smooth scar, which indicates the melon was fully mature before picking. Sniff for a sweet cantaloupe fragrance. **Persian.** As with cantaloupe, look for a clean stem end and raised netting (although it will be more sparse and less pronounced than a cantaloupe's net). As these melons ripen, the dark green rind turns light grayish-green and should give under gentle pressure. **Honeydew.** Choose a creamy, greenish-ivory melon with a smooth, waxy feel; don't expect a smooth stem end. Blossom end may be slightly soft. Also sniff for a mild, sweet melon fragrance; honeydews won't ripen much further if held at home. **Crenshaw.** Look for smooth, mottled-green rinds that have turned golden and are softening, especially at large end. You should detect a distinct melon fragrance.	Cantaloupe: May–September Persian: July–October Honeydew: June–October Crenshaw: July–October Casaba: August–December	In general, keep refrigerated. Crenshaws are especially perishable and should be used within 3 days; casabas will keep several weeks in a cool, dry place.

FRUIT	SELECTION	MONTHS OF PEAK AVAILABILITY	STORAGE
MELONS (cont'd.)	**Casaba.** The tough, wrinkly rind turns a definite yellow and the stem end is slightly soft when this melon is ripe; there's very little fragrance.		
NECTARINES	Choose fruit with a creamy or gold background color. Red blush is a variety characteristic and no indication of ripeness, but avoid fruit with green on its skin. Ripe fruit should yield to gentle pressure.	June–September	Keep at room temperature in a loosely closed paper bag until fully ripe; then place in a plastic bag and refrigerate.
ORANGES **Common varieties:** **Navel** (best for eating) **Valencia** (best for juice)	Select smooth-skinned fruit that's compact, fairly round, and heavy for its size.	Navel: November–May Valencia: February–November	Keep in a cool place.
PAPAYAS	Look for smooth-skinned fruit with as little green as possible on skin. Ripe fruit is slightly soft when pressed.	All year	Keep at room temperature until fully ripe; then place in a plastic bag and refrigerate. Do not wash until shortly before using.
PEACHES	Choose fruit with a creamy or gold background color. Red blush is a variety characteristic and no indication of ripeness, but avoid fruit with green on its skin. Ripe fruit should yield to gentle pressure.	May–September	Keep at room temperature in a loosely closed paper bag until fully ripe; then place in a plastic bag and refrigerate.
PEARS	Select pears that are plump, unbruised, and well-colored for their variety. When ripe, fruit yields to gentle pressure.	August–May, depending on variety	Keep at room temperature in a loosely closed paper bag until ripe; then place in a plastic bag and refrigerate.
PINEAPPLES	Choose pineapples that are fragrant and heavy for their size, with fresh, green tops. Avoid those with completely green skin; look for a yellow-orange blush.	All year	Keep at room temperature until fully ripe; then place in a plastic bag and refrigerate.
PLUMS/PRUNES	Buy plums and prunes that have deep, uniform color and are moderately firm, yielding slightly to pressure at the tip end.	May–September	Keep at room temperature in a loosely closed paper bag until fully ripe; then place in a plastic bag and refrigerate.
POMEGRANATES	Choose ruby-red fruit with skin that is completely intact (without cracks).	September–December	Keep refrigerated.
RASPBERRIES	Choose plump, well-colored raspberries; they should not have stem caps attached, and should show no signs of decay.	May–August	Pick through berries and discard any that are bruised or decaying; cover with plastic wrap and refrigerate for up to 2 days. Do not wash until shortly before using.
STRAWBERRIES	Select plump strawberries with fresh-looking stem caps and uniform red color.	April–September	Cover with plastic wrap and refrigerate for 2 to 3 days. Do not wash or hull until shortly before using.
TANGERINES/TANGELOS/MANDARINS	Choose glossy, well-colored fruit that is heavy for its size.	November–January	Keep refrigerated.
WATERMELONS	Look for whole watermelons with a yellowish (not white or light green) underside. Cut melon should have rich red flesh and dark brown or black seeds.	June–September	Keep refrigerated.

PREPARING FRUIT

Many cooks avoid buying fruits that call for special preparation techniques, thinking that they're too much trouble. But in truth, there's nothing difficult about preparing any fruit once you know how—and the sweet, juicy reward makes it all worthwhile.

The tools you'll need to prepare fruit are simple: a paring knife, a vegetable peeler, and a colander for washing will stand you in good stead for most purposes. Some more specialized devices are available too: there are grapefruit knives and citrus zesters, as well as gadgets for coring apples and pears or pitting cherries. Once in a while, you may even have use for a screwdriver—such as when piercing the eyes of a coconut and separating its meat from the shell.

In the illustrations below, we demonstrate three fruit preparation techniques: segmenting citrus fruits, cutting citrus zest, and making pineapple shells.

FRUIT PREPARATION TECHNIQUES

SEGMENTING CITRUS FRUITS

1 Slice off ends of fruit. Using a paring knife, remove peel, cutting deeply enough to remove all of white pith as well.

2 Working over a bowl to catch juice, cut toward center of fruit on both sides of white membrane—lift fruit segment out, leaving membrane intact.

TWO WAYS TO CUT CITRUS ZEST

With a vegetable peeler: Cut off thin colored layer; use a knife to cut into finer shreds or to chop.

With a citrus zester: Place sharper edge on fruit and pull down; fine strands of colored rind will come through.

HOW TO MAKE PINEAPPLE BOATS

1 Cut pineapple in half lengthwise. With curved grapefruit knife, cut around fruit on inside of each half, ¼ inch from edge.

2 With straight knife at 45° angle to pineapple, cut out wedges by slicing through core and fruit, but not through shell.

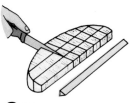

3 Slice core off each wedge and discard; cut wedges into 1-inch cubes.

4 Pile cubes back into pineapple, or mix with other fruit and pile back into shell. If made ahead, cover and refrigerate.

FOOD PROCESSING TECHNIQUES FOR FRUITS

Firm-ripe fruits give the best results in the food processor. You'll almost always get a few unevenly cut pieces, though; if you want fruit that's sliced or chopped perfectly evenly, use a knife.

Some fruits, such as apples, bananas, nectarines, peaches, and pears, turn brown when cut and exposed to air. If you won't be using these fruits immediately after processing, sprinkle them with lemon juice to prevent browning.

NOTE: Suggestions for filling the work bowl are based on standard machines with a 4-cup capacity. If you have a large-capacity processor, follow manufacturer's instructions for maximum amounts to process at one time.

When slicing or shredding, always empty the bowl when food reaches the fill line.

Chart Key

Metal blade Slicing disc Shredding disc

FOOD/ AMOUNT	FORM/ BLADE	BASIC PREPARATION	PROCESSING PROCEDURE/YIELD
APPLES **1 lb.** (about 3 small)	Sliced	Peel, if desired; cut into quarters and core.	Stack quarters in feed tube. Slice. Yield: 3–3½ cups.
	Chopped	Prepare as directed above.	Place up to half of pieces at a time in work bowl; chop, using on-off pulses, until as fine as desired. Yield: 3–3½ cups.
BANANAS **1 lb.** (2 medium-size)	Sliced	Peel; cut into lengths to fit vertically in feed tube.	Pack vertically in feed tube, cut ends down. Slice, using light pressure with pusher. Yield: 1½–2 cups.
CANDIED OR **PITTED DRIED** **FRUIT** **up to 2 cups**	Chopped	Reserve about ¼ cup sugar or flour from recipe for each ½ cup fruit.	Place fruit and sugar or flour in work bowl. Chop, using on-off pulses, until as fine as desired. Yield: ½ cup fruit plus ¼ cup flour or sugar = ½ cup chopped fruit.
CITRUS FRUIT **1 small lemon,** **1 medium-size** **lime, or 1** **medium-size** **orange**	Sliced	For best results, choose fruit which fits tightly in bottom of feed tube. Trim a small slice from each end. If fruit is too large to fit through bottom of feed tube, cut in half lengthwise.	Insert lemon, lime, or orange vertically through bottom of feed tube. Place cover over slicing disc; slice. If using halved fruit, don't stack halves; slice each separately. Yield: 1 small lemon = about ½ cup; 1 medium-size lime = about ½ cup; 1 medium-size orange = about 1 cup.
COCONUT **1¼–1½ lbs.**	Shredded	Pierce eyes; drain off milk. Place coconut in a shallow baking pan. Bake in a 350° oven for 30 minutes. Let cool. Hold coconut on a hard surface and hit with a hammer; separate flesh from shell with a screwdriver. Pare off brown skin, if desired, using a paring knife or a vegetable peeler; cut pieces to fit feed tube.	Pack in feed tube; shred. (Lift pusher slightly if coconut sticks.) Yield: about 4½ cups.
PEACHES OR **NECTARINES** **1 lb.** (3 medium-size)	Sliced	Peel, if desired; cut into quarters and remove pit.	Process as directed for Apples, sliced; use light pressure with pusher. Yield: 2½–3 cups.
PEARS **1 lb.** (about 3 small)	Sliced	For lengthwise slices, use small pears (ends trimmed, if necessary, to fit in feed tube). Peel, if desired; cut into quarters and core.	For lengthwise slices, pack pear quarters horizontally in feed tube, flat side down; slice. For crosswise slices, stack vertically in feed tube, alternating thick and thin ends; slice. Yield: about 3 cups.
PINEAPPLE **3 lbs.** (1 small)	Chopped	Trim ends of pineapple; then peel, remove eyes, cut into quarters, and core. Cut cored quarters into 1½-inch chunks.	Place up to half of pieces at a time in work bowl; chop, using on-off pulses, until as fine as desired. Yield: about 2½ cups.
STRAWBERRIES **1 lb.** (about 3 cups)	Sliced	Hull.	Stack washed and hulled berries horizontally in feed tube; slice, using very light pressure with pusher to avoid crushing fruit. Yield: about 2¼ cups.

BUYING & STORING VEGETABLES

Long overcooked and underrated, vegetables today have attained a new kind of popularity. Part of it is attributable to the growing awareness of our diet's role in maintaining general good health and fitness. But part of it, surely, is that we have realized how truly delicious vegetables can be when properly selected, carefully stored, and skillfully cooked.

Though many vegetables are available beyond their natural growing seasons, the choicest and most flavorful vegetables are those grown and harvested in season. Home-grown or local vegetables are the best—luscious red tomatoes from your own back yard, corn on the cob purchased at a farmer's roadside stand. And top quality isn't the only advantage of buying

VEGETABLES A TO Z

VEGETABLE SELECTION & MONTHS OF PEAK AVAILABILITY	AMOUNT (4 servings)	STORAGE
ARTICHOKES. Choose artichokes with tight, compact heads that feel heavy for their size. Surface brown spots (from frost) are harmless and indicate a meaty artichoke. Size is not an indication of quality. **March–May**	4 medium to large (2¾- to 4-inch diameter)	Place unwashed artichokes in a plastic bag and refrigerate for up to 1 week.
ASPARAGUS. Select firm, brittle spears that are bright green almost the entire length, with tightly closed tips. **March–June**	1½–2 lbs.	Wrap ends in a damp paper towel. Place unwashed asparagus in a plastic bag and refrigerate for up to 4 days.
BEANS, green, Italian, wax. Choose small crisp beans that are bright and blemish-free. **July–September**	1 lb.	Place unwashed beans in a plastic bag and refrigerate for up to 4 days.
BEANS, SHELLED—cranberry, fava, lima. Look for thick, broad, tightly closed pods that are bulging with large beans. If purchased shelled, beans should look plump and fresh. **Cranberry: August–October; fava: April–June; lima: July–September**	2½–3 lbs. unshelled or 1 lb. shelled	Place unwashed pods or shelled beans in a plastic bag and refrigerate for up to 4 days.
BEETS. Select small to medium beets that are firm and have smooth skins. Leaves should be deep green and fresh-looking. **June–October**	1½–2 lbs.	Cut off tops, leaving 1 to 2 inches attached. Do not trim roots. Reserve tops and cook separately (see **GREENS**). Place unwashed beets in a plastic bag; refrigerate for up to 1 week.
BELGIAN ENDIVE. Look for crisp, 4–6-inch-long heads that are creamy white tinged with light yellow at the tips. **September–May**	6–8 heads	Place unwashed endive in a plastic bag and refrigerate for up to 4 days.
BOK CHOY. Choose heads with bright white stalks and shiny dark leaves. Avoid heads with slippery brown spots; this indicates overchilling, which robs vegetable of flavor. **All year**	1¼–1½ lbs. (1 small to medium head)	Place unwashed bok choy in a plastic bag and refrigerate for up to 4 days.
BROCCOLI. Look for compact clusters of tightly closed dark green flowerets. Avoid heads with yellowing flowerets and thick, woody stems. **All year**	1–1½ lbs.	Place unwashed broccoli in a plastic bag and refrigerate for up to 5 days.
BRUSSELS SPROUTS. Choose small, firm Brussels sprouts that are compact and feel heavy for their size. They should be bright green and free of blemishes. **August–April**	1¼–1½ lbs.	Pull off and discard any limp or discolored leaves. Place unwashed sprouts in a plastic bag and refrigerate for up to 3 days.
CABBAGE, green, red, savoy. Choose firm heads that feel heavy for their size. Outer leaves should look fresh, have good color, and be free of blemishes. **All year**	1–1½ lbs. (1 small to medium head)	Place unwashed cabbage in a plastic bag and refrigerate for up to 1 week.
CABBAGE, napa (also called celery cabbage, Chinese cabbage). Look for fresh, crisp leaves free of blemishes. **All year**	About 1½ lbs. (1 medium-size head)	Place unwashed cabbage in a plastic bag and refrigerate for up to 4 days.
CARROTS. Select firm carrots that are smooth, well shaped, and brightly colored. Any tops should look fresh and be bright green. **All year**	1 lb. (3 or 4 medium-size)	Cut off and discard tops, leaving 1 to 2 inches attached to carrot. Place unwashed carrots in a plastic bag and refrigerate for up to 2 weeks.

vegetables at the peak of their season; prices are lowest then, too.

Whether you buy your produce at a large supermarket or at a small greengrocery, take time to choose the best vegetables your store offers. Sift through the mounds of oversize, tough green beans to find the thin, tender ones; avoid limp, tired celery, choosing instead the freshest, crispest bunch. A few moments spent in selecting superior produce can help transform an ordinary meal into a special occasion.

Some vegetables retain their peak flavor and texture longer than others. Root vegetables, such as carrots, potatoes, and onions, can be stored successfully for many weeks. In contrast, asparagus, corn on the cob, and leaf lettuce are among the most perishable.

In the following chart, you'll find tips for selecting the best produce and storing it to maintain peak condition. The chart also suggests appropriate cooking methods and seasonings for each vegetable. For detailed information on each of the suggested cooking methods, see pages 101–111. And for descriptions of the cutting and chopping techniques, turn to pages 96–97.

BASIC PREPARATION	SUGGESTED COOKING METHODS	SUGGESTED SEASONINGS
Prepare just before cooking. With a stainless steel knife, slice off stem. Remove and discard coarse outer leaves and cut off top third of artichoke. With kitchen shears, trim thorny tips of remaining leaves. Rinse well and plunge immediately into acidulated water (3 table-spoons vinegar or lemon juice per quart water).	Boil, steam, microwave	Melted butter, garlic butter, mayonnaise, hollandaise sauce
Snap off and discard tough ends. If desired, peel stalks with a vegetable peeler to remove scales. Plunge into a large quantity of cold water; lift out and drain. Leave spears whole or cut into slices.	Boil, steam, microwave, stir-fry, butter-steam, grill	Butter, tarragon, lemon juice, hollandaise sauce
Rinse beans; snap off and discard ends. Leave small beans whole; slice larger beans crosswise or diagonally, or cut into long French-style slivers.	Boil, steam, microwave, stir-fry, butter-steam, grill	Butter, chives, dill weed, thyme, crumbled bacon
Remove beans from pods and rinse.	Boil	Butter, savory, lemon juice
Scrub well but do not peel (to preserve their rich color, beets are usually cooked in their jackets). Leave roots, stems, and skin intact during cooking to prevent "bleeding." After cooking, let cool. Then cut off root and stem; slip off skins under cold running water.	Boil, microwave, butter-steam, bake	Butter, mustard butter, chives, dill weed, thyme, lemon juice, grated orange peel, dash of wine vinegar
Pull off and discard any wilted outer leaves; trim stem ends. Rinse under cold running water. To use in salads, separate individual leaves or slice crosswise. To cook, leave whole or cut in half lengthwise.	Boil	Butter, minced parsley, lemon juice, grated lemon peel, chopped toasted nuts
Plunge into a large quantity of cold water; lift out and drain. Cut leaves from stems (leaves cook faster). Slice stems crosswise and coarsely shred leaves.	Boil, steam, microwave, stir-fry, butter-steam	Butter, ginger, soy sauce
Rinse; cut off and discard base of stalks, leaving about 3½ inches of stalks. Peel bottom few inches of stalks, if desired. Cut lengthwise into spears. Leave spears whole and slash through bottom inch of stalks; or slice stalks crosswise, leaving flowerets whole.	Boil, steam, microwave, stir-fry, butter-steam	Butter, dill weed, rosemary, lemon juice
Trim stem ends and rinse. To ensure even cooking, cut a shallow "X" into end of each stem.	Boil, steam, microwave, butter-steam	Butter, basil, chives, dill weed, minced parsley, rosemary, thyme
Pull off and discard any wilted outer leaves. Rinse, cut in half lengthwise, and cut out core. Cut into wedges or shred.	Boil, steam, microwave, stir-fry, butter-steam	Butter, caraway seeds, dill weed
Pull off and discard any wilted outer leaves; rinse. Cut off and discard base. Cut cabbage in half lengthwise, then slice crosswise.	Microwave, stir-fry, butter-steam	Butter, ginger, soy sauce
Trim top and root ends. Scrub well; if desired, peel with a vegetable peeler and rinse. Cook whole; or slice, dice, shred, or cut into julienne strips.	Boil, steam, microwave, stir-fry, butter-steam, bake, grill	Butter, basil, chives, dill weed, ginger, mint, nutmeg, minced parsley, lemon juice, brown sugar

(Continued on next page)

VEGETABLES A TO Z

VEGETABLE SELECTION & MONTHS OF PEAK AVAILABILITY	AMOUNT (4 servings)	STORAGE
CAULIFLOWER. Choose firm, compact, creamy white heads. A yellow tinge and spreading flowerets indicate overmaturity. Any leaves should be crisp and bright green. **All year**	1¼–1½ lbs. (1 medium-size head)	Place unwashed cauliflower in a plastic bag and refrigerate for up to 1 week.
CELERY AND CELERY HEARTS. Look for rigid, crisp, green stalks with fresh-looking leaves. Avoid celery with limp or rubbery stalks. **All year**	1½ lbs. (1 medium-size bunch or 2 hearts)	Rinse and shake dry. Place in a plastic bag and refrigerate for up to 2 weeks.
CELERY ROOT (also called celeriac, celery knob). Select small to medium roots that are firm and relatively clean. Any tops should look fresh and be bright green. **October–April**	1–1½ lbs. (1 or 2 small roots)	Place unwashed roots in a plastic bag and refrigerate for up to 1 week.
CHAYOTE. Choose firm young chayotes that are free of blemishes. Color is not an indication of quality—chayotes range from pale to medium green. **October–March**	1½–2 lbs. (2 medium to large)	Store chayotes, unwrapped, in a cool (50°F), dry, dark place with good ventilation for up to 1 month. Or place chayotes in a plastic bag and refrigerate for up to 1 week.
CHICORY (also called curly endive). Look for fresh, crisp heads with tender, deep green outer leaves free of blemishes. **August–December**	1 lb. (1 large head)	Rinse under cold running water, then shake off excess. Dry greens. Wrap in a dry cloth or paper towel, place in a plastic bag, and refrigerate for up to 2 days.
CORN. It's best to buy and cook corn on the day it's picked. Look for fresh ears with green husks, moist stems, and silk ends that are free of decay and worm injury. When pierced with thumbnail, kernels should give a spurt of thin, milky juice. Thick liquid and tough skin indicate overmaturity. **May–September**	4 large or 8 small to medium ears (2 ears yield about 1 cup kernels)	Place unhusked ears in a plastic bag and refrigerate for up to 2 days.
CUCUMBERS—Armenian; English or European; lemon; marketer (most common variety); **pickling.** Choose firm dark green **marketer** and **pickling** cucumbers that are well shaped and slender. Soft, yellowing cucumbers are overmature. Select firm pale green **Armenian** and straight **English** or **European** cucumbers. Pale yellow-green **lemon** cucumbers should be small (2- to 3-inch diameter). **Armenian, lemon: July–October; English or European, marketer: All year; pickling: July–September**	1 medium-size **Armenian** or **English;** 2 small or 1 medium to large **marketer**	**Marketers** are waxed to prevent moisture loss and can be refrigerated whole, unwrapped, for up to 1 week; if cut, wrap in plastic wrap. Wrap other varieties, whole or cut up, in plastic wrap and refrigerate—**lemon** cucumbers for up to 5 days, others for up to 1 week.
EGGPLANT. Look for firm, heavy, shiny, deep purple eggplants with bright green stems. Dull color and rust-colored spots are signs of old age. **July–October**	1¼–1½ lbs. (1 large or 2 small to medium)	Place unwashed eggplant in a plastic bag and refrigerate for up to 5 days.
ESCAROLE (also called broad-leafed endive). Look for fresh, crisp heads with tender, deep green outer leaves and pale inner ones. **August–December**	1 lb. (1 large head)	Rinse under cold running water, pulling back outer leaves to expose gritty center; shake off excess water. Dry greens. Wrap in a dry cloth or paper towel, place in a plastic bag, and refrigerate for up to 2 days.
FENNEL (also called anise, finocchio). Look for firm, white bulbs with rigid, crisp stalks and feathery bright green leaves. **October–April**	3 lbs. (3 or 4 medium-size bulbs, each 3- to 4-inch diameter)	Place unwashed fennel in a plastic bag and refrigerate for up to 1 week.
GARLIC. Choose firm, dry bulbs with tightly closed cloves and smooth skins. Avoid bulbs with sprouting green shoots. **All year**	1 large head	Store unwrapped garlic in a cool (50°F), dry, dark place with good ventilation for 2 to 3 months.
GREENS—beet, collards, dandelion, kale, mustard, turnip. Look for fresh, tender leaves that are deep green and free of blemishes. Avoid bunches with thick, coarse-veined leaves. **Beet: June–October; collards, dandelion, kale, mustard: January–April; turnip: October–March**	1½ to 2 lbs.	Remove and discard wilted leaves. Rinse well under cold running water; shake off excess. Dry greens. Wrap in a dry cloth or paper towel and place in a plastic bag. Refrigerate **beet** and **turnip** greens for up to 2 days, **collards, dandelion, kale,** and **mustard** greens for up to 4 days.
HERBS. Look for herbs with allover green color. Yellowing leaves indicate herbs are old. **Cilantro, parsley: All year; basil, chervil, chives, dill weed, marjoram, mint, oregano, rosemary, sage, savory, tarragon, thyme: July–September**		Rinse under cold running water; shake off excess water. Wrap in a dry cloth or paper towel, place in a plastic bag, and refrigerate for up to 4 days (parsley for up to 1 week).

BASIC PREPARATION	SUGGESTED COOKING METHODS	SUGGESTED SEASONINGS
Remove and discard outer leaves and cut out core; rinse. Leave head whole or break into flowerets.	Boil, steam, microwave, stir-fry, butter-steam	Butter, chives, dill weed, nutmeg, minced parsley, lemon juice, mornay sauce, hollandaise sauce
Separate stalks and rinse thoroughly. Trim off leaves and base; cut out brown spots. To remove strings from outer stalks, pull strings with a knife from top of stalk down to base; discard. Dice stalks; or cut into slices or julienne strips. Rinse hearts and cut in half lengthwise.	Boil, steam, stir-fry, butter-steam	Butter, tarragon, thyme
Scrub with a vegetable brush; cut off and discard top and root ends. Peel away thick outer skin with a sturdy knife. Cut out pitted spots. Slice, dice, shred, or cut into julienne strips. To keep peeled or cut surfaces white, submerge immediately in a bowl of acidulated water (3 tablespoons vinegar or lemon juice per quart water).	Boil, butter-steam	Butter, dill weed, tarragon
Rinse well. Cut in half lengthwise. Or peel and slice crosswise or quarter lengthwise through seed (cooked seed is edible).	Boil, steam, butter-steam	Butter, basil, oregano, nutmeg, thyme, lemon juice, lime juice, orange juice
Separate leaves; leave whole or tear into bite-size pieces.	Best served raw	Salad dressings
Remove and discard husk and silk; trim stem end. To cut corn from cob, stand cooked or raw ear on end and slice straight down, leaving kernel bases attached to cob. If desired, scrape cob with back of a knife to remove remaining corn pulp and "milk."	Boil, steam, microwave, bake, grill	Butter, chili powder, oregano, lime juice
Rinse; if desired, peel with a vegetable peeler or score lengthwise with tines of a fork. To seed, cut cucumber in half lengthwise and scoop out seeds with a spoon. To use in salads or sandwiches: Slice whole cucumbers crosswise. To butter-steam: Peel, seed, and slice.	Butter-steam **Armenian, English, marketer;** do not cook **lemon** or **pickling** cucumbers	Butter, chervil, chives, dill weed, minced parsley
Rinse and pat dry. Cut off and discard stem end; peel, if desired. Cut into cubes or ½-inch-thick slices.	Bake	Garlic butter, basil, marjoram, oregano, minced parsley, thyme
Tear leaves into bite-size pieces.	Best served raw	Salad dressings
Rinse well. Trim stalks to within ¾ to 1 inch of bulb. Discard hard outside stalks and bulb base; reserve leaves for seasoning cooked bulb. Cut bulb lengthwise into halves or quarters; or dice or cut into julienne strips.	Boil, steam, stir-fry, butter-steam	Butter, fennel leaves, dash of whipping cream
To use as a seasoning, break into cloves. To peel, cut off root end of clove, crush clove with side of a knife blade, and peel skin away. Mince or press through a garlic press. To bake, leave unpeeled heads whole.	Bake	Needs no seasoning
Tear out and discard tough center ribs. Use leaves whole, or cut or tear into bite-size pieces.	Boil **collards, kale, mustard, turnip;** microwave **kale, mustard;** butter-steam **beet, turnip; dandelion** best served raw	Butter, oregano, lemon juice, dash of wine vinegar, crumbled bacon
Pull or cut off leaves, and chop or mince. Use as a seasoning or garnish.		

(Continued on next page)

VEGETABLES A TO Z

VEGETABLE SELECTION & MONTHS OF PEAK AVAILABILITY	AMOUNT (4 servings)	STORAGE
JICAMA. Choose firm, well-formed jicama that are free of blemishes. **October–June**	1 lb.	Store whole unwashed jicama at room temperature for 2 to 3 weeks. Wrap cut pieces in plastic wrap and refrigerate for up to 1 week.
KOHLRABI. Choose small, tender bulbs with fresh, green leaves; avoid those with scars or blemishes. **June–October**	4 small to medium bulbs	Cut off tops; reserve for other uses, if desired. Place unwashed kohlrabi in a plastic bag and refrigerate for up to 1 week.
LEEKS. Select leeks with clean, white bottoms and fresh-looking, crisp green tops. **October–May**	1½ lbs. (about 1 bunch)	Place unwashed leeks in a plastic bag and refrigerate for up to 1 week.
LETTUCE—bibb, Boston, butter, iceberg, red or green leaf, limestone, romaine. Choose heads of **iceberg** with fresh, green outer leaves; heads should give a little under pressure. Good **romaine** has crisp, deep green outer leaves without brown spots or decay. **Bibb, Boston, butter, red or green leaf,** and **limestone** lettuce should have tender, fresh-looking leaves free of tip burn and bruising. **All year**	1 small to medium head **iceberg** or **romaine;** 1 to 2 heads **butter;** or 1 large head **leaf**	Rinse before storing. To rinse **iceberg,** hold head, core side down, under cold running water; drain. Rinse **romaine, butter,** and **leaf** lettuce under running water, separating individual leaves. Dry well. Wrap in a dry cloth or paper towel and place in a plastic bag. Refrigerate **iceberg** and **romaine** for up to 5 days, **butter** and **leaf** lettuce for up to 2 days.
MUSHROOMS. Select smooth, plump mushrooms with caps closed around stems; avoid spotted mushrooms and those that have open caps with dark gills exposed. **All year**	1 lb.	Place unwashed mushrooms in a paper bag and refrigerate for up to 4 days. If desired, place a damp paper towel inside bag to help mushrooms retain moisture.
OKRA (also called gumbo). Select small to medium pods that are deep green and firm. Pods should be free of blemishes and flexible enough to bend easily. **July–October**	1 lb.	Place unwashed okra in a plastic bag and refrigerate for up to 3 days.
ONIONS, dry—boiling, mild red, shallots, mild white, yellow. Choose firm, dry onions with characteristically brittle outer skin. Avoid those with sprouting green shoots and dark spots. **All year**	1 lb.	Store whole onions, unwrapped, in a cool (50°F), dry, dark place with good ventilation for up to 2 months. Wrap cut pieces in plastic wrap and refrigerate for up to 4 days.
ONIONS, green (also called scallions). Choose green onions with bright green tops and clean, white bottoms. **All year**		Place unwashed onions in a plastic bag and refrigerate for up to 1 week.
PARSNIPS. Choose small to medium parsnips that are firm, smooth, and well shaped. Avoid large woody parsnips. **November–March**	1 lb.	Place unwashed parsnips in a plastic bag and refrigerate for up to 10 days.
PEAS, edible-pod—Chinese pea pods (also called snow or sugar peas), sugar snap peas. Look for firm, crisp, bright green pods. **February–June**	1 lb.	Place unwashed pods in a plastic bag and refrigerate for up to 3 days.
PEAS, green (also called shell peas). Select small, plump, bright green pods that are firm, crisp, and well filled with medium-size peas. **April–August**	2–2½ lbs. unshelled (1 lb. unshelled yields 1 cup shelled)	Place unwashed pods in a plastic bag and refrigerate for up to 3 days.
PEPPERS, green or red bell. Select bright, glossy peppers that are firm, well shaped, and thick walled; avoid those with soft spots or gashes. When allowed to ripen on the bush, green peppers turn brilliant red. **July–September**	3 or 4 medium to large	Place unwashed peppers in a plastic bag and refrigerate. Store **green peppers** for up to 5 days, **red peppers** for up to 3 days.
POTATOES, russet. Choose firm potatoes with reasonably smooth skins; avoid those with sprouting eyes, soft black spots, or green areas. **All year**	4 medium to large	Store potatoes, unwashed, in a cool (50°F), dry, dark place with good ventilation for up to 2 months or at room temperature for up to 1 week.
POTATOES, sweet (or yams). Choose sweet potatoes that are firm and well shaped with bright, uniformly colored skin. Two types are available. The one usually called **sweet potato** has light yellow flesh and a dry, mealy consistency when cooked; the second type, usually called **yam,** has orange flesh and is sweet and moist after cooking. **October–March**	4 medium to large	Store sweet potatoes, unwashed, in a cool (50°F), dry, dark place with good ventilation for up to 2 months or at room temperature for up to 1 week.

BASIC PREPARATION	SUGGESTED COOKING METHODS	SUGGESTED SEASONINGS
Scrub well and peel. Slice, dice, or cut into julienne strips for salads or to use in combination stir-fry dishes.	Stir-fry	Lemon or lime juice, soy sauce
Scrub young bulbs. Peel mature bulbs to remove tough outer skin. Use whole, slice, or dice.	Boil, butter-steam	Butter, chives, dill weed, lemon juice, dash of wine vinegar
Cut off and discard root ends. Trim tops, leaving about 3 inches of dark green leaves. Strip away and discard coarse outer leaves, leaving tender inner ones. Cut leeks in half lengthwise. Hold each half under cold running water, separating layers to rinse out dirt.	Boil, steam, microwave, stir-fry, butter-steam	Butter, chervil, minced parsley, tarragon, crumbled bacon
Tear leaves into bite-size pieces for salads. If desired, cut out core and shred **iceberg.**	Butter-steam **iceberg;** others best served raw	Salad dressings
To clean, wipe with a damp cloth or mushroom brush, or rinse briefly under cold running water; pat dry. Trim stem base. Use whole, slice lengthwise through stem, or chop.	Microwave, stir-fry, butter-steam	Butter, minced parsley, tarragon, thyme, dash of dry sherry
For long, slow cooking, trim stem ends, then rinse and slice okra; pods contain a milky liquid that will help thicken stews and gumbos. *For more quickly cooked dishes,* leave pods whole to contain liquid. Rinse pods and trim stem ends carefully to avoid piercing pods.	Boil, steam	Butter, chives, minced parsley, lemon juice
Trim ends from **red, white, and yellow onions** and **shallots;** peel outer skin. Leave whole, quarter, slice, or chop. To peel small **boiling onions,** pour boiling water over onions; let stand for 2 to 3 minutes, then drain. Trim ends; peel and discard outer skin. Cut a shallow "X" into each stem end to ensure even cooking and keep onion intact.	Microwave, stir-fry, butter-steam, bake **mild red, mild white, yellow;** boil, steam, microwave **boiling onions**	Butter, minced parsley, thyme, brown or granulated sugar
Rinse and pat dry. Trim root ends; strip off and discard wilted outer leaves. Trim brown or dried areas from tops. Slice or cut into julienne strips for salads or to use in combination stir-fry dishes.	Stir-fry	Salad dressings, ginger, soy sauce
Trim tops and root ends. Peel with a vegetable peeler and rinse. Leave whole, dice, slice, or cut into sticks or julienne strips.	Boil, steam, microwave, stir-fry, butter-steam, bake	Butter, basil, tarragon, thyme, lemon juice, brown sugar
Break off both ends; remove and discard strings. Rinse.	Boil, steam, microwave, stir-fry, butter-steam	Butter, soy sauce
Remove peas from pods and rinse.	Boil, steam, microwave, stir-fry, butter-steam, grill	Butter, basil, chervil, chives, mint, nutmeg, minced parsley, rosemary, tarragon, thyme
Rinse; remove stem, seeds, and pith. Leave whole, cut in half lengthwise, slice, dice, or cut into julienne strips.	Stir-fry, butter-steam, bake	Basil, oregano, dash of wine vinegar
Scrub well and dry. To bake, pierce in several places and leave whole. To keep peeled or sliced potatoes white, submerge in a bowl of cold water immediately after cutting.	Microwave, bake, grill	Butter, chives, paprika, minced parsley, crumbled bacon, sour cream
Scrub well and dry. To bake, pierce in several places and leave whole.	Boil, steam, microwave, bake	Butter, lemon or orange juice, grated lemon or orange peel, brown sugar

(Continued on next page)

VEGETABLES A TO Z

VEGETABLE SELECTION & MONTHS OF PEAK AVAILABILITY	AMOUNT (4 servings)	STORAGE
POTATOES, thin-skinned (red or white "new" potatoes). Look for firm, well-shaped potatoes with fairly smooth skins; avoid those with sprouting eyes or yellow spots. **All year**	1½ lbs. (6 to 8 small)	Store potatoes, unwashed, in a cool (50°F), dry, dark place with good ventilation for up to 1 month. Store unwashed at room temperature or in the refrigerator for up to 1 week.
RADISHES, daikon. Choose firm, white, small to medium daikon, 1–1½ inches in diameter. **All year**	1 large (about 1 lb.)	Place unwashed daikon in a plastic bag and refrigerate for up to 10 days.
RADISHES, red. Look for smooth, crisp, firm radishes with good red color. Bright green tops indicate freshness. **All year**	1–1½ bunches	Place unwashed radishes in a plastic bag and refrigerate for up to 1 week.
RUTABAGAS. Choose small to medium rutabagas that are smooth and firm and feel heavy for their size. Lightweight rutabagas may be woody. **October–March**	1½–2 lbs.	Store rutabagas, unwashed, in a cool (50°F), dry, dark place with good ventilation for up to 2 months. Store unwashed at room temperature or in the refrigerator for up to 1 week.
SHALLOTS—See **ONIONS, dry**		
SORREL. Select young, fresh-looking leaves that are free of blemishes. **July–October**	1 lb. (about 10 cups leaves)	Wrap unwashed sorrel in a dry cloth or paper towel, place in a plastic bag, and refrigerate for up to 2 days.
SPINACH. Choose bunches having crisp, tender, deep green leaves, with few yellow leaves or blemishes. **All year**	1½ lbs. (about 2 bunches)	Discard wilted leaves. Remove and discard tough stems and midribs. Plunge into cold water; lift out and drain. For salads, dry well. Wrap in a dry cloth or paper towel, place in a plastic bag, and refrigerate for up to 3 days. To cook, do not dry; cook in water that clings to leaves.
SPROUTS, bean and alfalfa. Select small, tender examples of both varieties. Bean sprouts should be crisp and white with beans attached. **All year**	1 lb. bean sprouts	Place unwashed sprouts in a plastic bag and refrigerate for up to 4 days.
SQUASH, spaghetti. Squash should have a hard, thick shell and feel heavy for its size. **August–February**	2 lbs.	Store whole squash, unwashed, at room temperature for up to 2 months.
SQUASH, summer—crookneck, pattypan, zucchini. Select firm, small to medium squash with smooth, glossy, tender skin. Squash should feel heavy for their size. **June–September**	1–1½ lbs.	Place unwashed squash in a plastic bag and refrigerate for up to 5 days.
SQUASH, winter—acorn, banana, butternut, Hubbard, pumpkin. Choose squash that have hard, thick shells and feel heavy for their size. Flesh should be thick and bright yellow-orange. **September–March**	1½–2 lbs.	Store whole squash, unwashed, in a cool (50°F), dry, dark place with good ventilation for up to 2 months. Wrap cut pieces in plastic wrap and refrigerate for up to 5 days.
SUNCHOKES (also called Jerusalem artichokes). Choose tubers that are firm and free of mold. **October–April**	1–1½ lbs.	Place unwashed tubers in a plastic bag and refrigerate for up to 1 week.
SWISS CHARD. Look for bunches with fresh, glossy, dark green leaves and heavy white or red stems. **July–October**	1½–2 lbs.	Place unwashed chard in a plastic bag and refrigerate for up to 3 days.
TOMATOES. Choose tomatoes that are smooth, well formed, and firm but not hard. Color varies according to variety and ripeness. Tomatoes that are picked ripe are richly colored; those picked before ripening are paler in color. **July–September**	1–1½ lbs. (4 to 6 small)	Store unwashed tomatoes at room temperature, stem end down, until slightly soft. Refrigerate very ripe tomatoes, unwrapped, for up to 4 days.
TURNIPS. Choose firm, small to medium turnips (2- to 3-inch diameter) that have smooth skin and feel heavy for their size. **October–March**	1½–2 lbs. (about 4 medium-size)	Remove tops; if desired, cook tops separately (see **GREENS**). Place unwashed turnips in a plastic bag and refrigerate for up to 1 week.
WATERCRESS. Select vivid green leaves; avoid wilted and yellowed leaves. **All year**	1 medium to large bunch or 2 small bunches	Rinse under cold running water. Stand stems in a container of cold water; then cover tops with a plastic bag. Refrigerate for up to 2 days.
YAMS—See **POTATOES, sweet**		

BASIC PREPARATION	SUGGESTED COOKING METHODS	SUGGESTED SEASONINGS
Scrub well and dry. Boil, steam, or pierce and bake small **red potatoes** whole; cut larger, long **white potatoes** into quarters before cooking. To keep peeled or sliced potatoes white, submerge in a bowl of cold water immediately after cutting.	Boil, steam, bake, grill	Butter, caraway seeds, dill weed, minced parsley, rosemary, crumbled bacon
Rinse, trim stem and root ends, and peel. Slice or shred to use in salads, soups, or combination stir-fry dishes.	Stir-fry	Dash of white rice vinegar, soy sauce
Rinse well; cut off and discard tops and roots. Use whole; or slice, shred, or quarter.		Salad dressings
Rinse and peel with a vegetable peeler. Leave whole; or quarter, slice, dice, or cut into julienne strips.	Boil, steam, stir-fry, butter-steam, bake	Butter, caraway seeds, cinnamon, dill weed, lemon juice, brown sugar
Remove and discard stems and midribs. Plunge into a large quantity of cold water; lift out and drain. To reduce color loss and acidity, blanch leaves before cooking. Or serve raw in salads.		Sliced green onion, crumbled bacon
Keep leaves whole, tear into bite-size pieces, or shred.	Boil, steam, microwave, stir-fry, butter-steam	Butter, basil, mint, nutmeg, oregano, grated lemon peel, crumbled bacon
Rinse **bean sprouts;** discard discolored ones. Drain. Rinse and drain **alfalfa sprouts.** Use raw in salads, sandwiches, or other dishes.	Microwave, stir-fry, butter-steam **bean sprouts;** do not cook **alfalfa sprouts**	Butter, ginger, soy sauce **(bean sprouts)**
Rinse; do not peel. To bake, pierce shell in several places; leave whole. To microwave, cut in half lengthwise and remove seeds.	Microwave, bake	Butter, basil, oregano, minced parsley
Trim ends and rinse. Do not peel. Leave whole, dice, or cut into slices or julienne strips.	Boil, steam, microwave, stir-fry, butter-steam, grill	Butter, basil, oregano, minced parsley
Rinse. Cut **acorn** or **butternut** squash or **pumpkin** in half lengthwise; cut **banana** or **Hubbard** squash into serving-size pieces. Remove and discard seeds and fibers. Bake unpeeled; for other cooking methods, peel and cut into cubes, spears, or slices.	Boil, steam, bake **all varieties;** microwave **acorn, banana, butternut;** butter-steam **banana, Hubbard, pumpkin;** grill **banana, Hubbard**	Butter, allspice, cardamom, cinnamon, nutmeg, brown sugar
Scrub well or peel with a vegetable peeler. Submerge immediately in a bowl of acidulated water (3 tablespoons vinegar or lemon juice per quart water) to prevent discoloration. Leave whole, slice, or dice.	Boil, steam, butter-steam	Butter, tarragon, lemon juice
Plunge into a large quantity of cold water; lift out and drain. Cut leaves from stems (leaves cook faster). Slice stems crosswise and shred leaves.	Boil, steam, microwave, stir-fry, butter-steam	Butter, basil, nutmeg, oregano, crumbled bacon
To peel, submerge tomatoes in boiling water for 30 seconds to 1 minute, then plunge immediately into cold water; lift out and slip off skins. Or hold tomato on a fork over a flame until skin splits; then peel. To seed, slice in half crosswise and squeeze out seeds. Leave whole; or slice, chop, or cut into wedges.	Bake	Basil, chives, dill weed, oregano, minced parsley
Rinse. Bake whole turnips unpeeled; peel for other cooking methods. Leave whole; or dice, slice, or cut into quarters or julienne strips.	Boil, steam, microwave, stir-fry, butter-steam, bake	Butter, basil, caraway seeds, brown sugar, crumbled bacon
Remove tough stems. Use leaves and tender part of stems in salads or soups, tucked into sandwiches, or as a garnish.		Salad dressings

PREPARING VEGETABLES

For the beginning cook, it isn't always easy to know what's meant by terms such as "mincing" or "julienne strips." And even those with many hours of experience in the kitchen may appreciate a few pointers on preparing leeks for cooking or cutting raw corn off the cob.

Here, then, is an illustrated guide to some of the techniques commonly used in preparing vegetables. Once you've mastered these, you'll feel confident in your ability to follow virtually any vegetable recipe. Then you can unleash your imagination, and start to create your own tempting vegetable dishes.

VEGETABLE PREPARATION TECHNIQUES

SLICING

To slice a round vegetable such as an onion or potato, cut it in half and lay halves, cut side down, on a cutting board. Gripping one half with your fingers, and curling your fingertips under toward your palm, cut straight down through vegetable at a right angle to board.

DIAGONAL SLICING

To diagonally slice long vegetables, cut them crosswise on the diagonal. (With long, thin vegetables, such as asparagus or green beans, you can diagonally slice several at a time.)

CUTTING JULIENNE STRIPS

To cut vegetables such as zucchini, carrots, turnips, or potatoes into julienne strips (similar in size to wooden matchsticks), first cut vegetable, if necessary, into 2- to 3-inch lengths. Cut a thin lengthwise strip off one side and lay vegetable on flat side. Cut into ⅛-inch-thick slices, stack 2 or 3 slices at a time, and cut slices into ⅛-inch-thick strips.

DICING

Cut as directed for julienne strips, but cut strips, a handful at a time, crosswise into dice. For larger dice, start with ¼- or ½-inch-thick slices, then cut crosswise to make ¼- or ½-inch cubes.

CHOPPING

Hold top of knife blade at both ends. Chop with steady up-and-down movements, scraping chopped vegetables into a heap, as necessary, with knife blade.

MINCING

Push chopped vegetables into a heap. Keeping tip of knife blade on cutting board, and using it as a pivot, lift heel of knife in up-and-down movements to finely chop vegetables.

SHREDDING

To shred cabbage or iceberg lettuce, cut head in half through core. Cut out and discard core from each half. Place each half, cut side down, on cutting board; cut crosswise into 1/8- to 1/4-inch-thick slices.

PEELING TOMATOES

Begin by blanching tomatoes; then plunge into cold water to cool. Slide tip of a sharp knife beneath skin, then strip off skin. Cut out and discard core from stem end.

SEEDING TOMATOES

Cut tomato in half crosswise. Gently squeeze each half to remove seeds and juice. Tomatoes are now ready for chopping or slicing.

CUTTING RAW CORN OFF THE COB

Slice down length of cob with a sharp knife, leaving kernel bases attached. For creamy corn, scrape cob with back of knife to remove corn pulp and "milk."

PREPARING EDIBLE-POD PEAS

Snap or cut off one end of pea pod and pull off attached string. Repeat at opposite end to remove other string.

PREPARING LEEKS

Trim off root ends and all but about 3 inches dark green leaves. Discard coarse outer leaves. Insert knife through white part just below leaves; split leek lengthwise through leaves. Rinse well, separating layers to wash out all dirt.

ROLL-CUTTING ZUCCHINI

Make a diagonal slice straight down through zucchini; give it a quarter turn and slice diagonally again. Continue turning and slicing until zucchini is completely sliced.

SEEDING BELL PEPPERS

First cut a 1/4-inch slice off stem end. Hold slice in both hands, thumbs beneath stem; push on stem to snap it out. Tear through seed membranes inside pepper; pull out seeds.

PITTING AVOCADOS

Cut avocado in half lengthwise around pit. Cup avocado in both hands and twist in half. Holding half with pit in one hand, carefully thrust knife into pit and twist out.

FOOD PROCESSING TECHNIQUES FOR VEGETABLES

For best results, use produce that's firm and crisp. It's normal to get a few unevenly cut pieces; if you want perfectly cut pieces, use a knife.

To shred just one long vegetable (such as a carrot) or slice it crosswise, cut into 2 or 3 even lengths, or enough to fit snugly when packed vertically in the feed tube.

For neat, even slicing, remember the following tips. At the grocery store, keep in mind the size of your machine's feed tube and learn to select foods which will fit snugly with the least amount of trimming. For standard processors, this

means choosing a small tomato instead of a large one, a long, narrow potato instead of a round, fat one. Processors with large feed tubes accommodate bigger pieces.

Before you slice, consider that rounded vegetables, such as tomatoes and mushrooms, cut best if you remove a small slice from one end or side, then set the food flat over the slicing disc.

We give directions for making julienne strips by cutting vegetables twice with the slicing disc. If you have a French fry disc or one that produces julienne strips, follow the manufacturer's instructions.

NOTE: Suggestions for filling the work bowl are based on standard machines with a 4-cup capacity. If you have a large-capacity food processor, follow manufacturer's instructions for maximum amounts to process at one time.

When slicing or shredding, always empty the bowl when food reaches the fill line.

Chart Key

Metal blade   Slicing disc

Shredding disc

FOOD/ AMOUNT	FORM/ BLADE	BASIC PREPARATION	PROCESSING PROCEDURE/YIELD
BEANS, green, Italian, or wax 1 lb.	French-cut	Trim ends; cut beans into lengths to fit horizontally in feed tube.	Stack horizontally in feed tube; slice. Yield: about 4 cups.
BEETS, cooked (4 or 5 small)	Sliced	Trim stem and root ends; peel. If beets are too large to fit in feed tube, cut in half lengthwise.	Insert one beet through bottom of feed tube. Place cover over slicing disc; pack tube with more beets. Slice. Yield: about 2½ cups.
	Shredded	Prepare as directed above.	Stack in feed tube; shred. Yield: about 2½ cups.
CABBAGE, green, red, or napa 1 lb. (1 small head)	Shredded	Core; cut lengthwise into quarters or eighths to fit vertically in feed tube.	Pack vertically in feed tube; shred using slicing disc. Yield: green or red = about 5 cups, lightly packed; napa = about 6 cups, lightly packed.
	Chopped	Core; cut lengthwise into quarters, then crosswise into 2-inch chunks.	Place up to half of pieces at a time in work bowl; chop, using on-off pulses, until as fine as desired. Yield: about 4½ cups, lightly packed.
CARROTS 1 lb. (3 or 4 medium-size)	Sliced	Trim ends; peel, if desired. Cut into lengths to fit vertically in feed tube.	Pack vertically in feed tube, alternating thick and thin ends; slice. Yield: about 3½ cups.
	Julienne strips	Trim ends; peel, if desired. Cut into lengths to fit horizontally in feed tube.	Pack horizontally in feed tube, alternating thick and thin ends; slice. Stack slices; turn stack on its side, long, thin edges down. Tightly fit stack into bottom of feed tube with pusher in place (hold cover at an angle so carrots don't fall out). Carefully place cover over disc and slice. (Process one stack at a time.) Yield: about 3½ cups.
	Shredded	Trim ends; peel, if desired. Cut into lengths to fit vertically in feed tube.	Pack vertically in feed tube, alternating thick and thin ends; shred. Yield: about 4 cups, lightly packed.
CELERY 3 large stalks	Sliced	Trim ends; remove strings, if desired. Cut into lengths to fit vertically in feed tube.	Nest curved part of stalks together; pack vertically in feed tube. Slice. Yield: about 2 cups.
	Chopped	Trim ends; cut into 1½-inch lengths.	Place in work bowl; chop, using on-off pulses, until as fine as desired. Yield: about 2 cups.

FOOD/ AMOUNT	FORM/ BLADE	BASIC PREPARATION	PROCESSING PROCEDURE/YIELD
CELERY ROOT 1 lb. (1 small)	Sliced	Trim ends, peel, and cut into quarters lengthwise to fit vertically in feed tube.	Pack in feed tube; slice. Use, or place in acidulated water (3 tablespoons lemon juice to 4 cups water) to prevent browning. Yield: 4 cups.
	Julienne strips	Prepare as directed above.	Slice as directed above. Stack slices, then turn stack on its side—thin, flat edges down. Continue as directed for Carrots, julienne strips. (If feed tube is large, place 2 stacks side by side.) Slice; use, or submerge in acidulated water (see above). Yield: about 3½ cups.
CUCUMBER 1 small	Sliced	Trim ends; peel or score if desired. Cut into lengths to fit vertically in feed tube.	Place vertically in feed tube, cut end down; slice. Yield: about 1¼ cups.
FENNEL 1 lb. (1 medium-size bulb)	Sliced	Trim stalks just above bulb; trim bulb base. Cut bulb in half lengthwise; trim sides, if necessary, to fit vertically in feed tube.	Place vertically in feed tube; slice. Yield: about 4 cups.
GARLIC up to 1 head	Minced	Separate into cloves; peel cloves.	With motor running, drop through feed tube, one clove at a time; continue processing until minced. Yield: 1 large clove = 1 teaspoon.
GINGER, fresh 1- by 1-inch piece	Chopped or minced	Peel, if desired; cut into quarters.	With motor running, drop through feed tube; continue processing until as fine as desired. Yield: about 2 tablespoons.
HERBS		*See* Parsley.	
JICAMA 1 lb. (1 small)	Shredded	Trim ends; peel. Trim sides, if necessary, to fit in feed tube.	Place in feed tube; shred. Yield: about 4 cups, lightly packed.
LEEKS 1 lb. (2 medium-size)	Sliced	Trim root ends and all but 3 inches of dark green tops. Split lengthwise; rinse and dry. Cut into lengths to fit vertically in feed tube.	Pack vertically in feed tube; slice. Yield: about 4½ cups.
LETTUCE, iceberg 1 lb. (1 small head)	Shredded	Prepare as directed for Cabbage, shredded.	Process as directed for Cabbage, shredded. Yield: about 5 cups, lightly packed.
MUSHROOMS 1 lb.	Sliced	Trim stem bases. Remove a thin slice from one side of enough mushrooms to cover slicing disc at bottom of feed tube (1–3 mushrooms).	Arrange sliced mushrooms in bottom of feed tube over disc, with cut sides down and stems pointing in. Stack more mushrooms on top, stems in; slice. Yield: about 4½ cups.
	Chopped	Trim stem bases.	Place up to ½ lb. at a time in work bowl. Chop, using on-off pulses, until as fine as desired. Yield: about 5 cups.
ONIONS, dry (red, white, or yellow) 1 small	Sliced	Trim ends; peel. If too large to fit through bottom of feed tube, cut in half lengthwise.	Insert whole or halved onion vertically through bottom of feed tube. Place cover over slicing disc; slice. Yield: about 1½ cups.
	Chopped or minced	Trim ends; peel, and cut into quarters (or eighths, if large).	Place in work bowl; chop, using on-off pulses, until as fine as desired. Yield: about 1 cup coarsely chopped, about ½ cup minced.
ONIONS, green 1 bunch (7–9 medium-size)	Sliced	Trim root ends; do not trim tops. Rinse and pat dry.	With tongs, grasp tops of as many onions as can be held firmly at one time. With motor running, insert root ends down into feed tube. Slice until tongs are halfway into feed tube. Stop machine. Reserve remaining tops for other uses, if desired. Repeat. Yield: about 1 cup.
	Chopped	Trim root ends and green tops from onions. (Reserve tops for other uses, if desired.) Then cut white part of each onion into 1-inch lengths.	Place in work bowl. Chop, using on-off pulses, until as fine as desired. Yield: about ½ cup.

(Continued on next page)

FOOD PROCESSING TECHNIQUES FOR VEGETABLES

FOOD/ AMOUNT	FORM/ BLADE	BASIC PREPARATION	PROCESSING PROCEDURE/YIELD
PARSLEY (and other leafy herbs) up to 2 cups lightly packed sprigs or leaves	Chopped	Rinse well; discard tough stems. Work bowl, blade, and herbs should be as dry as possible.	Place in work bowl; chop, using on-off pulses, until as fine as desired. Yield: ½ cup sprigs or leaves = ¼ cup.
PEPPER, green or red bell 1 medium-size	Sliced	Cut in half lengthwise; remove seeds and stem.	Place one half, stem end down, in feed tube; slice. Repeat. Yield: about 1¼ cups.
	Chopped	Prepare as directed above; cut into 2-inch chunks.	Place in work bowl; chop, using on-off pulses, until as fine as desired. Yield: about 1 cup.
POTATOES, thin-skinned or russet 1 lb. (about 4 small thin-skinned or 2 small russet)	Sliced	Peel if desired. If necessary, trim to fit feed tube. Trim a thin slice off one end of each potato so it will sit flat over slicing disc.	Place in feed tube, one at a time, trimmed end down; slice. Use sliced potatoes immediately or submerge in cold water to prevent browning. Yield: about 3 cups.
	Julienne strips	Prepare as directed above.	Slice as directed above. Then process as directed for Celery root, julienne strips. Use immediately or submerge in cold water. Yield: about 3 cups.
	Shredded	Prepare as directed above.	Place in feed tube; shred. Use immediately or submerge in cold water. Yield: about 4 cups lightly packed.
RADISHES 1 bunch (about 12)	Sliced	Trim ends.	Pack vertically in feed tube; slice. Yield: about 1¼ cups.
SHALLOTS ¼ lb. (5 medium-size)	Chopped or minced	Trim ends; peel.	Place in work bowl; chop, using on-off pulses, until as fine as desired. Yield: about 1 cup coarsely chopped, about ½ cup minced.
SQUASH, zucchini 1 lb. (3 medium-size)	Sliced	Trim ends; cut into lengths to fit vertically in feed tube.	Pack vertically in feed tube; slice. Yield: about 5 cups.
	Julienne strips	Trim ends; cut into lengths to fit horizontally in feed tube.	Process as directed for Carrots, julienne strips. Yield: about 3½ cups.
	Shredded	Trim ends; cut to fit vertically in feed tube.	Pack vertically in feed tube; shred. Yield: about 4 cups, lightly packed.
TOMATOES 1 lb. (about 4 small)	Sliced	Core. Trim a thin slice from end of one tomato so it will sit flat over slicing disc. If too large to fit vertically through bottom of feed tube, cut in half lengthwise.	Insert trimmed tomato (cut end down) through bottom of feed tube. Place cover over slicing disc; pack feed tube with more tomatoes. Slice, using light pressure with pusher. Yield: about 3 cups.
	Chopped	Core; cut lengthwise into quarters (or eighths, if large) and seed.	Place up to ½ lb. at a time in work bowl; chop, using on-off pulses, until as fine as desired. Yield: about 2½ cups.
TURNIPS 1 lb.	Sliced	Trim ends. Peel; trim sides to fit feed tube, if necessary.	Insert one turnip through bottom of feed tube, then place cover over slicing disc. Pack feed tube with more turnips and slice. Yield: about 4 cups.

COOKING VEGETABLES

Once you've decided which vegetable to serve, how should you cook it? If you're undecided, take a look through the next 11 pages for inspiration. We've covered a range of basic cooking techniques: boiling, steaming, stir-frying, butter-steaming, baking, and grilling. There's a microwave chart, as well.

Some vegetables, such as the versatile carrot, are suitable for all these cooking methods. Others are a bit more limited—for example, you may serve kale boiled or butter-steamed, but it doesn't take well to steaming or stir-frying. But for any vegetable you choose, you'll find at least a few cooking choices.

To ensure that your vegetables cook just right, each chart is accompanied by an explanation of the cooking method, directions for testing doneness, and serving instructions. If you're a novice cook, be sure to read this information carefully before you begin.

A final note: Remember that the first step toward delicious cooked vegetables comes well before you pull out your steamer or switch on the oven. For the best cooked vegetables, you need to start with high-quality produce—plump, crisp bell peppers; bright, juicy tomatoes; crunchy carrots. Overripe or blemished vegetables will never taste as good as really fresh, perfect ones, no matter how carefully you cook them.

When you shop, follow our selection tips on pages 88 to 95; they'll help you choose the freshest and finest vegetables available.

BOILING & STEAMING FRESH VEGETABLES

Before boiling or steaming fresh vegetables, check the chart beginning on page 88 for tips on selection, storage, and basic preparation. Keep in mind that whole or cut-up vegetables cook more evenly if they're uniform in size and shape.

To boil vegetables. Bring designated amount of water to a boil over high heat; add vegetables. When water returns to a boil, cover pan if specified in chart, reduce heat to medium (water should boil throughout cooking time), and begin timing.

To steam vegetables. Cookware shops have various utensils for steaming, but the simplest and least expensive is a collapsible metal steaming basket, available in two sizes to fit into ordinary pans.

If you have a metal colander and a pan big enough to hold it, that's another possibility. Whatever you use, it should accommodate whole vegetables such as potatoes in a single layer, or cut-up vegetables or small vegetables such as peas in an even layer no deeper than 1½ to 2 inches.

Place steaming rack in pan; pour in water to a depth of 1 to 1½ inches (water should not touch bottom of rack). Bring to a boil over high heat; then place vegetables on rack. Cover pan, reduce heat to medium (water should boil throughout cooking time), and begin timing. If necessary, add boiling water to pan to maintain water level throughout cooking time.

To test for doneness. Cooking time depends on freshness and maturity of vegetables. Test after minimum cooking time; if necessary, continue to cook, testing frequently, until vegetables are done to your liking. Most cooked vegetables should be just tender when pierced; potatoes and beets should be tender throughout. Leafy vegetables should appear wilted and have bright color.

To serve. Immediately drain vegetables, if necessary, reserving any liquid to use in soups, stock, or sauces. To serve vegetables hot, season to taste with salt and pepper; or choose one or more of the seasonings suggested in the chart beginning on page 88. To serve vegetables cold, immediately plunge them into cold water; when cool, drain again.

VEGETABLE For amount for 4 servings, see chart on pages 88–95	Container	BOILING Amount of Water	Time	STEAMING Time	TEST FOR DONENESS
ARTICHOKES Whole (medium-size)	5–6-qt. pan, covered	3–4 qts. plus 2 tablespoons vinegar	30–45 minutes	25–35 minutes	Stem end tender when pierced
ASPARAGUS Spears	Wide frying pan, covered	1 inch	7–10 minutes	8–12 minutes	Tender when pierced
Slices (½–1 inch)	Wide frying pan, covered	½ inch	2–5 minutes	5–7 minutes	Tender when pierced

(Continued on next page)

BOILING & STEAMING FRESH VEGETABLES

VEGETABLE For amount for 4 servings, see chart on pages 88–95	Container	BOILING Amount of Water	Time	STEAMING Time	TEST FOR DONENESS
BEANS, green, Italian, wax Whole	3-qt. pan, covered	1 inch	5–10 minutes	10–15 minutes	Tender-crisp to bite
Pieces (1–2 inches)	3-qt. pan, covered	1 inch	4–7 minutes	8–12 minutes	Tender-crisp to bite
BEANS, shelled Cranberry, Fava	3-qt. pan, covered	1½ inches	20–25 minutes	Do not steam	Tender to bite
BEANS, lima	3-qt. pan, covered	1½ inches	12–20 minutes	Do not steam	Tender to bite
BEETS Whole (2–3-inch diameter)	4–5-qt. pan, covered	Water to cover	20–45 minutes	Do not steam	Tender throughout when pierced
BELGIAN ENDIVE Halved lengthwise	Wide frying pan, covered	½ inch	5–7 minutes	Do not steam	Stem end tender when pierced
BOK CHOY—See **SWISS CHARD**					
BROCCOLI Spears	Wide frying pan, covered	1 inch	7–12 minutes	15–20 minutes	Stalk tender when pierced
Pieces (1 inch)	Wide frying pan, covered	½ inch	3–6 minutes	8–15 minutes	Tender when pierced
BRUSSELS SPROUTS Whole (medium-size)	3-qt. pan; cover during last half of cooking time	1 inch	7–10 minutes	15–25 minutes	Stem end tender when pierced
CABBAGE, green, red, savoy Wedges	Wide frying pan; cover after 2 minutes	1 inch	8–12 minutes	9–14 minutes	Tender when pierced
CARROTS Whole, baby	Wide frying pan, covered	½ inch	5–10 minutes	8–12 minutes	Tender when pierced
Whole, large	Wide frying pan, covered	1 inch	10–20 minutes	12–20 minutes	Tender when pierced
Slices (¼ inch)	Wide frying pan, covered	½ inch	5–10 minutes	5–10 minutes	Tender when pierced
CAULIFLOWER Whole (medium-size)	4–5-qt. pan, covered	1 inch	15–20 minutes	20–25 minutes	Stem end tender when pierced
Flowerets	Wide frying pan, covered	½ inch	5–9 minutes	10–18 minutes	Stem end tender when pierced
Slices (¼ inch)	Wide frying pan, covered	½ cup	3–5 minutes	7–12 minutes	Tender-crisp to bite
CELERY Slices (1 inch)	Wide frying pan, covered	½ inch	5–10 minutes	8–10 minutes	Tender when pierced
CELERY HEARTS Halved lengthwise	Wide frying pan, covered	½ inch	8–12 minutes	10–14 minutes	Tender when pierced
CELERY ROOT Whole (medium-size)	3-qt. pan, covered	Water to cover	40–60 minutes	Do not steam	Tender when pierced
CHAYOTE Halved lengthwise	Wide frying pan, covered	2 inches	30–35 minutes	35–40 minutes	Tender when pierced
Slices (¼ inch)	Wide frying pan, covered	½ inch	7–9 minutes	18–22 minutes	Pale green throughout and soft to bite

VEGETABLE For amount for 4 servings, see chart on pages 88–95	Container	BOILING Amount of Water	Time	STEAMING Time	TEST FOR DONENESS
CORN ON THE COB	4–5-qt. pan, covered	2–3 qts.	3–5 minutes	8–10 minutes	Tender when pierced
FENNEL 3–4-inch diameter, halved lengthwise	Wide frying pan, covered	½–1 inch	8–10 minutes	18–22 minutes	Tender when pierced
Slices (½ inch)	Wide frying pan, covered	½ inch	5–8 minutes	10–12 minutes	Tender-crisp to bite
GREENS **Collards, kale, mustard, turnip** Leaves, coarsely chopped	4–5-qt. pan, covered	1 inch	5–15 minutes	Do not steam	Tender to bite
KOHLRABI Whole (medium-size)	3-qt. pan, covered	1 inch	30–40 minutes	Do not steam	Tender when pierced
Slices (¼–½ inch)	Wide frying pan, covered	½ inch	12–25 minutes	Do not steam	Tender when pierced
LEEKS 1-inch diameter, halved lengthwise	Wide frying pan, covered	½ inch	5–8 minutes	5–8 minutes	Tender when pierced
OKRA Whole (medium-size)	3-qt. pan, covered	Water to cover	5–10 minutes	15–20 minutes	Tender when pierced
ONIONS, small white boiling Whole (1 to 1½- inch diameter)	3-qt. pan, uncovered	Water to cover	15–20 minutes	20–25 minutes	Tender when pierced
PARSNIPS Whole (medium-size)	Wide frying pan, covered	1 inch	10–20 minutes	15–25 minutes	Tender when pierced
Slices (¼ inch)	Wide frying pan, covered	½ inch	5–10 minutes	7–15 minutes	Tender when pierced
PEAS, edible-pod	5-qt. pan, uncovered	3 qts.	30 seconds	3–5 minutes	Tender-crisp to bite
PEAS, green Shelled	3-qt. pan, covered	½ inch	5–10 minutes	8–12 minutes	Tender to bite
POTATOES, red or white thin-skinned Whole (3-inch diameter)	3-qt. pan, covered	1–2 inches	20–30 minutes	30–35 minutes	Tender throughout when pierced
Slices (½ inch)	3-qt. pan, covered	½–1 inch	8–10 minutes	8–10 minutes	Tender when pierced
POTATOES, sweet (or yams) Whole (3-inch diameter)	3-qt. pan, covered	2 inches	20–30 minutes	30–40 minutes	Tender throughout when pierced
RUTABAGAS Whole (3- to 4-inch diameter)	4–5-qt. pan, covered	2 inches	25–35 minutes	30–45 minutes	Tender when pierced
Slices (½ inch)	Wide frying pan, covered	½–1 inch	7–10 minutes	9–12 minutes	Tender when pierced
SPINACH Leaves (whole)	4–5-qt. pan, covered	Water that clings to leaves	2–4 minutes	3–5 minutes	Wilted appearance, bright color
SQUASH, summer **Crookneck, pattypan,** **zucchini** Whole	3-qt. pan, covered	1 inch	8–12 minutes	10–12 minutes	Tender when pierced
Slices (¼ inch)	3-qt. pan, covered	½ inch	3–6 minutes	4–7 minutes	Tender when pierced

(Continued on next page)

BOILING & STEAMING FRESH VEGETABLES

VEGETABLE For amount for 4 servings, see chart on pages 88–95	Container	BOILING Amount of Water	Time	STEAMING Time	TEST FOR DONENESS
SQUASH, winter **Acorn, banana, butternut, Hubbard,** **pumpkin** Slices (½ inch)	Wide frying pan, covered	½ inch	7–9 minutes	9–12 minutes	Tender when pierced
SUNCHOKES Whole (medium-size)	3-qt. pan, covered	1 inch	10–20 minutes	15–20 minutes	Tender when pierced
Slices (¼–½ inch)	Wide frying pan, covered	½ inch	5–10 minutes	12–15 minutes	Tender when pierced
SWISS CHARD Stems, cut into ¼- inch slices, and leaves, shredded	Wide frying pan, covered	¼ inch	Stems: 2 minutes; add leaves and cook 1–2 more minutes	Stems: 3 minutes; add leaves and cook 2–4 more minutes	Tender-crisp to bite
TURNIPS Whole (2- to 3-inch diameter)	4–5-qt. pan, covered	2 inches	20–30 minutes	25–35 minutes	Tender when pierced
Slices (½ inch)	Wide frying pan, covered	½ inch	6–8 minutes	7–9 minutes	Tender when pierced
YAMS—See **POTATOES, sweet**					

MICROWAVING FRESH VEGETABLES

When it comes to cooking fresh vegetables, the microwave is truly a wonder worker. Vegetables cook in minutes, often without any liquid whatsoever. The bonuses to you are garden-fresh flavors and crispness, along with maximum retention of vitamins and minerals.

For information on selecting, storing, and preparing vegetables, see the chart beginning on page 88. Keep in mind that whole or cut-up vegetables microwave more evenly if they're of uniform size and shape. **Cook all vegetables on HIGH (100%) power.**

Covering vegetables. To hold in steam, cover the cooking dish either with the lid of the casserole or with heavy-duty plastic wrap (use only those wraps specifically described on the package as being for use in the microwave; light-weight plastic wraps may split during cooking and melt into the food). *Caution:* **When uncovering a dish after cooking, be sure to start at the edge farthest from you; escaping steam can cause burns.**

When you need only minimum moisture retention—for mushrooms and onions, for example—wax paper is an ideal cover.

Potatoes, squash, and corn on the cob, left whole and unpeeled or unhusked, can be microwaved without any wrapping other than the natural one. Pierce potato skins before cooking to allow steam to escape (unpierced potatoes may explode).

Cooking & standing time. Cooking time depends on the freshness, moisture content, maturity, and quantity of the vegetable. (If you double the amount of vegetable, in-crease the initial cooking time by about 60 percent.) Remove the vegetables from the microwave after the shortest suggested cooking time and let stand for the recommended time before testing for doneness (see below). If the vegetables are still too crisp for your liking, microwave them further in 1-minute increments.

Testing for doneness. Most cooked vegetables should be tender-crisp when pierced; if overcooked, they'll dry out and become tough. Potatoes should give slightly when squeezed. Leafy vegetables should appear wilted and have bright color.

To serve. Season to taste with salt and pepper after cooking; or choose one or more of the seasonings suggested in the chart beginning on page 88.

MICROWAVING FRESH VEGETABLES

VEGETABLE/ AMOUNT	CON- TAINER	PREPARATION	COOKING TIME (CT) STANDING TIME (ST)
ARTICHOKE Whole 1 medium (6–8 oz.)	10-oz. cus- tard cup	Prepare as directed on page 89. Place arti- choke upside down in container. Pour in ¼ cup water and cover with heavy-duty plastic wrap.	**CT:** 5–7 minutes Before standing, lower leaves should be easy to pull away from stems with a slight tug; stem should be tender when pierced. **ST:** 5 minutes, covered
2 medium	9-inch round baking dish	Same as above; use ½ cup water.	**CT:** 8–10 minutes **ST:** 5 minutes, covered
3 medium	9-inch round baking dish	Same as above; use ¾ cup water.	**CT:** 9–11 minutes **ST:** 5 minutes, covered
4 medium	9-inch round baking dish	Same as above; use 1 cup water.	**CT:** 13–15 minutes **ST:** 5 minutes, covered
ASPARAGUS Spears 1 bunch (1 lb.)	7- by 11-inch baking dish	Prepare as directed on page 89. Place asparagus so tips are toward center of dish. Add 3 tablespoons water and cover with heavy-duty plastic wrap.	**CT:** 5 minutes Rearrange spears halfway through cooking, bringing center pieces to edge of dish; cover again. **ST:** 5 minutes, covered
Slices 1 bunch (1 lb.)	1½-qt. casserole	Prepare as directed on page 89. Cut asparagus into 1-inch slices. Add 2 table- spoons water and cover with lid or heavy- duty plastic wrap.	**CT:** 4–7 minutes Stir after 3 minutes; cover again. **ST:** 4–5 minutes, covered
BEANS, green, Italian, wax Pieces 1 lb.	1½-qt. casserole	Prepare as directed on page 89. Cut beans into 1-inch pieces. Add ½ cup water and cover with lid or heavy-duty plastic wrap.	**CT:** 12–15 minutes Stir after every 5 minutes; cover again. **ST:** 5 minutes, covered Degree of tenderness depends on variety used and maturity of beans.
BEETS Whole 2 bunches (6 medium)	2-qt. casserole	Prepare as directed on page 89. Arrange beets in dish. Add 1 to 1½ cups water and cover with lid or heavy-duty plastic wrap.	**CT:** 14–16 minutes Rearrange after 7 minutes, bringing outside beets to center of casserole; cover again. **ST:** 5 minutes, covered Let cool until easy to handle, then peel.
BOK CHOY 1 bunch (1¼–1½ lbs.)	2-qt. casserole	Prepare as directed on page 89. Cut white stems crosswise into ¼-inch slices and place in casserole with 2 tablespoons water; cover with lid or heavy-duty plastic wrap. Cut leaves into 1-inch strips and add after 3 minutes cooking time.	**CT:** 7–8 minutes Stir in leaves after 3 minutes; cover again. **ST:** 2 minutes, covered
BROCCOLI Spears 1 bunch (1¼–1½ lbs.)	9- by 13-inch baking dish or 12-inch flat plate	Prepare as directed on page 89; cut into uniform spears. Peel skin off bottom 2 inches of stalks; then rinse spears and place so flowerets are toward center of dish and stalk ends are toward outside. Add 2 tablespoons water. Cover with heavy-duty plastic wrap.	**CT:** 8–10 minutes *If using baking dish,* rearrange spears half- way through cooking, bringing center pieces to edge of dish; cover again. *If using plate,* rotate plate ¼ turn halfway through cooking. **ST:** 4 minutes, covered
Pieces 1 bunch (1¼–1½ lbs.)	2-qt. casserole	Prepare as directed on page 89; cut into uniform spears. Peel skin off bottom 2 inches of stalks; then rinse spears and cut into 1-inch pieces. Sprinkle with 1 table- spoon water and cover with lid or heavy- duty plastic wrap.	**CT:** 5–6 minutes Stir after 3 minutes; cover again. **ST:** 4 minutes, covered
BRUSSELS SPROUTS 1 lb. (about 24 medium)	1½-qt. casserole	Prepare as directed on page 89. If Brussels sprouts are not of uniform size, cut larger ones in half. Add 2 tablespoons water and cover with lid or heavy-duty plastic wrap.	**CT:** 6–7 minutes Stir after 3 minutes; cover again. **ST:** 3–5 minutes, covered

(Continued on next page)

MICROWAVING FRESH VEGETABLES

VEGETABLE/ AMOUNT	CONTAINER	PREPARATION	COOKING TIME (CT) STANDING TIME (ST)
CABBAGE, green, red, savoy Shredded 1 lb. (6 cups)	2- to 3-qt. casserole	Prepare as directed on page 89. Add 2 tablespoons water and cover with lid or heavy-duty plastic wrap.	**CT:** 4–6 minutes Stir after 2 minutes; cover again. **ST:** 3 minutes, covered
Wedges 1 lb. (1 small head)	9- to 10-inch baking dish or pie plate	Prepare as directed on page 89. Arrange wedges like spokes, with large core ends toward edge of dish. Sprinkle with 2 tablespoons water and cover with lid or heavy-duty plastic wrap.	**CT:** 6–8 minutes Rotate dish ¼ turn after 3 minutes. **ST:** 2–3 minutes, covered
CARROTS Whole 1 lb. (1-inch diameter)	7- by 11-inch baking dish	If carrots are very tapered, cut off root ends to prevent ends from cooking faster than tops. Prepare as directed on page 89. Add ¼ cup water and cover with heavy-duty plastic wrap.	**CT:** 6–7 minutes Rotate each carrot ½ turn after 3 minutes; cover again. **ST:** 5 minutes, covered
Slices 1 lb. (1-inch diameter)	1-qt. casserole	Prepare as directed on page 89. Cut carrots into ¼-inch thick slices. Add 3 tablespoons water and cover with lid or heavy-duty plastic wrap.	**CT:** 8–9 minutes Stir after 4 minutes; cover again. **ST:** 5 minutes, covered
CAULIFLOWER Whole 1¼–1½- lb. head (1 medium)	1–1½-qt. casserole	Prepare as directed on page 91. Place stem side down. Add 2 tablespoons water and cover with lid or heavy-duty plastic wrap.	**CT:** 10–11 minutes Turn over after 7 minutes; cover again. Before standing, stem end should be tender when pierced. **ST:** 5 minutes, covered
Flowerets 1¼–1½-lb. head (1 medium)	1½-qt. casserole	Prepare as directed on page 91. Break cauliflower into flowerets; cut larger ones in half lengthwise. Add 2 tablespoons water. Cover with lid or heavy-duty plastic wrap.	**CT:** 6–8 minutes Stir after 4 minutes; cover again. **ST:** 4 minutes, covered
CORN ON THE COB 1–6 ears	None	Be sure corn is completely enclosed in husk; secure ends with string or rubber bands. Or remove husk and silk and wrap each ear individually in heavy-duty plastic wrap. Arrange on paper towels on microwave floor; place 1 ear in center of oven, 2 ears side by side, 3 in a triangle, 4 ears in a square, 5 ears—place 4 in a line and 1 across top; 6 ears—place 4 in a line, 1 across top, and 1 across bottom.	**CT:** 3–4 minutes per ear Turn ears over halfway through cooking. **ST:** 2–3 minutes
KALE 1 bunch (about 1¼ lbs.)	3-qt. casserole	Rinse and coarsely chop greens. *Do not add water.* Cover with lid or heavy-duty plastic wrap.	**CT:** 7–8 minutes Stir after 3 minutes; cover again. **ST:** 2 minutes, covered
LEEKS 1½ lbs.	8-inch square baking dish	Prepare as directed on page 93. Rinse and arrange in a single layer. *Do not add water.* Cover with heavy-duty plastic wrap.	**CT:** 5 minutes **ST:** 5 minutes, covered
MUSHROOMS 1 lb.	2-qt. casserole	Prepare as directed on page 93. Cut lengthwise into ¼-inch slices. Add 2 tablespoons water, or 2 tablespoons butter or margarine cut into 6 pieces. Cover with lid or wax paper.	**CT:** 4–6 minutes Stir after 2 minutes; cover again. **ST:** 2 minutes, covered
ONIONS, dry Slices 1 lb.	1-qt. casserole	Prepare as directed on page 93. Slice ¼ inch thick and separate into rings. Add 2 tablespoons water or 2 tablespoons butter or margarine cut into 6 pieces. Cover with lid or wax paper.	**CT:** 5–6 minutes Stir after 2 minutes; cover again. (To make onions sweet, cook for 10 minutes, stirring after every 3 minutes; cover again.) **ST:** 5 minutes, covered
Whole (small boiling onions) 8–12	1-qt. casserole	Peel as directed on page 93. *Do not add water.* Cover with lid or heavy-duty plastic wrap.	**CT:** 4–6 minutes Stir after 2 minutes; cover again. **ST:** 5 minutes, covered

VEGETABLE/ AMOUNT	CON- TAINER	PREPARATION	COOKING TIME (CT) STANDING TIME (ST)
PEAS, edible-pod 1 lb.	2-qt. casserole	Prepare as directed on page 93. Rinse. *Do not add water.* Cover with lid or heavy-duty plastic wrap.	**CT:** 4–5 minutes Stir after 2 minutes; cover again. **ST:** 4 minutes, covered
PEAS, green Unshelled About 2½ lbs. (to yield 2½ cups shelled)	1½-qt. casserole	Prepare as directed on page 93. Add ¼ cup water and cover with lid or heavy-duty plastic wrap.	**CT:** 8–12 minutes Stir after 5 minutes; cover again. **ST:** 5 minutes, covered
POTATOES, russet 1–6 potatoes (8 oz. *each*)	None	Scrub potatoes; pierce skin on 4 sides with a fork or knife. Place on paper towels on microwave floor. Arrange at least 1 inch apart as follows: 1 potato in center of oven 2 potatoes side by side 3 potatoes in a triangle 4 potatoes like spokes 5 potatoes like spokes 6 potatoes like spokes	**CT:** 4–5 minutes 6–8 minutes 8–10 minutes 10–12 minutes 12–15 minutes 15–20 minutes ·Turn potatoes over halfway through cooking. After cooking, potatoes should give slightly when squeezed. **ST:** 5–10 minutes, wrapped in a clean towel or in foil
POTATOES, sweet (or yams) 1–6 fairly round potatoes (about 8 oz. *each*)	None	Prepare and arrange as for russet potatoes (see above). 1 sweet potato 2 or 3 sweet potatoes 4 or 5 sweet potatoes 6 sweet potatoes	**CT:** 4–5 minutes 6–7 minutes 8–12 minutes 12–16 minutes Follow directions for russet potatoes (above). **ST:** 5–10 minutes, wrapped in a clean towel or in foil
SPINACH 1 lb.	3-qt. casserole	Prepare as directed on page 95. *Do not add water.* Cover with lid or heavy-duty plastic wrap.	**CT:** 5–7 minutes Stir after 3 minutes; cover again. **ST:** 2 minutes, covered
SQUASH, summer Crookneck, pattypan, zucchini 1 lb.	1½-qt. casserole	Prepare as directed on page 95. Slice squash ¼ inch thick. Add 2 tablespoons butter or margarine cut into 6 pieces. Cover with lid or heavy-duty plastic wrap.	**CT:** 6–7 minutes Stir after 3 minutes; cover again. **ST:** 3 minutes, covered
SQUASH, winter Acorn or butternut 2 medium (1½ lbs. *each*)	10- to 12-inch flat plate	Prepare as directed on page 95. Cut in half lengthwise and remove seeds. Place squash, hollow side up, on plate with fleshy portion toward edge of dish. Spread cut surfaces with 1 to 2 tablespoons butter or margarine. Cover with heavy-duty plastic wrap.	**CT:** 10–12 minutes Rotate plate ¼ turn after 5 minutes. **ST:** 5 minutes, covered
SWISS CHARD 1 bunch (1¼–1½ lbs.)	2-qt. casserole	Prepare as directed on page 95. Cut white stems crosswise into ¼-inch slices and place in casserole with 2 tablespoons water; cover with lid or heavy-duty plastic wrap. Cut leaves into 1-inch strips and add after 3 minutes cooking time.	**CT:** 7–8 minutes Stir in leaves after 3 minutes; cover again. **ST:** 2 minutes, covered
TURNIPS 1 lb. (2 or 3 medium)	1½-qt. casserole	Prepare as directed on page 95. Cut into ½-inch cubes. Add 3 tablespoons water and cover with lid or heavy-duty plastic wrap.	**CT:** 7–9 minutes Stir after 3 minutes; cover again. **ST:** 3 minutes, covered

STIR-FRYING & BUTTER-STEAMING FRESH VEGETABLES

Stir-frying and butter-steaming are similar techniques that quickly produce cooked vegetables with tender-crisp texture, bright color, and rich, natural flavor. Whether you stir-fry or butter-steam in a wok or frying pan, the basic procedure is the same.

To stir-fry or butter-steam. Prepare vegetables (see chart beginning on page 88); then cut as indicated in chart below. Place a wok or wide frying pan over high heat; when wok is hot, add salad oil or butter (depending on method of cooking) and cut-up vegetables. Cook, uncovered, stirring constantly, for time given in chart. Add specified amount of liquid; then cover and cook, stirring occasionally, for time indicated in chart. Add a few drops of additional liquid or water if vegetables appear dry.

Note that several vegetables—fennel, lettuce, mushrooms, onions, and spinach—have such a high moisture content that you won't need to add any liquid during cooking. Don't cover the pan when cooking fennel and mushrooms; they'll be ready to serve after just a few minutes of uncovered cooking.

We do not suggest stir-frying those vegetables that taste better when cooked in butter.

Two secrets to success. *Never crowd the wok or frying pan.* Cook no more than 5 cups cut-up vegetables in a 12- to 14-inch wok or 10-inch frying pan. To prepare more servings than you can cook at one time, have ready the total amount of cut-up vegetables you'll need and cook in two batches. The cooking process is so fast that you can keep the first portion warm, without flavor loss, while the second portion cooks.

Use highest heat so the vegetables begin cooking at once: a slow start means slow cooking. As the vegetables cook, all or most of the liquid evaporates; because there's no cooking liquid to drain off, vitamins and minerals are retained.

Testing for doneness. Cooking time will vary, depending on the freshness and maturity of the vegetables and on individual preference. Taste after the minimum cooking time; if you prefer a softer texture, continue cooking, tasting frequently, until vegetables are done to your liking.

To serve. Season to taste with salt and pepper; or choose one of the seasonings suggested in the chart beginning on page 88.

VEGETABLE 4–5 cups cut-up vegetable	SALAD OIL OR to stir-fry	BUTTER OR MARGARINE to butter-steam	TIME to cook and stir, uncovered	BROTH (regular-strength chicken or beef) OR WATER	TIME to cook, covered
ASPARAGUS Cut into ½-inch diagonal slices	1 tbsp.	2 tbsps.	1 minute	1–2 tbsps.	2–3 minutes
BEANS, green, Italian, wax Cut into 1-inch pieces	1 tbsp.	2 tbsps.	1 minute	4 tbsps.	4–7 minutes
BEET GREENS Shredded	Do not stir-fry	2 tbsps.	1 minute	1–2 tbsps.	2–3 minutes
BEETS Cut into ¼-inch slices	Do not stir-fry	2 tbsps.	1 minute	6 tbsps.	5–6 minutes
BOK CHOY See **SWISS CHARD**					
BROCCOLI Cut into ¼-inch slices	1 tbsp.	2 tbsps.	1 minute	3–5 tbsps.	3–5 minutes
BRUSSELS SPROUTS Cut in half lengthwise	Do not stir-fry	2 tbsps.	1 minute	3–5 tbsps.	3–5 minutes
CABBAGE, green, red, savoy Shredded	1 tbsp.	2 tbsps.	1 minute	2 tbsps.	3–4 minutes
CABBAGE, napa Cut white part into 1-inch slices; shred leaves and add during last 2–3 minutes of cooking time	1 tbsp.	2 tbsps.	1–2 minutes	2 tbsps.	4–5 minutes
CARROTS Cut into ¼-inch slices	1 tbsp.	2 tbsps.	1 minute	2–3 tbsps.	3–5 minutes
CAULIFLOWER Flowerets, cut into ¼-inch slices	1 tbsp.	3 tbsps.	1 minute	3–4 tbsps.	4–5 minutes
CELERY Cut into ¼-inch slices	1 tbsp.	2 tbsps.	1 minute	1–2 tbsps.	1–3 minutes

VEGETABLE 4–5 cups cut-up vegetable	SALAD OIL OR to stir-fry	BUTTER OR MARGARINE to butter-steam	TIME to cook and stir, uncovered	BROTH (regular-strength chicken or beef) OR WATER	TIME to cook, covered
CELERY ROOT Cut into ¼-inch slices	Do not stir-fry	2 tbsps.	1 minute	3–4 tbsps.	2–4 minutes
CHAYOTE Cut into ¼-inch slices	Do not stir-fry	3 tbsps.	1 minute	4–6 tbsps.	6–8 minutes
CUCUMBERS, Armenian, English, marketer Cut into ¼-inch slices	Do not stir-fry	2 tbsps.	1 minute	1 tbsp.	2–2½ minutes
FENNEL Cut into ¼-inch slices	1 tbsp.	2 tbsps.	2–3 minutes	No liquid necessary	No covered cooking necessary
KOHLRABI Cut into ⅛-inch slices	Do not stir-fry	3 tbsps.	1 minute	7 tbsps.	6–8 minutes
LEEKS White part only, cut into ¼-inch slices	1 tbsp.	2 tbsps.	1 minute	3–4 tbsps.	3 minutes
LETTUCE, iceberg Shredded	Do not stir-fry	2 tbsps.	30 seconds	No liquid necessary	2–3 minutes
MUSHROOMS Cut into ¼-inch slices	1 tbsp.	2 tbsps.	3–4 minutes	No liquid necessary	No covered cooking necessary
ONIONS, dry Cut into ¼-inch slices	1 tbsp.	2 tbsps.	1 minute	No liquid necessary	3–4 minutes
PARSNIPS Cut into ¼-inch slices	2 tbsps.	4 tbsps.	1 minute	6–8 tbsps.	4–6 minutes
PEAS, edible-pod	1 tbsp.	2 tbsps.	3 minutes	1 tbsp.	½ minute
PEAS, green Shelled	1 tbsp.	2 tbsps.	1 minute	3–4 tbsps.	2–3 minutes
PEPPERS, green or red bell Cut into 1-inch pieces	1 tbsp.	2 tbsps.	1 minute	2–3 tbsps.	3–5 minutes
RUTABAGAS Cut into ¼-inch slices	1 tbsp.	2 tbsps.	1 minute	4–5 tbsps.	5–6 minutes
SPINACH Leaves, whole or coarsely chopped	1 tbsp.	2 tbsps.	30 seconds	No liquid necessary	2–3 minutes
SPROUTS, bean	1 tbsp.	2 tbsps.	1 minute	1 tbsp.	½–1½ minutes
SQUASH, summer **Crookneck, pattypan, zucchini** Cut into ¼-inch slices	1 tbsp.	2 tbsps.	1 minute	2–4 tbsps.	3–4 minutes
SQUASH, winter **Banana, Hubbard, pumpkin** Cut into 1-inch cubes	Do not stir-fry	2 tbsps.	1 minute	3–5 tbsps.	6–8 minutes
SUNCHOKES Cut into ¼-inch slices	Do not stir-fry	2 tbsps.	1 minute	2–3 tbsps.	3–5 minutes
SWISS CHARD Cut stems into ¼-inch slices; shred leaves and add during last 2–3 minutes of cooking time	1 tbsp.	2 tbsps.	1 minute	1 tbsp.	3½–4½ minutes
TURNIP GREENS Shredded	Do not stir-fry	2 tbsps.	1 minute	1–2 tbsps.	3–5 minutes
TURNIPS Cut into ¼-inch slices	1 tbsp.	2 tbsps.	1 minute	4–5 tbsps.	4–5 minutes

BAKING & ROASTING FRESH VEGETABLES

Certain vegetables cook to perfection in the oven. Baking or roasting accentuates the naturally mellow-sweet flavor and preserves the nutritional value of vegetables such as corn, potatoes, and squash. At the same time, the dry oven heat tames the pungency of other vegetables such as garlic and onions.

Oven-cooking vegetables. When you tuck vegetables into the same oven with beef or chicken, you save energy—your own included. The vegetables require minimal preparation and cook with little or no at-

tention. Some vegetables—onions and potatoes, for example—can be roasted alongside the meat in the pan drippings. In this case, use the oven temperature specified for roasting the meat and add 20 to 30 minutes to the cooking time listed in the chart for the vegetables.

Never overcrowd the oven; the heat needs ample room to circulate. As long as you observe this rule, you can bake ten potatoes as quickly as one.

To adapt the following chart for convection oven baking, lower the oven

temperature by 25° or 50°F; test for doneness at the minimum suggested time.

To serve. Season baked or roasted vegetables to taste with salt and pepper; or choose one or more of the seasonings suggested in the chart beginning on page 88. *Exception:* Don't serve roasted garlic as you would other vegetables. Pluck garlic cloves from the head and squeeze each to release the cooked garlic. Serve on dinner rolls, cooked meat, or other vegetables.

VEGETABLE/ PREPARATION	OVEN TEMPERATURE (°F)	TIME	TEST FOR DONENESS
BEETS—2- to 3-inch diameter Scrub beets; pat dry. Do not peel. Wrap each beet in heavy-duty foil.	375°	1–1¼ hours	Tender when pierced
CARROTS—Medium-size Scrub well or peel; cut into 1-inch diagonal slices. Arrange in a shallow layer in a baking dish; generously dot with butter or margarine.	325°, covered	40–50 minutes; stir several times	Tender when pierced
CORN ON THE COB—Large ears Remove husk and silk. Rub kernels with butter or margarine. Wrap each ear in heavy-duty foil.	375°	30–35 minutes	Tender when pierced
EGGPLANT—Large Scrub; pat dry. Cut into ½-inch-thick slices; brush all sides with salad oil. Arrange in a single layer in a shallow baking pan.	425°–450°, uncovered	20–30 minutes	Well browned and tender when pierced
GARLIC—Large heads Place whole, unpeeled heads in a greased dish.	325°, uncovered	1 hour	Tender when pierced
ONIONS, dry—Medium-size Peel; stand upright in a close-fitting baking dish. Drizzle with melted butter or margarine.	350°, uncovered	30–45 minutes; baste several times with butter	Tender when pierced
PARSNIPS—Medium-size Peel; cut into ½- by 3-inch sticks. Arrange in a shallow layer in a baking dish; generously dot with butter or margarine.	325°, covered	45–60 minutes; stir several times	Tender when pierced
PEPPERS, green or red bell—Large Cut lengthwise into quarters; discard stem and seeds. Rinse. Arrange, skin side down, in a greased, close-fitting dish; drizzle with salad or olive oil.	375°, uncovered	40–45 minutes	Tender when pierced
POTATOES, russet or thin-skinned—Medium-size Scrub; pat dry. Pierce skin in several places; rub with butter or margarine. Place on oven rack (potatoes shouldn't touch each other).	400°, uncovered	50–60 minutes	Soft when squeezed
POTATOES, sweet (or yams)—Medium-size Scrub; pat dry. Pierce skin in several places; rub with butter or margarine. Arrange in a single layer on a rimmed baking sheet.	400°, uncovered	45–50 minutes	Soft when squeezed
RUTABAGAS—Medium-size Peel; cut into ¼-inch slices. Arrange in a shallow layer in a baking dish. Generously dot with butter or margarine; sprinkle lightly with water.	400°, covered	30–45 minutes	Tender when pierced

VEGETABLE/ PREPARATION	OVEN TEMPERATURE (°F)	TIME	TEST FOR DONENESS
SQUASH, spaghetti—Medium-size Rinse; pierce in several places. Place on a rimmed baking sheet.	350°, uncovered	1½ hours; turn over after 45 minutes	Shell gives to pressure
SQUASH, winter Acorn, butternut—Medium-size Cut in half lengthwise. Scrape out seeds and stringy portions. Place, cut side down, in a greased baking dish.	400°–450°, uncovered	30–40 minutes	Flesh tender when pierced
Banana, Hubbard—Large pieces Cut into serving-size pieces. Scrape out seeds and stringy portions. Place, cut side down, in a greased baking dish.	400°–450°, uncovered	30–40 minutes	Flesh tender when pierced
Pumpkin—9–11 pounds Cut in half lengthwise. Scrape out seeds and stringy portions. Place, cut side down, on a greased rimmed baking sheet.	350°, uncovered	1–1¼ hours	Flesh tender when pierced
TOMATOES—Medium-size Core and cut in half crosswise; squeeze out juice and seeds. Place, cut side up, in a baking dish. Drizzle with olive oil or salad oil.	400°, uncovered	20–25 minutes	Soft throughout

GRILLING FRESH VEGETABLES

It's a simple matter to grill vegetables on the barbecue alongside the main course. You can prepare the vegetables ahead of time and have the wrapped packets waiting to put on the grill when the fire is ready.

To grill. Rinse vegetables thoroughly but do not pat dry—water that clings creates enough moisture to steam most vegetables. Place up to 4 servings of the vegetable on a sheet of heavy-duty foil (wrap potatoes and corn on the cob individually). Evenly dot with butter or margarine, using 2 tablespoons for every 4 servings.

Wrap vegetables tightly in foil and place on a grill 4 to 6 inches above a solid bed of medium coals. Cook, shifting packets occasionally so vegetables cook evenly; test for doneness at minimum suggested time.

To serve. Season to taste with salt and pepper; or choose one or more of the seasonings suggested in the chart beginning on page 88.

VEGETABLE	TIME	TEST FOR DONENESS
ASPARAGUS Spears	15–20 minutes	Tender when pierced
BEANS, green, Italian, wax Whole	20 minutes	Tender-crisp to bite
CARROTS Cut into 1-inch slices	25–30 minutes	Tender when pierced
CORN ON THE COB Remove husk and silk; wrap individually	15–20 minutes	Tender when pierced
PEAS, green Shelled	20 minutes	Tender to bite
POTATOES, red or white thin-skinned Small whole; pierce skin	50–55 minutes	Tender throughout when pierced
POTATOES, russet Medium-size whole; pierce skin, wrap individually	1 hour	Soft when squeezed
SQUASH, summer Crookneck, pattypan, zucchini Cut into 1-inch slices	20–25 minutes	Tender when pierced
SQUASH, winter Banana, Hubbard Peel; cut into 1- by 6-inch spears	25–30 minutes	Tender when pierced

INDEX

METRIC CONVERSION TABLE

TO CHANGE	TO	MULTIPLY BY
ounces (oz.)	grams (g)	28
pounds (lbs.)	kilograms (kg)	0.45
teaspoons	milliliters (ml)	5
tablespoons	milliliters (ml)	15
fluid ounces (fl. oz.)	milliliters (ml)	30
cups	liters (l)	0.24
pints (pt.)	liters (l)	0.47
quarts (qt.)	liters (l)	0.95
gallons (gal.)	liters (l)	3.8
Fahrenheit temperature (°F)	Celsius temperature (°C)	5/9 after subtracting 32